CW00921734

The Japan Culture Book

英語で日本文化の本

Written by Miura Fumiko
三浦史子 著

Translated by Alan Gleason
アラン・グリースン 訳

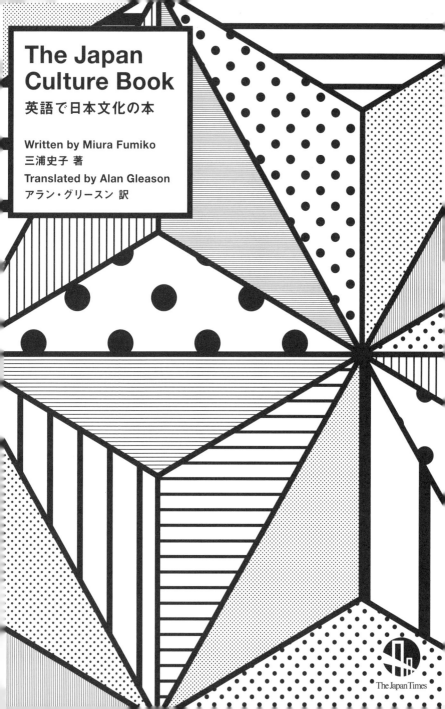

The Japan Times

PREFACE

日本の読者のみなさんへ
To Japanese Readers

みなさんは海外の人との会話で、日本文化が話題になったとき、会話がうまくかみあわなかった経験はありませんか？　それは「英語力が足りない」ばかりが理由でしょうか。もしかするとベースとなる認識のどこが異なるのか、お互いにわからないせいかもしれません。

そこで本書では、3つの観点から「日本文化」の解説をこころみました。

ひとつめは、「日本では当たり前だけれど、英語圏などにはない概念」に注目しました。わざわざ説明が必要だとは、気づかないことがあるからです。

2つめとして、日本についての「ステレオタイプ」を知っておくことを提案します。

たとえ相手の先入観が大きな誤解に思えたとしても、あらかじめ踏まえておけば、言われたときにジョークで返す余裕も生まれますし、またそれぞれの方の、実感としての「日本文化」について、説明しやすくなるのではないでしょうか。得意分野の話なら、「これが真髄だ」と主張したい部分があるかもしれません。あるいは育った地方の特徴や、変わりつつある状況なども話題にできるでしょう。

「日本文化」といっても実際は多様で、海外の文化とも影響し合って、常に変化し続けているものです。本書では便宜上、前近代の様式を色濃く残しているものに対して、「伝統的」という言葉を使っていますが、伝統文化と呼ばれるものも、ほとんどが近代以降に大きくアレンジされています。政府や企業などが、一種のブランド戦略として、日本の決まったイメージを積極的に作り出している場合もあります。本書では、なるべくそうしたステレオタイプの成立事情にせまりつつ、各章のテーマに関するさまざまな論説を紹介しました。

関連しますが、3つ目のポイントとして、日本における文化の多様性の一端を紹介するようにつとめました。

読者のみなさんには、本書の内容をご自身の認識に合わせて再編しつつ、会話に生かしていただければ幸いです。そして、日本の音楽や映画、ファッション、アニメ、小説……、なんでも好きなものについて感じている魅力や、また実際のやり方──たとえば武道の技や料理のレシピなどを伝えることは、楽しい会話のもうひとつのポイントではないでしょうか。

著者

To English Readers

海外の読者のみなさんへ

This book is primarily designed as an English-language learning resource for Japanese readers, but we hope that other readers interested in Japan will also enjoy it.

In these pages we introduce Japanese culture with three focuses in mind.

First, we focused on concepts that are common in Japan but not in some other cultures. Without being aware of those differences, Japanese and non-Japanese may not even realize when they are talking past each other.

A second focus of our discussion is stereotypes about Japan. Stereotypes often produce serious misconceptions, yet they are always going to appear. By identifying such generalizations from the outset, we can learn to joke about them, and perhaps find it easier to exchange honest opinions about what "Japanese culture" really means to each of us.

The reality, of course, is that "Japanese culture" is a diverse thing that has undergone constant changes while being influenced by, as well as influencing, other cultures. For convenience we use the word "traditional" in this book when we refer to things that retain a strong flavor of pre-modern Japan. In fact, however, most elements of what is called "traditional culture" have been adapted into their present form since the modern era began.

As in other countries, governments, corporations and the like in Japan often try to manufacture and sell images of their nation as a branding strategy. Here we offer a variety of perspectives on each subject, and part of that involves examining how such stereotypes came into being.

Our third focus, which relates to this issue, is the sheer diversity of culture in Japan, which we have tried to provide at least a taste of in this book.

We hope that readers will find this a useful guide that expands your interest in Japanese culture—hopefully without creating any new stereotypes!

The Author

READER'S GUIDE
本書の構成と使い方

本書はテーマごとに12章に分かれた、それぞれ短いトピック（項目）によって構成されています。章の最初のページには、テーマの概論がありますが、実際にはどこから読んでもかまいません。カフェで、学校で、職場で、文化交流のパートナーとして、いつでもこの本を参照し、表現をピックアップしたり、自由にアレンジしたりして、ご自身の会話にお役立てください。

In the chapters of this book, the English text is arranged to match the Japanese text on the preceding page, except for the omission of Notes, WORLD CAFÉ (see below), and a few other parts. Japanese personal names are spelled in Japanese order, family name first.

1. Texts

左右ページで日本語と英語の対訳になっています。逐語訳ではなく、ネイティブ・スピーカーにとって自然なように意訳していたり、日本に詳しくない人に向けて、言葉を加えたりしている部分があります。

The English text is not translated word for word from the Japanese, but written to convey the same meaning in natural English. It also contains supplementary expressions for non-Japanese readers to help make certain words or concepts more understandable.

2. Keywords

別のページ（同じ章のなかとは限らない）に、項目名として登場する言葉が、探しやすいように色分けしてあります。これらは日本文化を語るうえで、頻出するキーワードでもあります。

Keywords that appear in topic titles on other pages are color-coded in the text for easy reference.

3. Notes

日本語の内容を補足する注釈です。海外の友人から突っ込んだ質問をされたときには、これらを糸口に調べてみてはいかがでしょうか。

Notes in the Japanese main text provide additional information for Japanese readers interested in further study for conversational purposes; these have not been translated into English.

4. Vocabulary

英語の単語やイディオム、むずかしい表現に対する注釈です。

The Vocabulary section defines English words, idioms and expressions for Japanese readers.

5. Comment

個性豊かな日本人キャラクターたちによるコメントです。ご自身の意見や思いを言葉にする上でのご参考に。

Comments appear as quotes from different Japanese characters, each with their own point of view.

私がご案内します。
I'll be your
guide today.

Mika

文化の神髄を
伝えたいですね。
That's the essence
of Japanese culture!

Jiro

僕の地元では、
ちょっと違うんだ。
In my hometown,
things are a bit
different.

Ryota

6. COLUMN

項目の内容から発展させた話題を展開しているコーナーです。

Each Column expands on a topic discussed in the main text.

7. WORLD CAFÉ

日本語のコラムです。おもに、日本の文化が海外でどのように受けとめられているかを紹介しています。

WORLD CAFÉ columns explain to Japanese readers how their country's culture has been introduced and spread overseas; these have not been translated into English.

CONTENTS

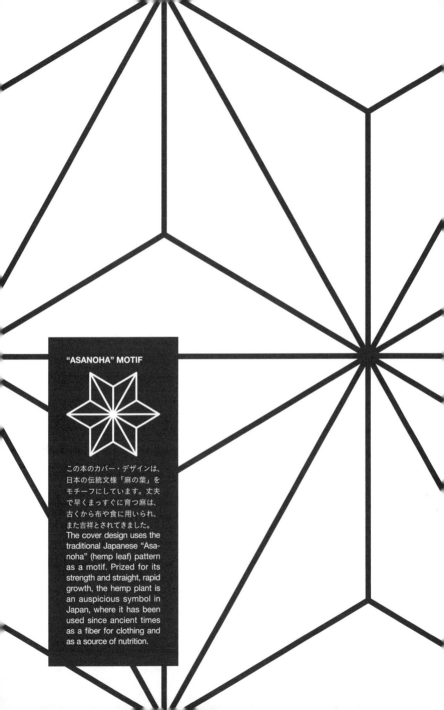

"ASANOHA" MOTIF

この本のカバー・デザインは、
日本の伝統文様「麻の葉」を
モチーフにしています。丈夫
で早くまっすぐに育つ麻は、
古くから布や食に用いられ、
また吉祥とされてきました。
The cover design uses the
traditional Japanese "Asanoha" (hemp leaf) pattern
as a motif. Prized for its
strength and straight, rapid
growth, the hemp plant is
an auspicious symbol in
Japan, where it has been
used since ancient times
as a fiber for clothing and
as a source of nutrition.

01

MUSIC
音楽

01 現代日本の音楽事情

日本の伝統的な音楽は、西洋音楽とは**音**や**音階**、**リズム**などの感覚が大きく異なっています。ところが、現代の日本で多くの人に親しまれているのは、欧米の影響が強い日本のポップス（**J-ポップ**）です。テレビではミュージシャンが歌い、私たちはカラオケ※1 で歌います。

それらのポップスは、ミュージシャンのファッションやダンスも含めて、欧米から輸入した文化のようでありながら、じつは音階や歌い方などの、どこかに日本的な音楽の要素が混ざっていたりします。そこがおもしろいという外国人もいますね。

日本らしさを前面に出した**演歌**というジャンルのポピュラー音楽もあって、特に高齢層に人気があります。演歌歌手は、よく**着物**を着ています。

東京などの都市には、コンサートのできるホールや小さなライブハウスが無数にあって、世界各地のさまざまな音楽が演奏されています——ジャズやロック、**邦楽**、**西洋クラシック**、ワールド・ミュージック……海外アーティストもこれまでたくさん演奏ツアーにやって来ました。

都会で電車に乗ると、イヤホンを付けている人の割合が多いでしょう。日本は、79 年にヘッドフォンステレオ「ウォークマン」を世に出した国です。今は座席に隣合わせて座っていても、それぞれ好みの曲を聴いているのが、当たり前の時代になりましたね。

ところで、古くからの**民謡**はというと、民謡歌手が唄って全国に普及した曲がある一方で、各地方の生活の場からは消えていっています。

新しい試みをひとつ、紹介しましょう。誰でも参加できる共同作曲のワークショップ※2 が、最近、美術館などで開催されています。楽器を弾かない人も、何でもいいから好きな音で——たとえば「手を 3 回たたく」とか、「携帯電話の着信音を鳴らす」といったフレーズを順番に「作曲」し、それをつなげて新曲ができるのです。

Notes

※1 カラオケは1971年、井上大佑の発明とされるが、フィリピンでは同国のアル・ロザリオが特許を主張し、最高裁で認められている。　※2 作曲家・野村誠が考案したメソッド「しょうぎ作曲」("*Shogi* Composition" by Nomura Makoto)。

⁰¹ Japan's Music Scene Today

Traditional Japanese music differs quite a bit from Western music in its **sounds**, musical **scales**, and **rhythms**. Today, however, more Japanese are familiar with the country's distinctive brand of pop music, commonly called **J-pop**, in which you can hear a strong Western influence. Musicians perform it on television and everyone sings it at karaoke. While on the surface J-pop may appear to be a Western import like the fashions and dances that go with it, in fact it contains elements of Japanese music—in the scales it uses and the way it is sung, for example. To some foreigners, that is precisely what makes J-pop interesting.

Another genre of popular music in Japan, *enka*, has a pronounced Japanese flavor and appeals particularly to an older audience. Enka singers often perform wearing **kimono**.

In large cities like Tokyo, there are countless venues, from concert halls to tiny clubs, where you can hear music from everywhere on the planet—jazz, rock, *hogaku*, **Western classical music**, world music, and more. Many overseas artists have come to Japan to give concerts.

When you ride the trains in Japan, you will notice that a large proportion of passengers are wearing earphones. It was a Japanese company that introduced the world to the personal stereo—the Walkman—in 1979. We now live in an era when it's completely normal for people to sit next to each other while they listen by themselves to their own favorite music.

Meanwhile, *minyo* (traditional folk tunes) no longer figure in the daily lives of various locales as they once did. Yet certain of these tunes are familiar to people throughout the country thanks to versions sung by professional minyo singers.

Recently, some artists have been trying out new ways to make music accessible to everyone. In workshops held at art museums and the like, participants make music together by "composing" short linked passages in turn. Even without playing a musical instrument, anyone can join in creating a new tune, for example by "clapping three times" or ringing one's cell phone.

Vocabulary

quite a bit｜かなりたくさん、相当
musical scale｜音階
distinctive｜独特の
on the surface｜表面上は
a large proportion of ...｜…のかなりの部分

tune｜曲、節、メロディー
figure｜現れる
certain of ...｜ある一定の…、とある…
compose ...｜…を作曲する
musical instrument｜楽器

02 邦楽

明治時代以前に、日本で形づくられた音楽の総称[3]。江戸時代までは身分によって聴く音楽が違い、それぞれ作曲家も演奏家も、使う楽器まで異なりました。そのジャンルの多様さは、世界にもあまり類を見ないほどだといいます。邦楽はおもに家元制度（P. 186 参照）によって、流派ごとに伝承されてきて、楽譜はないか、あってもかき方が統一されていませんでした。明治以降は、近代化とともに邦楽が軽視され、学校の音楽の授業でも「ドレミ」は教えても、自国の音楽についてまともに扱われないという状態が続いていましたが、近年は邦楽が見直されています。また、和楽器を使った現代音楽やロック、ジャズ、オルタナティブ[4]などの曲も増えています。

Notes

※3 洋楽と呼ばれる現代の欧米のポピュラー音楽に対して、現代日本のポピュラー音楽（J-ポップ）を「邦楽」と呼ぶこともある。そのため、伝統音楽は「純邦楽」（pure hogaku）とも呼ばれる。

※4 商業的な型にはまらない音楽活動。alternative（型にはまらない、代わりの）からきている。

03 日本の音と尺八

尺八は、細い種類の竹の形を生かした縦笛で、穴は 5 つだけ。単純な楽器ですが、穴の上に指をちょっとかざしたり、舌やのどひこを震わせたり、あごを前後左右に振ったりして（ビブラートのようになる）音の高さや表情を変えます。西洋音階では「ド」ならド、「レ」ならレの音を、正確に出すことが求められますが、**邦楽**ではそうとは限りません。むしろ、**音階**に分けられない、微妙な音色を味わうところに真髄があるのです。

1960 年代頃、**武満徹**などの前衛音楽に尺八が使われ、近代の西洋音楽の概念を打ち破るものとして脚光を浴びました。

尺八は中国から伝来したといわれますが、現在の中国で同じものは使われていないそうです。名前は一尺八寸（約 54.5 センチメートル）の標準サイズからきています。13～19 世紀、「虚無僧」という禅宗の一派の僧が、宗教のために尺八を吹きながら、諸国行脚したことでも知られます。

Comment

尺八は稽古してみると、奥が深い楽器だといいますよ。単純な竹の筒だけに、一本一本の竹や、演奏者の個性が出やすいのです。

People who study the shakuhachi will tell you that it is a profound instrument. This simple bamboo tube readily expresses the unique character of each piece of bamboo and every individual player.

02 Hogaku

Hogaku is a general term for music that evolved in Japan up to the Meiji period (1868-1912). Through the preceding Edo period (1603-1868), not only did people listen to different types of music according to their social status, but the composers, performers, and musical instruments varied as well, giving rise to a diversity of musical genres rarely seen, some scholars claim, in other parts of the world. Most forms of hogaku have been passed down via different schools under the *iemoto* system (see p. 187), and they all use different notation systems, or none at all.

From the Meiji period on, hogaku fell into neglect as the country modernized. Although things have changed for the better in recent years, schools used to teach the Western do-re-mi scale while ignoring Japan's own musical traditions. Today, more and more artists in rock, jazz, alternative, and other contemporary genres use Japanese instruments in their music.

Vocabulary

school｜流派、派	notation system｜記譜法

03 Japanese Sounds and the Shakuhachi

The shakuhachi is an end-blown flute that utilizes the shape of a single thin stalk of bamboo. It's a simple instrument with just five finger holes, but the pitch and timbre can be altered by partially covering the holes, making the tongue or uvula quiver, or moving the chin to produce a kind of vibrato. In Western classical music, the musician is required to reproduce notes exactly as written, but with **hogaku** this is not always the case. Indeed, savoring subtle tone colors that cannot be divided into a **scale** is the very essence of hogaku. In the 1960s, the shakuhachi featured prominently in the avant-garde music of people like **Takemitsu Toru**, a postwar composer who shattered the conventions of modern Western music.

It's said that the shakuhachi was introduced to Japan from China, though no instruments like it are used in China today. The name refers to the shakuhachi's standard length of 1.8 *shaku* (*hachi* means "eight"). It's also famous as a religious instrument played by the *komuso*, itinerant priests of a sect of **Zen** Buddhism who were active from the 13th through 19th centuries.

Vocabulary

pitch｜音の高さ	subtle tone colors｜微妙な音色
timbre｜音色	itinerant｜放浪している
make the tongue or uvula quiver｜舌やのどひこを震わせる	

コラム 虫聴き

夏から秋にかけた夜には、松虫、鈴虫、コオロギなど、多くの虫の鳴き声が聞かれますが、日本ではこの草間のささやかな声が、とても好まれます。江戸時代の**浮世絵**に、『東都名所 道灌山虫聞之図』※5（歌川廣重）といって、「虫聴き」という庶民の娯楽を描いたものがあります。当時は家族で小高い丘などに出かけて、虫の声を聴きながら酒肴を楽しむ習慣があったのです――今はすたれてしまいましたが。自宅で虫の声を楽しむため、屋台をかついで鈴虫などを売り歩く「虫売り」もいました。こうした自然の音を愛でる趣味が、日本の音楽につながっているのではないか……とは、明治の頃からよくいわれる説です。たしかに**邦楽**には、**能**※6 や**歌舞伎**などの演劇でも見られるように、声の音楽が多く、高くて渋い声の音色を重視し、音が消えていく余韻を好むのも特徴です。

Notes

※5　長谷川雪旦の『江戸名所図会』挿絵を元に描かれた。　※6　能の音楽は「謡曲（ようきょく）」。歌舞伎では「長唄」や「常磐津節（ときわずぶし）」、「清元節（きよもとぶし）」等。文楽では「義太夫節（ぎだゆうぶし）」。室内で三味線を伴奏に歌う音楽には、地唄や端唄（はうた）、小唄等がある。また、仏典に節をつけた宗教音楽を「声明（しょうみょう）」という。

04 箏（そう）

箏（一般に「こと」と呼ばれる）※7 は日本の伝統楽器。カマボコのような形の木製弦楽器で、胴の長さは170〜190センチメートル、弦は通常13本で、床に置いて演奏します。弾き方は、楽器の手前に座り、左手では弦を上からおさえて、ツメを付けた右手の3本の指――親指、人さし指、中指――で弦を弾きます。弦の下にある支柱を動かすと、音程を調整することができます。

箏は奈良時代に中国大陸から伝来しましたが※8、日本では大がかりな器楽ではなく、室内楽や、家庭のなかでプライベートに演奏される楽器として発展しました。今では、箏を演奏することには、ちょっと昔の「**着物を着た女性のたしなみ**」といったイメージがあります。

→

COLUMN **Mushi-kiki**

In Japan from summer to early fall, the night air is filled with the chirping of various kinds of crickets, and many people find this chorus-like sound appealing. The Edo-period **ukiyo-e** woodblock print *Listening to Insects, Mount Dokan*, from the series *Famous Places in the Eastern Capital* by Utagawa Hiroshige, depicts the once-popular pastime of *mushi-kiki*, or listening to crickets. At the time, it was common to take excursions into the hills for the purpose of savoring those sounds while eating and drinking. *Mushi-uri*, or insect peddlers, would walk around selling crickets and other insects so people could listen to the chirping in their own homes. Since the Meiji period, some people have promoted the notion that this fondness for natural sounds had an influence on Japanese music. Like forms of Japanese theater such as **Noh** and **Kabuki**, **hogaku** features a lot of vocal music characterized by high-pitched, elegantly austere tones and a fondness for lingering notes that can be heard as the sound fades.

Vocabulary

chirp ｜ (虫や鳥が) 鳴く	peddler ｜ 行商人
cricket ｜ コオロギ、松虫、鈴虫等	high-pitched ｜ 高音の
woodblock print ｜ 木版画	austere ｜ 飾り気のない
depict ｜ 描く	lingering ｜ なかなか消えない

04 **Koto**

The koto is a traditional Japanese wooden stringed instrument with a semi-cylindrical body 170 to 190 cm long. It typically has 13 strings and is played resting on the floor. The player sits in front of it and presses the strings with the left hand while plucking them with the right, using finger picks attached to the thumb, index finger, and middle finger. Bridges underneath the strings can be moved to adjust the tuning. The koto was an instrument introduced from the Chinese mainland during the Nara period (710-794). In Japan, it evolved not as a concert instrument but as a vehicle for chamber music or private performances in the home. Today, koto performances have a slightly old-fashioned image as a "pastime enjoyed by ladies in **kimono**."

→

←
箏には弦をたたいたり、こすったりなどのおもしろい技法もあり、そうした微妙な音色を楽しむ曲が作られています。代表的な箏曲には、17世紀に作られた『六段の調』や、フランスのヴァイオリニスト、ルネ・シュメーが演奏に加わって有名になった『春の海』（1929／宮城道雄・作曲）などがあります。

最近では、箏と西洋楽器で合奏することもめずらしくなくなってきました。そんな時は、たいてい箏を台の上に乗せて、弾き手はその前に立つか、椅子に座って演奏します。

Notes

※7 「箏」が常用漢字でないので、新聞では「琴」の字で代用されるが、琴を「きん」と発音すると箏とは別の楽器になる。琴（七弦琴）は長さ125センチメートルの胴に七本の弦を張ったもので、柱がなく、右手にはツメをつけないで弾く。『源氏物語』の光源氏は琴の名手。　※8 日本固有の和琴（わごん）もある。

吉田兄弟　The Yoshida Brothers, 2006

05　三味線

三味線は、リュートやバンジョーなどに似た弦楽器。四角い胴には犬や猫の皮が張られ、絹糸[9]で出来た3本の弦をバチではじきます[10]。16世紀頃、中国の三弦が、沖縄を経由して（沖縄では「三線（さんしん）」[11] となる）伝来したのがルーツといわれますが、江戸時代には町人の生活に密着した、日本でもっともポピュラーな楽器となりました。三味線はポータブルだし、メロディの演奏もできれば、打楽器のようにも演奏できる、バラエティ豊かな楽器。それで、**歌舞伎**や**文楽**の伴奏、**芸者**のいるお座敷の音楽、**民謡**や家庭音楽と、さまざまな場に合わせた三味線音楽が作られ、流派ごとに違う形に改良されました。

近年、高橋竹山などの奏者の活躍をきっかけに、バチを叩き付けるように

→

Actually, playing the koto involves some interesting techniques, such as hitting or scraping the strings, and there are compositions that make the most of the delicate variations in timbre these give rise to. Well-known koto pieces range from "Rokudan no Shirabe" ("Music of Six Steps"), which was written in the 17th century, to "The Sea in Spring," composed in 1929 by Miyagi Michio and later recorded with Miyagi on koto and Renee Chemet of France on violin.

Nowadays it's not uncommon to hear ensemble performances featuring the koto with Western instruments. In these settings the koto is usually placed on a raised platform, and the player stands in front of it or sits in a chair.

Vocabulary

stringed instrument｜弦楽器［名詞形は string で「弦」］	middle finger｜中指
	adjust the tuning｜調律する
semi-cylindrical｜半円筒形の	chamber music｜室内楽
pluck …｜（楽器の弦）をかき鳴らす	pastime｜趣味、娯楽
thumb｜親指	scrape｜（楽器）をこすって音を出す
index finger｜人さし指	

05 Shamisen

The shamisen is a stringed instrument similar to a lute or banjo. It has a squarish body covered with dog or cat skin and three silk strings that are plucked with a plectrum. The shamisen is said to derive from the Chinese *sanxian*, which was introduced to Japan around the 16th century via Okinawa (where it evolved into the *sanshin*). During the Edo period it became the most popular musical instrument in the country and an established part of the lives of the townspeople. It is extremely versatile, thanks to its portability and the fact that it can both carry a melody and be struck like a percussion instrument. Accordingly, a tremendous variety of shamisen music has been composed for such purposes as accompaniment to **Kabuki** and **Bunraku** plays, performances by **geisha** at banquets, **minyo** (folk songs), and music in the home. The instrument itself has been modified in a number of ways for different schools and styles.

With the emergence of such charismatic performers as Takahashi Chikuzan, the style of shamisen music known as *Tsugaru-jamisen* has attained hit status in recent years. Tsugaru-jamisen's percussive technique produces a contemporary sound, and young performers like

→

弾く津軽三味線がポピュラーになりました。その奏法には現代的な響きがあり、上妻宏光、吉田兄弟などの若手奏者は、ロックやオルタナティブともいえる分野を切り拓いています。

Notes

※9 三味線の種類によっては、ナイロン、テトロン製を用いることもある。　※10 「さわり」(timbre) が付いていて、ノイズのような残響音が出ることも三味線の弦楽器としての特徴。　※11 三線には蛇の皮が張られていて、「さわり」はない。

Comment

津軽三味線の名演奏には、なんというか、グルーヴを感じるんだ。YouTube で聞いてみてください。
There are some very groove-heavy performances of Tsugaru-jamisen available on
YouTube. Check them out!

06 和太鼓

日本の太鼓の総称。木でできた胴に皮が張ってあり、バチでたたきます（手でたたくものは鼓といいます）。和太鼓には古代からの歴史があり、現代では、祭礼や歌舞伎、能、神社仏閣の儀式などに使われています。なかでも太鼓が人々の生活に密着しているシーンといえば、夏の盆踊りでしょう（P. 124 参照）。踊りの輪の中心に組まれたやぐらの上で、大太鼓が指揮を執るような役割をしています。

太鼓は長らく音楽の主体となることはありませんでしたが、近年、太鼓の大きさによって音が違うことを利用して、その組み合わせで音楽を創る、創作和太鼓がさかんになりました。佐渡の「鼓童」などの創作和太鼓グループは海外でも人気です。また、宮本やこ率いるニューヨークの「鼓舞」は、和太鼓とタップダンスのビートを組み合わせたパフォーマンスを展開しています。

←

Agamatsu Hiromitsu and the Yoshida Brothers are pioneering a new way of playing the instrument that could even be described as rock or alternative music.

Vocabulary

squarish｜ほぼ四角の、角ばった	portability｜携帯できること
plectrum｜（三味線の）バチ、（箏などの）爪、（ギターの）ピック	accordingly｜それゆえ、したがって
	attain hit status｜人気になる
derive from …｜…に由来する	pioneer …｜…の先がけとなる、…を開拓する
versatile｜用途の広い、多目的な	

06 Wa-daiko

Wa-daiko (literally "Japanese drums") are made of skins stretched over a wooden frame and struck with drumsticks (hand-beaten drums are called *tsuzumi*). Wa-daiko have existed since ancient times, and today they are used on many occasions—for festivals, **Kabuki, Noh**, religious ceremonies, and so forth. One event at which the wa-daiko is still a fixture in Japanese life is the Bon-odori (see p. 125), the folk dance performed every summer during the O-bon festival. A giant wa-daiko sits atop a wooden scaffold around which people dance, and it is the drummer who sets the rhythm for the dancers.

For a long time the wa-daiko served mainly to accompany other instruments, but in recent years "creative wa-daiko," percussion music utilizing the diverse sounds produced by drums of different sizes, has gained a following. Creative wa-daiko groups such as Sado Island's Kodo are popular abroad as well as in Japan. The New York ensemble Cobu, led by Miyamoto Yako, gives performances that combine wa-daiko rhythms with tap dancing.

Vocabulary

stretched over …｜…に張られた	wooden scaffold｜特設舞台、やぐら
be struck｜たたかれる［原形は strike］	gain a following｜さかんになる、支持を得る
drumstick｜ドラムスティック、バチ	

左：「第5回ティーンズ和太鼓コンテスト」より
Left: From the 5th Teens Wa-Daiko Contest, 2009
Photo courtesy of Turtle Co., Ltd.

07 日本のリズムと民謡

邦楽には、拍（ビート）がない曲もあります。ひとりで自由に歌うタイプの民謡に多く[12]、フレーズの長さがまちまちになります。拍はなくてもリズムがないわけではなくて、歌い方のパターンにリズムがあります——たとえば、フレーズの途中で張り上げた声を、フレーズの終わりでは必ず上下に細かく揺らしながら弱めていくなど。また邦楽では、拍のある曲でも、一拍の長さが決まっていなくて、伸びたり縮んだりすることがよくあります[13]。西洋近代のリズム感を音楽の基本と考えると、まるで不正確なようですが、邦楽ではむしろここが聴きどころです。たとえば、曲が終わる直前の音をちょっと伸ばして、緊張感を高めて、曲に微妙な表情を付けたりします。

Notes

※ 12　追分節、舟歌、馬子歌（まごうた、馬のひづめを伴奏にした歌）等に多い。また、民謡だけでなく、雅楽の声楽曲や、仏教音楽の声明などにもみられるリズム様式。　※ 13　拍が伸び縮みする音楽は、日本だけでなく、世界の民俗音楽に共通したものが珍しくない。

Comment

たとえば北海道の江差追分（えさしおいわけ）は、ビートがないから、手拍子はできません。あなたの国にも、こういう伝統的な音楽は残っていますか？
You can't clap along to a no-beat minyo tune like the "Esashi Oiwake" of Hokkaido.
Does traditional music like that survive today in your country, too?

08 雅楽

宮廷や神社で演奏されている雅楽は、言葉の意味を直訳すると「宮廷風の優雅な音楽」。千数百年の歴史があります。宮内庁には、雅楽を演奏する楽団があって、天皇家の行事や、サミットで各国の来賓をもてなすときに、平安時代の装束を着て演奏します。雅楽を代表する『越天楽（えてんらく）』のような華やかな器楽曲は、5〜9 世紀に、文化の中心地だった中国大陸から輸入した音楽がルーツ。ベトナムや韓国にも似た音楽が残っています。楽器はおもに 8 種類。篳篥（ひちりき）や笙（しょう）などの管楽器のほか、弦楽器、打楽器を使います。雅楽にはほかに、舞が主体となる伴奏音楽[14]や、日本古来の歌曲などもあります。東儀秀樹という雅楽の奏者は、雅楽器とピアノやシンセサイザーとのコラボレーションなどに取り組んで注目を集めています。

Notes

※ 14　雅楽と舞が合わさったものを「舞楽」という。

07 Japanese Rhythm and Minyo

Some **hogaku** songs have no beat. Minyo designed to be sung solo and unaccompanied often have phrases of highly varying lengths. Although they may lack a fixed beat, the songs do retain a rhythm in the pattern in which they are sung. There may be loud cries between phrases, and the voice always trails off with a distinctive vibrato-like effect at the end of each phrase. Even in hogaku that has a beat, the length of a single beat may not be fixed, growing shorter or longer in the course of the same song. If you happen to believe that the modern Western sense of rhythm is a fundamental of music, then this may all seem wrong, but it is an important component of hogaku. The note immediately before the end of a song may be extended, for example, to heighten the tension and add to the expressive subtlety of the tune.

Vocabulary

beat｜拍、ビート	trail off｜次第に消える
be unaccompanied｜伴奏がない	vibrato-like effect｜ビブラートのような効果
phrase｜フレーズ、楽句	component｜要素
loud cry｜大きな声、張り上げた声	immediately before ...｜...の直前の

08 Gagaku

Gagaku is music performed in such venues as the Imperial Court and Shinto shrines; the word literally means "courtly, elegant music." Its history stretches back well over a thousand years. There is a group of musicians within the Imperial Household Agency who perform gagaku in Heian-period costumes at certain court functions and state banquets. Gorgeous instrumental pieces like the celebrated "Etenraku" have their roots in music introduced between the fifth and ninth centuries from China, which was then the cultural epicenter of Asia. Similar kinds of music still exist in Vietnam and Korea as well. In general, eight instruments are used to perform gagaku. They include wind instruments like the *hichiriki* and *sho*, as well as stringed instruments and percussion. Gagaku is also used as a musical accompaniment to dance and ancient Japanese classical songs.

　　The gagaku performer Togi Hideki has attracted attention with his collaborations between gagaku instruments and pianos or synthesizers.

Vocabulary

Imperial Court｜宮廷	epicenter｜中心地
Imperial Household Agency｜宮内庁	wind instrument｜管楽器
function｜儀式、行事	musical accompaniment｜伴奏
state banquet｜（サミットで）各国の来賓をもてなす祝宴、イベント	

⁰⁹ 日本の五音音階

西洋音階（全音階）が「ドレミファソラシ」の7音階なのに対し、**邦楽**ではおもに4種類の5音階が使われています。2音少ないから、限定的な音しか出せない……というわけでなく、音を抑えたり、にじり上げたりして、表情を変えるタイプの音楽[15]なのです。

なかでも多くの日本人にとって一番自然に聞こえるのは、**民謡**によく使われている「民謡音階」（ド、♭ミ、ファ、ソ、♭シ）[16]ですが、じつはこの音階は朝鮮、中央アジア、トルコ、ハンガリーなどの民俗音楽と共通しているそうです。

その他、沖縄の「琉球音階」もアジア各地に広く分布していますし、**雅楽**に使われている「律音階」は中国から入ってきました。こうした共通点から、日本人の音感に、シルクロードの歴史が垣間見えるという人もいます。また、音楽の発展の仕方に、地域を越えた普遍性があるととらえることもできるのです。

『さくらさくら』などの「都節音階（みやこぶし）」は、江戸時代にさかんに使われた音階。私たちにとっては日本情緒を感じさせますが、これはおそらく律音階が変化したもので、インドネシアや韓国にも近いものがあるといいます。

日本が西洋化をめざした明治時代以降は、ドレミファソラシから4番目と7番目を抜いて、日本でなじみやすい五音にした「四七抜き音階（ヨナ）」の曲[17]が作られるようになりました。このヨナ抜きと同じ音階は、世界中でみられます。スコットランド民謡の『蛍の光』は好例ですね。海外でも大ヒットしたポピュラーソング『上を向いて歩こう』も、ヨナ抜き音階をベースにしています。

Notes

※15 音楽学者・小泉文夫によると、歴史上ある時期から「ハーモニー」を切り捨てた音楽なので、そのように発達した（世界の民俗音楽の中で、特別なことではない）。 ※16 「八木節」、「こきりこ節」、「安来節」等の音階。 ※17 長調ドレミソラ／短調ラシドミファ。『あかとんぼ』、『月の砂漠』、『チューリップ』等。

Comment

学生時代、バックパックでヒマラヤを旅していたとき、聞こえてきた祭りの曲が、日本の曲のような懐かしい響きだったんだ。あれは不思議な気分だったな。
When I was a student backpacking in the Himalayas, I heard a festival song that reminded me in the most nostalgic way of a Japanese song. That was a truly weird sensation!

09 Japan's Pentatonic Scales

As opposed to the majority of Western music, which is largely based on seven-pitch scales like the diatonic (do-re-mi) scale, most **hogaku** uses pentatonic (five-pitch) scales, mainly of the four types described below. You might think that lacking the extra two notes would result in a limited sound palette—but actually there is plenty of expressive variation afforded through pitch bending.

The pentatonic scale that sounds most natural to typical Japanese ears is the **minyo** (folk song) scale, made up of the notes do, mi♭, fa, so, si♭ (for example, C-E♭-F-G-B♭). In fact, the same scale is found in folk music in other parts of the world, including Korea, central Asia, Turkey, and Hungary. Another pentatonic scale, the Ryukyu scale of Okinawa, can be heard in much of Asia, while the *ritsu* scale used in **gagaku** originally came from China. Some people see this as evidence that the Japanese sense of pitch can be traced to the Silk Road. Or it may simply point to the universal nature of music's development around the world.

The *miyako-bushi* scale heard in songs like "Sakura, Sakura" was popular during the Edo period. It has a peculiarly Japanese feel, but it's probably a variation of the *ritsu* scale, and similar scales can be found in such places as Indonesia and Korea.

In the Meiji period, when Japan first sought to westernize, composers began to use the *yonanuki* scale, a pentatonic scale easy on the Japanese ear that is produced by removing the fourth (*fa*) and seventh (*si*) notes from the diatonic Western scale. Scales similar to the yonanuki can be found all over the globe—a good example is the famous Scottish song "Auld Lang Syne." The pop tune "**Sukiyaki**," which was a major international hit, is also based on the yonanuki scale.

Vocabulary

as opposed to ... | …に対し
diatonic scale | 全音階 [いわゆる「ドレミファソ ラシ (ド)」のこと]
pentatonic scale | 5 音階
sound palette | 音調の幅

expressive variation | 表現のバリエーション
sense of (musical) pitch | 音感
seek to do | …しようとする [seek の過去形は sought]
westernize | 西洋化する

¹⁰ 日本における西洋クラシック音楽

ポピュラー音楽に比べると、CD を買うようなファンの人口はぐっと少ないものの、西洋クラシック音楽は、多くの日本人にとって意外と耳馴染みがあります。小中学校の音楽の授業で、バッハやモーツァルト、ベートーヴェンの曲を聴きますし、レストランやテレビ番組などの BGM でも、クラシック音楽がよく使われているからです。またピアノは、子どもの習い事としても人気です。

日本には現在、30 ほどのプロ・オーケストラ※18 があります。1980 年代に、大阪のザ・シンフォニーホール、東京のサントリーホールなど、音響のいいクラシック専用ホールが開館してからは、一流の演奏が聴ける環境になりました。海外のオーケストラが来日すると、チケットがとても高くなってしまうのですが……。1997 年には東京に、新国立劇場※19 という初の歌劇場もできました。

また、指揮者の小澤征爾やピアニストの内田光子など、海外で活躍するクラシック演奏家も数多くいます。

Notes

※ 18 ヨーロッパには、歌劇場での活動を主とする専属オーケストラが多数あるが、日本にはない（ホール専属のオーケストラは少数ある）。　※ 19 新国立劇場は、オペラやバレエなども上演可能な複数の舞台をもつ劇場。

Comment

中学生の頃に、『のだめカンタービレ』っていう、主人公がピアニストをめざしている漫画が流行ってね、それからクラシックの CD を、自分で選んで聴くようになったの。
When I was in middle school there was a hit manga, *Nodame Cantabile*, whose heroine was a girl studying to be a concert pianist. Reading it inspired me to go out and pick up my first CD of classical music.

¹¹ 武満徹

20 世紀後半の日本を代表する作曲家（1930〜96）。琵琶、**尺八**とオーケストラを組み合わせた『ノヴェンバー・ステップス』(1967) などの現代音楽で、世界に衝撃を与えました。一方で、**黒澤明**監督の『乱』(1985) をはじめ 100 曲を超える映画音楽、テレビや舞台の音楽など、ジャンルによらない作曲活動を展開しました。

¹⁰ Western Classical Music in Japan

Although the CD-purchasing fan base is far smaller than that of popular music, a surprisingly large number of Japanese are partial to Western classical music. Children listen to the likes of Bach, Mozart, and Beethoven during music classes in elementary school, and classical music often plays in the background at restaurants and on TV shows. Many Japanese children also receive piano lessons. There are currently around 30 professional orchestras in Japan. In the 1980s, with the opening of a number of dedicated classical music venues with superior acoustics, such as The Symphony Hall in Osaka and Suntory Hall in Tokyo, Japanese fans at last had access to environments conducive to listening to top-class performances. However, when overseas orchestras do come to Japan, the tickets are very expensive. In 1997 the country's first opera house opened at the New National Theatre in Tokyo.

Many Japanese classical music performers, including conductor Ozawa Seiji and pianist Uchida Mitsuko, are active on the global stage.

Vocabulary

dedicated ... venue ｜ …専用会場
superior acoustics ｜ すぐれた音響

have access to ... ｜ …を手に入れる
conducive to ... ｜ …に貢献する、…をもたらす

漫画『のだめカンタービレ』23 巻
二ノ宮知子・作（講談社）
The manga *Nodame Cantabile* vol. 23
by Ninomiya Tomoko

¹¹ Takemitsu Toru

One of the leading Japanese composers of the late 20th century, Takemitsu Toru (1930-96) shocked the world with contemporary music like his *November Steps* (1967), a composition for *biwa*, **shakuhachi**, and orchestra. Refusing to restrict himself to any single genre, he wrote music for over 100 movies, television shows, and stage productions, including the score for **Kurosawa Akira**'s film *Ran* (1985).

Vocabulary

contemporary music ｜ 現代音楽

refuse to restrict *oneself* to ... ｜ …内にとどまらない

12 坂本龍一

日本の音楽家。1952 年生まれ。俳優として出演もしている映画『戦場のメリークリスマス』（P. 218 参照）や『ラストエンペラー』のテーマ曲をはじめ、海外では特に映画音楽の作曲家として知られています。しかしその音楽活動の幅は広く、坂本が最初に注目されたのは、1978 年に結成された 3 人組テクノポップ・グループ「イエロー・マジック・オーケストラ（YMO）」の先鋭的な活動でした（キーボード担当）。ポピュラー音楽で活動をスタートしたミュージシャンにはめずらしく、有名な芸術大学の修士課程を修了するというアカデミックな経歴を持つことから、「教授」の愛称でも親しまれています——実際には教授はしていませんが。以降、実験的な電子音楽、民族音楽の要素を取り入れたポップス、オペラなど、ジャンルを超えた作品を発表・演奏・プロデュース。環境・平和活動にも取り組んでいます。

13 上を向いて歩こう（スキヤキ・ソング）

1961 年に坂本九が歌って、世界中で大ヒットした日本のポピュラーソング。作曲は中村八大、作詞は永六輔。アメリカなどでは『スキヤキ』[20] というタイトルで発売されましたが、これは日本料理の名前で、元のタイトルとは関係ありません。オリジナルの歌詞は、ひとりで夜道を歩きながら、こらえる涙がこぼれないように、『上を向いて歩こう』——これが原題——としている歌。現在まで世界各地で、数多くのアーティストに繰り返しカヴァーされてきました。「前を向いて歩こう。涙がこぼれてもいいじゃないか」[21] という替え歌が、私のお気に入りです。

Notes

※ 20 ベルギーやオランダでは『忘れ得ぬ芸者ベイビー』のタイトルで発売された。
※ 21 詞は「寿 [kotobuki]」という 2 人組ミュージシャンのボーカル、ナビィ。

14 演歌

演歌はポピュラー音楽のなかでも、少し昔の「日本の心」とされる情緒を前面に出したジャンルです。演歌歌手は着物を着ていることが多く、歌詞の内容はおもに、悲恋や人生などを歌った切ないものです。「小節」といって一音を高低に揺らす、小唄や民謡のような歌い方に特徴があります。
演歌の音階は、意外に民謡と同じものは少なく、明治時代に使われ始めた

→

¹² Sakamoto Ryuichi

A Japanese musician born in 1952, Sakamoto is perhaps best known overseas for his movie-related compositions, including the theme music for the films *Merry Christmas, Mr. Lawrence* (see p. 219) and *The Last Emperor*, both of which he also appeared in as an actor. But the scope of his musical activity extends much further than that. He first drew attention as a founding member (on keyboards) of the techno-pop trio Yellow Magic Orchestra (YMO), which formed in 1978. Unusual for a musician who launched his career in popular music, Sakamoto graduated from a prestigious arts college with an M.A., a background that earned him the nickname "the professor" (although he has never actually worked as a professor). He has since recorded, performed, and produced music that crosses a spectrum of genres, from experimental electronic music to pop with folk music elements to opera. Sakamoto has also been involved in environmental and peace activities.

Vocabulary

M.A. ｜文学修士［Master of Arts の略］	**experimental** ｜実験的な
cross a spectrum of genres ｜ジャンルをまたぐ	

¹³ "Ue wo Muite Aruko" ("Sukiyaki")

Sung by Sakamoto Kyu in 1961, this Japanese pop tune became a huge international hit. Composed by Nakamura Hachidai with lyrics by Ei Rokusuke, it was released in the U.S. and elsewhere under the title "Sukiyaki"—the name of a Japanese dish that has nothing to do with the song. The lyrics tell of a man who "looks up while walking" (that is the meaning of the Japanese title) alone at night so his tears won't fall. The song has been covered by numerous artists overseas. I personally like the parody whose lyrics go, "Let's look straight ahead while walking. Who cares if our tears fall?"

Vocabulary

be released ｜発売される	**Who cares if ...?** ｜…だとしても関係ない、…でも
under the title ... ｜…というタイトルで	いいじゃないか

¹⁴ Enka

Enka is a genre of Japanese popular music that highlights "traditional Japanese sentiments" of yesteryear. Enka singers usually wear **kimono** and the lyrics lean toward heartbreaking love affairs and hard life

→

ヨナ抜き音階の曲がほとんどだそうです。演歌は伝統的な日本のイメージが強いものの、じつは 1960 年代頃に成立した、比較的新しいジャンルなのです。その当時は、美空ひばりという伝説的な演歌歌手がいました。

現在、演歌ファンは高齢層が中心で、若い人はほとんど演歌を聴かなくなりました。しかし、新しい動きもあります。2008 年、アメリカ人演歌歌手ジェロがデビュー。日本人の祖母をもちアフリカ系でもある彼は、ヒップホップのファッションで、「日本のブルース」と解釈した独特の演歌の世界を切り拓いています。

ところで、日本の演歌は、エチオピアでも聴かれているそうです。ヨナ抜き音階の演歌には、意外と遠い国でも受け入れられる要素があるのでしょうか。

15 J-ポップ

J-ポップは、日本のポピュラー音楽の総称。90 年代頃からの言葉で、**演歌**などを含まず、欧米のロックやポップスの影響が強い音楽に限定して使う場合もあります。

サザンオールスターズ Southern All Stars

日本のポップスは 70 年代頃から、日本語の歌詞のサビの部分などに、英語の歌詞をはさみ込むのが一般的になりました。そして、ダンスや和声、リズム感、バックコーラスなどが欧米のポピュラー音楽のようであっても、じつは日本の**民謡**と同じ**音階**の曲[※22]だったり、歌い方にこぶしが入っていたり（P. 26 参照）、ちょっとした民俗的な要素が感じられるところがあります。外国人にとって、そこは好き嫌いが分かれますね。

代表的なアーティストについては、名前をしぼるのが難しいですが、70 年代から活躍するシンガーソングライターの井上陽水や松任谷由実（彼らの音楽は当時、「ニューミュージック」と呼ばれていました）、「サザンオールスターズ」というバンドの曲のいくつかは、すでに日本のスタンダートになっています。

50 年来、ずっとアメリカやイギリスの音楽シーンを追いかけてきた日本のポップスですが、近年、J-ポップに魅かれて欧米から来日するミュージシャ

experiences. Other characteristics of enka include the *kobushi*, a vibrato-like technique used in **minyo** and other traditional forms of vocal music. Surprisingly, enka rarely employ the minyo **scale**; most of the tunes are based on the yonanuki scale that first came into use in the Meiji period. Although many people regard enka as traditionally Japanese, as a genre it only became established around the 1960s. One of the most renowned traditional enka singers from that period was Misora Hibari.

These days, enka fans tend to be elderly, and few young people listen to songs in this style. However, there have been some intriguing developments lately. In 2008 an African-American enka singer named Jero made his debut. With his hip-hop fashions, Jero, whose grandmother was Japanese, has pioneered a unique new enka look and sound that he describes as "Japanese blues."

Japanese enka reportedly has a following in Ethiopia. Perhaps there is something about enka with its yonanuki scale that helps it catch on in distant countries.

Vocabulary

highlight ... | …を強調する、目立たせる	renowned | 有名な、高名な
regard *A* as *B* | A を B と見なす	intriguing | 興味深い、面白い

[15] **J-Pop**

As a general term for Japanese popular music, "J-pop" has been in use since around the 1990s. Often it refers to music (excluding **enka**) that is strongly influenced by Western rock or pop music.

Since around the 1970s, it has been common to sprinkle English words in Japanese pop lyrics, particularly in the climactic parts. But even if the dancing, harmonies, rhythms, backing vocals and so on resemble those of Western pop, the tunes sometimes contain a taste of native Japanese music as well. A melody may be in the same **scale** as **minyo**, for example, or the singing may feature the kobushi vibrato (or more precisely, melisma) technique. Non-Japanese listeners seem to be divided between those who like these qualities and those who don't.

With so many artists placed in the J-pop category, it's hard to pick a few major standouts. But a list of musicians whose tunes have become Japanese standards would have to include Inoue Yosui and Matsutoya Yumi, both singer-songwriters of the genre then known as "New Music," and the band Southern All Stars—all of them active since the 1970s.

For half a century, Japanese pop has been playing catch-up with the music scene in places like the U.S. and the U.K., but recent years have

➔

ンが出てきました。たとえばアメリカ出身のギタリスト、マーティ・フリードマン（ジャンルはヘヴィーメタル）や、バンド「MONKEY MAJIK」のメンバーでカナダ出身のメイナード・プラント。日本語の歌詞も歌うプラントは、子どもの頃カナダで放送されていた日本のテレビドラマ『西遊記』で、「ゴダイゴ」という日本のバンドが歌うテーマ曲に大きな影響を受けたそうです（その曲のタイトルがバンド名の由来になりました）。

また、バンド「少年ナイフ」や「きゃりーぱみゅぱみゅ」など、海外にファンを増やしている日本のミュージシャンもいます。

Notes

※ 22　キャンディーズの歌った『春一番』(1976)、安室奈美恵の歌った『Sweet 19 Blues』(1996) 等。似ている理由は、20 世紀に欧米のポップスも、アフリカ起源の音階の影響を受けて、民謡音階やヨナ抜き音階と似た 5 音音階が普及したせいという説もある（チャビー・チェッカーの『Let's Twist Again』やザ・ビートルズの『Yellow Submarine』も民謡音階と構成音が同じ）。

16 アイドル

現代の日本で、一般の人の憧れの対象としてプロデュースされる、若手の歌手や俳優は「アイドル」と呼ばれ、自発的な音楽性・メッセージ性の強い「アーティスト」とは、分けてとらえられることがあります。アイドルには爽やかな清潔感が求められ、グループでの活動が多いのも特徴です。

男性アイドルグループの代表は、ジャニーズ事務所という芸能事務所に所属する「SMAP」、「嵐」など。彼らは 10 代の頃にデビューし、30〜40 代になった現在では、メンバーがそれぞれ番組司会やニュースキャスターなどの分野に進出しています。

女性アイドルは、未成熟で「隣の女の子」のような親しみやすいキャラクターが人気です。90 年代デビューの「モーニング娘。」以来、大人数のグループが流行り始め、「AKB48」のメンバーは 48 人以上います（メンバーは時々入れ替わります）。

こうした日本のアイドルは、海外では台湾やシンガポールなど、特にアジア地域にファンを増やしています。

Comment

インドネシアでは、JKT48 っていう、AKB48 の姉妹ユニットが結成されたんだって。AKB は東京の秋葉原から採ったネーミングだから、JKT はジャカルタってことだね。
I hear that in Indonesia, they've formed an AKB sister unit called JKT48. Just as AKB is named after the Akihabara district of Tokyo, JKT stands for Jakarta.

←

seen musicians from Western countries drawn to Japan by a fascination with J-pop, like American heavy-metal guitarist Marty Friedman or Maynard Plant, a member of the Japan-based band Monkey Majik who comes from Canada but sings in Japanese. Plant says he has been strongly influenced by the theme song, performed by the Japanese band Godiego, of the Japanese TV drama *Saiyuki* (*Monkey*), which was broadcast in Canada when he was a child (the theme song, "Monkey Magic," was the inspiration for the band's name). Other Japanese musicians, such as Kyary Pamyu Pamyu and the band Shonen Knife, have won devoted followings overseas.

少年ナイフ Shonen Knife　　Photo: Shibata Akira

Vocabulary

melisma｜メリスマ [1 音節に複数の音符をあてて装飾的に歌うこと]	play catch-up with ...｜…を追いかける
	drawn to ...｜…に魅きつけられた

¹⁶ Idols

In Japan, young singers and actors produced with the aim of winning the adoration of the general public are referred to as "idols," and are regarded as distinct from "artists" who write their own songs or have a more active hand in the creative process. Idols, who frequently perform in groups, are expected to maintain a fresh, unsullied image. Many of the most famous male idol groups, including SMAP and Arashi, are affiliated with the talent agency Johnny & Associates. These groups debuted when their members were in their teens, and now that they are in their thirties or forties they are expanding into such fields as program emceeing and newscasting.

As for female idols, those with innocent, unthreatening "girl-next-door" personalities are the most marketable. Since the 1990s debut of Morning Musume, there has been a boom in girl groups with very large memberships. The mega-popular AKB48 has more than 48 members (from time to time some are replaced). These and other Japanese idols enjoy a growing fan base overseas, especially in other Asian countries like Taiwan and Singapore.

Vocabulary

with the aim of ...｜…という目的で	unthreatening｜圧迫的ではない
unsullied｜汚されていない	mega-popular｜大人気の
be affiliated with ...｜…に所属している	

02

ART
美術

01 日本の美術事情

海外で日本美術といえば、**浮世絵**や屏風絵がまっさきに挙がるイメージで しょう。これらは 19 世紀後半、日本の開国とともに欧米に渡って、フラン スなどでブームになった経緯があります（P. 58 参照）。また当時は、陶磁 器や漆器といった**工芸品**も、各地の万国博覧会で紹介されて、大量に輸出 されました。

一方、日本が西洋の「ファインアート」[1] という概念に出会ったのもその頃 で、これは「美術」[2] という言葉に翻訳されました。

美術の文字通りの意味は、「美と技術」あるいは「美の技術」で、英語の （ファイン）アートとの意味のずれがよく議論になっています。ともあれ、 日本ではそれから「美術」とは何か、また「日本の美術」とは何か、という 問いが始まりました。

江戸時代までの日本では、豪華な絵はおもに権力者に仕える絵師たちが、 ふすまや屏風などに描いていましたが、やがて近代の欧米に倣（なら）って、アー ティストが自発的に絵画や彫刻を創作する「美術」と、食器やインテリア 用品など生活上の用途をもった「工芸」が、ジャンル分かれしていきました。

時代は下って 1960 年代前後、欧米では禅を中心とする第二の日本ブーム が起きます。この時は日本の書やいけばなが、各国の美術の抽象表現と、 互いに影響し合いました（P. 186 参照）。

そうした日本美術のイメージにおさまらないものとしては、たとえば太古の **縄文土器**の、野性的な魅力が認識されてきています。

現代のアーティストには、没後も若い世代に支持される**岡本太郎**、音楽で も有名な**オノ・ヨーコ**、アニメのようなスタイルを用いて、日本美術の理論 化に取り組んできた**村上隆**などがいます。

また、画壇とは無縁のアーティストにも人気者がいて、なかでも 1970 年代 に亡くなった**山下清**は、多くの人に愛されています。

Notes

※1　実用や娯楽を離れて、芸術的価値のみを追求する絵画や彫刻等（建築を含む考え方もある）。現代では、 商業美術（イラストレーション、デザイン等）との区分けが薄れつつある。音楽、詩、演劇、ダンス等、日 本でいう「芸術」を含むこともある。

※2　英語の「fine art」、ドイツ語「Kunstgewerbe」を訳した等の説がある。「fine art」を「純粋美術」と 訳すこともある。

01 Visual Arts in Japan

When people outside of Japan talk about Japanese art, the first images that come to mind are most likely **ukiyo-e** prints and folding-screen paintings. These are the kinds of works that made their way to the West and kindled a boom in France and elsewhere when Japan re-opened its doors to trade in the second half of the 19th century. Pottery, lacquerware, and other **crafts** also found favor at international expositions and were exported in great quantities.

It was around this same time that Japan encountered the Western concept of "fine art," translated into Japanese as *bijutsu*. The word can be parsed as either "beauty and technique" or "the technique of beauty"; in any case art critics for some time have debated the degree to which its meaning diverges from that of "(fine) art." From the outset, questions have arisen over just what *bijutsu*—and Japanese *bijutsu* in particular—really is.

Until the end of the Edo period (1603-1868), artists working mostly under hire to powerful personages created resplendent paintings on folding screens or sliding doors. But in the Meiji era (1868-1912), Japan began to follow the lead of the modern Western art world in distinguishing between "art"—painting, sculpture, and so on, spontaneously created by the artist—on the one hand, and "crafts" with practical functions—dishes, furnishings, and the like—on the other.

Nearly a century later, a second "Japan boom," primarily **Zen**-inspired, occurred in the West around the 1960s. This time such arts as **calligraphy** and **ikebana** began to influence, and be influenced by, abstract art forms in other countries (see p. 187).

Japan is also home to creative works that do not fit the prevailing image of Japanese art. Ancient **Jomon pottery**, for example, has a wild, powerful appeal that attracts enthusiasts on its own terms.

Amid the ranks of contemporary artists, the late **Okamoto Taro** remains a hero to many younger Japanese. **Ono Yoko** is known for her music as well as her art, and **Murakami Takashi**, who employs an anime-like style in his work, has developed his own maverick theory of Japanese aesthetics. Some outsider artists with few if any ties to the established art world have also earned recognition, such as **Yamashita Kiyoshi**, who died in the 1970s but is still a beloved figure today.

Vocabulary

folding-screen painting ｜屏風絵	resplendent ｜華麗な、まばゆい
kindle a boom ｜ブームを起こす	abstract art ｜抽象美術
lacquerware ｜漆器	prevailing ｜支配的な、一般的な
be parsed as ... ｜（文法的に）…と説明される	on *one's* own terms ｜独自に、そのもので

02 浮世絵

「浮世絵」は江戸時代[3]のイラストレーション。肉筆画もありますが、量産されたカラフルな木版画（錦絵）が、浮世絵の代名詞になっています。

江戸時代の浮世絵版画は、今でいう雑誌や新聞のようなもので、美人画や人気歌舞伎役者の肖像、名所風景、春画など、世相を反映するさまざまなモチーフが描かれました。

19世紀後半の欧米で人気を得て、浮世絵は日本美術の代表格になりました（P. 58参照）。最初は陶磁器（P. 42参照）の包み紙として渡ったものが、フランスである画家の目にとまり、評判になったといわれています。彩色が鮮やか[4]で、彫りの精巧な木版画を、彼らは見たことがなかったのです[5]。

欧米で主流だった写実的な絵と違って、浮世絵の人や物は平面的に描かれていますが、風景画には、西洋の影響と考えられる遠近法がみられます。近世の庶民生活がいきいきと記録されている点も、今日では浮世絵の価値を高めています。

葛飾北斎（1760〜1849）は、大胆な構図や色使いで、特に評価の高い浮世絵師です。ほかには、歌川廣重、喜多川歌麿、東洲斎写楽などの絵師がよく知られています。

Notes

※3 明治時代にも、文明開化の様子等が描かれた。　※4 退色しやすく、ボストン美術館にある非公開のスポルディング・コレクション等をのぞき、当時の色が残っているものは稀。　※5 ヨーロッパでは15世紀以降、銅版画が普及。　※6 富士山が見える風景のシリーズ『富嶽三十六景』(36 Views of Mount Fuji) のうち、大波の間に富士を望む『神奈川沖浪裏』(The Great Wave off Kanagawa)。

Comment

ハワイに行ったとき、「北斎は、大波の絵（図版 P. 59）をハワイに来て描いた[6]」と言う人がいました。荒唐無稽に思えましたが、そんな話が生まれるくらい、彼の絵が親しまれているんですね。だけど北斎自身は、世界的スターになるとは知らずに亡くなっているんですよ。

When I visited Hawaii, someone told me, "Hokusai came here to paint his picture of the big wave." Though the claim sounded like nonsense, it did show just how familiar people outside of Japan are with his work. However, Hokusai himself died without knowing that he was on his way to world stardom.

03 光琳と若冲

18世紀頃の古都・京都は、とても創造的な場だったようで、数々の優れた絵師を輩出しています。

もっとも有名なのは尾形光琳（1658〜1716）。富裕な町人などを顧客に、洗練されたさまざまな調度品をプロデュースしました。なかでも『燕子花

→

02 Ukiyo-e

Literally "pictures of the floating world," ukiyo-e are illustrations produced during the Edo period. Although some ukiyo-e were painted, the term has become synonymous with the colorful, mass-produced woodblock prints called *nishiki-e*.

Ukiyo-e prints were the magazines or newspapers of their day, covering current topics and trends. The motifs ranged from portraits of beautiful women and **Kabuki** actors to views of famous places and the erotica known as *shunga*.

Owing to the acclaim it received in the West during the latter half of the 19th century, ukiyo-e came to be recognized as one of the leading genres of Japanese art. Legend has it that the prints first caught the eye of a French painter when they were used as wrapping paper for ceramics (see p. 43) imported from Japan. People in Europe had never seen woodcuts with such brilliant colors and precise workmanship.

In contrast to the realistic style of most Western art at the time, ukiyo-e portrayed human figures and objects in a flat plane. Landscapes, however, showed some evidence of Western influence in their use of perspective. These days ukiyo-e are also prized as a vivid record of the lives of ordinary people in early-modern Japan.

A standout among ukiyo-e artists is Katsushika Hokusai (1760-1849), revered for his bold compositions and colors. Other masters include Utagawa Hiroshige, Kitagawa Utamaro, and Toshusai Sharaku.

Vocabulary

become synonymous with ... | …と同義語になる	perspective | 遠近法
woodblock print | 木版画	standout | 傑出した人物
acclaim | 称賛、喝采	revered for ... | …で評価が高い
woodcut | 木版（画）	bold composition | 大胆な構図、構成

03 Korin and Jakuchu

Eighteenth-century Kyoto appears to have been a fertile environment for creativity, as it spawned a good number of exceptional painters.

The most celebrated of these was Ogata Korin (1658-1716), who painted or produced all manner of sophisticated decorative furnishings, mainly for wealthy merchants. *Irises* and *Red and White Plum Blossoms* (image on p. 39), both gorgeous screen paintings on gold backgrounds, are two of his most admired works.

Paintings on folding screens were a format imported from China, but in Japanese hands they evolved from single-screen compositions into huge

➔

←
図』、『紅白梅図』（写真／右）といった、ゴージャスで装飾的な金地の屏風絵は、よく知られています。

屏風絵は中国から伝わったものですが、日本では一枚ごとの縁をなくし、大画面に絵を描くようになりました。光琳が影響を受けた俵屋宗達（生没年不明、16〜17世紀）[7]の『風神雷神図』という屏風絵も、日本人なら誰でも目にしたことがある名画で、光琳をはじめ、多くの絵師が模写しています。

一方、光琳が没した年に生まれた伊藤若冲（1716〜1800）は、近代以降あまり顧みられていませんでしたが、最近、「奇想の画家」として再評価ブームが起こっています。彼は40歳のときに、青物問屋の主人から転向した、無派の画家です。動植物を細密に、幻想を織り混ぜて描いた『動植綵絵』や『樹花鳥獣図屏風』が代表的な作品です。

Notes

---

[7] 書や陶芸で有名な本阿弥光悦（1558〜1637）や上記の宗達、光琳から影響を受けた江戸時代の酒井抱一等、同傾向の造形表現をする者が、今では合わせて「琳派」と呼ばれている（徒弟関係はない）。

04 日本画

「日本画」[8]は、伝統絵画の流れをくむ絵画のジャンルで、岩絵の具（顔料）や膠などを使って、おもに和紙や絹に描きます。天然の岩絵の具には、孔雀石、ラピスラズリをくだいた高価なものもありますが、20世紀後半からは、粉末ガラスの「新岩絵の具」が普及しました。

日本画の源流は、10世紀頃に起こった「大和絵」にさかのぼります。これは中国伝来の「唐絵」が日本流に発展したもので、屏風や襖の大画面に、四季の花鳥などが描かれました。また12世紀には、大和絵のスタイルによる『源氏物語絵巻』（図版 P. 90）など、絵巻物[9]の名作が生まれました。

その後の日本には、長く土佐派、狩野派、**浮世絵**の各派など、顧客の身分ごとに分かれた絵の流派がありました。なかでも狩野派は、武家に仕えて15〜19世紀の約400年間、絶大な勢力をふるった絵師の集団です。

現在の日本画[10]というジャンルが誕生したのは、近代になってからのこと[11]。西洋の油絵が「洋画」といわれて、日本で本格的に描かれるようになる[12]と、すたれつつある伝統技法を生かした絵画が、「日本画」と呼ばれるようになったのです。そして日本画は、西洋式に額に入れて飾られるようになりました。

→

←

multi-panel displays. Korin was much influenced by Tawaraya Sotatsu, a 16th-to-17th century painter whose *Wind God and Thunder God*, a folding-screen tour-de-force familiar to every Japanese, was replicated by Korin and many other artists.

Born in the same year that Korin died, Ito Jakuchu (1716-1800) suffered neglect for much of the modern era, but in recent years he has come back into fashion as a "painter of outrageous fancies." Unaffiliated with any school, Jakuchu quit his job as a grocery wholesaler at age 40 to devote himself to art. Such works as *Colorful Realm of Living Beings* and *Birds and Animals in the Flower Garden* blend meticulous renderings of plants and animals with Jakuchu's unique flights of imagination.

Vocabulary

fertile environment｜作品をたくさん生み出す環境	be replicated by ...｜…に模写される
spawn ...｜…を生む	suffer neglect｜軽視される
all manner of ...｜あらゆる種類の…	unaffiliated with ...｜…に属さない
evolve from ...｜…から発展する	meticulous rendering｜細部にまで注意を払った
tour-de-force｜傑作、力作［フランス語］	表現

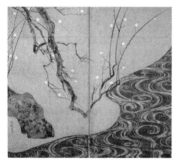 

⁰⁴ Nihonga

Nihonga (literally "Japanese painting") is a term for art that utilizes the materials and techniques of traditional painting in Japan. Nihonga are usually painted on washi paper or silk using pigments mixed with a glue binder. Traditionally these were natural mineral pigments, including expensive items like crushed malachite and lapis lazuli, but the latter part of the 20th century saw the increased use of synthetic pigments made of powdered glass.

The Nihonga style has its origins in *Yamato-e* (a more archaic term for "Japanese painting"), a genre inspired by Chinese painting that first appeared around the 10th century. Yamato-e typically depicted flowers, birds, and other natural motifs through the four seasons in large compositions on

→

当時の日本画は、花鳥風月や美人が代表的なモチーフで、輪郭線があって陰のない平面的な描き方が特徴でした。しかし現代の日本画には、写実画も抽象画もあり、ジャンルとしての特色が薄れてきています。

Notes

※8 広義には江戸以前の絵画も日本画というが、「日本絵画」等と区別することが多い。　※9 絵巻物は東アジアで多く作られた。　※10 代表的な日本画家は、横山大観、田中一村、平山郁夫 等。　※11 日本画の成立には、美術史家のフェノロサや岡倉天心が寄与した。二人は後に、米ボストン美術館で日本美術を紹介。天心は『The Book of Tea（茶の本）』等の著作でも知られる。　※12 江戸時代にも蘭画として油絵が描かれていた。

05 水墨画

墨※13 一色の濃淡で、筆を使って和紙に描く絵を「水墨画」（または墨絵）といいます。13 世紀頃、禅を通じて中国から伝わりました。

一方、墨で文字を書く芸術は「書」といいますが、東アジアには「書画」という言葉があって、書と絵画はもともと同じジャンルでした。ひとつの画面に書と画が両方入っていることもあり、14 世紀頃の禅寺では、絵の上部に漢詩を寄せ書きすることが流行しました。

室町時代の禅僧・雪舟（1420〜1506）は、水墨画の巨匠として知られています。中国で学んだ雪舟は、やがて独自の水墨表現を展開し、後の日本画壇に大きな影響を与えました。

Notes

※13 墨は中国発祥。すす、にかわ、香料を練って固形の墨（inkstick）をつくる。すずりの上で水と合わせてすった黒い液も墨という。　※14 中国の謝赫（5 世紀前後）は、画論書『古画品録』において、絵画に必要な 6 つの要旨を提示した。その最初に挙げられた「気韻生動（qiyun shengdong）」は、絵画の生命感や迫力、あるいは人々を感動させる力を指すと考えられる。

Comment

雪舟といえば、子どもの頃から絵が好きで、描いたねずみが「本物と見間違えられた」という逸話があります。日本には、「絵には生命観が宿っていないといけない」といった考え方があるように思いますね※14。いや、これは世界に共通する絵の見方でしょうか？

Speaking of Sesshu, the story goes that he loved drawing pictures even as a child, and once produced a mouse so lifelike it was mistaken for the real thing. Japanese people seem to feel that "a painting must be imbued with life." Perhaps this is something everybody around the world can agree on?

←

folding screens or sliding doors (see p. 283). The 12th century saw the emergence of masterpieces in the Yamato-e style painted on horizontal picture scrolls, such as the *Illustrated Handscroll of **The Tale of Genji***.

For some centuries afterward, Japanese painting was divided into various schools—Tosa, Kano, and those of the **ukiyo-e** world being the most noteworthy—that differed from one another in the relative social status of their patrons. Of these, the Kano School, which benefited from the patronage of the samurai class, held sway among painters for some 400 years, from the 15th to the 19th century.

The category of Nihonga is actually a product of the modern era. As Japanese artists began fully adopting Western oil painting techniques, the word was coined to identify "Japanese-style paintings" employing the traditional methods that had fallen out of fashion, and to contrast them with *Yoga* or "Western-style paintings." Eventually Nihonga, too, came to be framed and hung on walls in the Western manner.

The early Nihonga of the Meiji period commonly portrayed natural motifs or beautiful women in a flat, unshaded style with distinct outlines. Contemporary Nihonga, however, include realist and abstract works, and the definition of the term has grown somewhat ambiguous.

Vocabulary

pigment｜顔料
glue binder｜膠等の接着剤
malachite｜孔雀石［鉱物］
synthetic｜合成の

hold sway｜権勢をふるう
be coined｜新たに作られる
eventually｜最後には、ついには
ambiguous｜あいまいな

⁰⁵ Sumi-e

Sumi-e, also called *suiboku-ga*, are monochrome brush paintings in black *sumi* ink of varying shades on washi paper. The art was introduced to Japan from China, along with **Zen** Buddhism, around the 13th century.

Sumi ink is also used for calligraphy, or ***sho***, and as the word *sho-ga* ("calligraphy and painting") suggests, these modes of expression were originally treated as one art form in East Asia. A single painting might contain both text and imagery. At Zen temples in the 14th century it was the fashion to add some lines of Chinese poetry at the top of a sumi painting.

The Muromachi-era Zen monk Sesshu (1420-1506) is a giant among sumi painters. After studying the art in China, he developed a distinctive style that significantly influenced Japanese art to come.

Vocabulary

brush painting｜筆を使って描く画

significantly｜非常に

06 床の間と掛軸

床の間（床(とこ)）とは、**茶室**など畳の部屋の一角を柱や壁で区切って、掛軸や花（P. 190 参照）、置物などを展示するコーナーです。床の間[15] の起源は諸説ありますが、神聖な場所という雰囲気をもっています。

掛軸（掛物）は、書画を高級な布や紙の上に貼って仕立てたもので、中国の発祥といわれています。丸めて保管や持ち運びができ、茶事（P. 188 参照）を行うときなどは、季節やテーマに合わせて取り替えます[16]。

Notes

※ 15 「間（ま）」は部屋や仕切られた空間の他、はっきり仕切りのないへだたり、あいだの空間や時間も意味するが、海外では美術作品の余白等について、日本語から採った「ma」と説明されることがある。

※ 16 昨今は、従来の様式を離れた、壁飾りとして使える掛軸も工夫されている。

『楼閣山水蒔絵水注』（17～18 世紀）。マリー・アントワネットのコレクションと同系統の規格。
Pair of Ewers with Pavilions in Landscape (17th-18th c.), maki-e ornamentation, same style as a pair in the Marie Antoinette collection
Kyoto National Museum Collection

07 工芸

漆器、陶磁器、染織、刀剣などの精巧な技術を誇る日本の工芸品は、早くから海外でコレクションの対象になってきました。

漆器は、漆の木の樹液で木製品などを塗装したもので、艶があり、数千年[17] もつほど丈夫になります。アジア各地で同様のものがみられますが、樹液の種類が違うと特質も変わります。黒や朱色の漆器に、金粉で模様を描く「蒔絵」は、日本独自の技法です。

大航海時代の 17～18 世紀には、漆器が「ジャパン」と呼ばれるほど、大量に欧米に輸出されました。マリー・アントワネットの蒔絵コレクションなど、当時の高級調度品が各地に残されています。その後、19 世紀のジャポニスムの時代にも、蒔絵人気が再燃しました。

一方、陶磁器では、やはり 17 世紀から輸出が始まった伊万里（有田焼）と

→

06 Tokonoma and Kakejiku

The *tokonoma* is an alcove or corner of a **tearoom** or other tatami-floored room, separated from the rest of the room by a pillar or wall, in which scrolls, flowers (see p. 191), and other artistic objects are displayed. There are a number of theories about the origins of the tokonoma, but it retains the air of a sacred space.

The *kakejiku* hanging scroll that graces a tokonoma features a painting or calligraphic work mounted on high-quality cloth or paper. Originating in China, the kakejiku is a convenient display medium that can be rolled up for storage or transport. The scroll hung in a tokonoma may be replaced on such occasions as tea ceremonies (see p. 189) to evoke different seasons or themes.

Vocabulary

(hanging) scroll ｜掛軸	storage ｜保管
grace ... ｜…を美しく飾る	evoke ... ｜…を呼び起こす

07 Crafts

Japan is justly proud of the exquisite workmanship that goes into its crafts—notably lacquerware, ceramics, dyeing, weaving, and swordmaking. The country's handicrafts have long been coveted by collectors overseas.

Applied to wood, the sap of the lacquer tree imparts a soft sheen while acting as a preservative that has enabled Japanese lacquerware to last for thousands of years. Though similar lacquers are used throughout Asia, their properties vary with the type of tree. Japan's lacquerware, or *shikki*, is renowned for original techniques like *maki-e*, decorative patterns made with gold powder sprinkled on a jet black or deep vermilion background.

During the Age of Discovery of the 17th and 18th centuries, Japan exported lacquerware to the West in such quantities that the work acquired the name "japan." Some of the most sublime lacquerwork of the day can be found overseas, Marie Antoinette's collection of maki-e being a legendary example. Maki-e enjoyed a resurgence of popularity during the Japonisme boom of the 19th century.

In the realm of Japanese ceramics, the highest name recognition abroad surely belongs to Imari porcelain (also called Arita ware), exports of which began in the 17th century. Early pieces featured images painted in blue on a white background, but eventually Imari became associated with colorful pictures with red and gold highlights.

Japan boasts over 100 centers of ceramics production, each with its

→

いう磁器[18] が有名です。伊万里といえば、初期のものは白地に青一色でしたが、やがて赤や金を配した豪華な絵が付けられるようになりました。

ほかにも日本には、陶磁器の産地が 100 以上あり、それぞれに特色が異なります。たとえば千年ほどの歴史をもつ備前焼は、釉薬（ゆうやく）を使わず、褐色の土の持ち味をそのまま生かした陶器[19] です。

Notes

※ 17 世界最古の漆器は、日本の縄文時代約 9000 年前のもの。日本・中国産漆樹の主成分はウルシオール（urushiol）。漆には防虫効果や耐熱性もある（P. 232 参照）。紫外線には弱い。また乾く前はかぶれやすい。
※ 18 江戸時代におもに有田で作られて、伊万里港で積み出された磁器のこと。国内では現在、「古伊万里」と呼ばれている。近代以降は、焼き物を産地名で呼ぶのが一般的になったので、有田で焼かれる磁器は有田焼と呼ばれるようになった。　※ 19 備前焼は、陶器と磁器の中間的な炻器（せっき／ stoneware）にも分類される。

Comment

現代アートの作家は、作品ごとに素材を変えることもありますが、工芸作家は、陶なら陶の素材と技法にこだわります。ある若い陶芸作家の作品は、一見、斬新なデザインに見えて、じつは江戸時代以来失われていた高度な技法を、掘り起こしたんだそうです。
Whereas contemporary artists may readily switch between materials for different works, craft artists are particular about the materials and techniques they use. I've seen work by one young potter who appears be experimenting with innovative designs when in fact he is reviving classic techniques that fell out of use back in the Edo period.

08 民芸

1920 年代に起こった民芸運動[20] とは、民衆の手仕事による日用品を「民芸」と名付けて、そのなかに「用の美」を見いだそうとする運動です。

作家の手による鑑賞のための**工芸**品でもなく、また大量生産の工業製品にも押されて時代遅れになりつつあった雑器に、思想家の柳宗悦（そうえつ／むねよし）らが新たな価値づけをして、今までにない使い方や、新しいデザインをプロデュースしたのです。

民芸運動は、**茶道**（わび茶）において日用雑貨を茶道具に転用する「見立て」の精神や、また 19 世紀イギリスのウィリアム・モリスらが推進した、アーツ・アンド・クラフツ運動[21] とも通じるところがあります。

時を経るにつれ、「民芸品」といえば地方の素朴なみやげものというイメージになりましたが、近年、もとの思想性が見直されつつあります。

Notes

※ 20 民芸運動には、イギリスの陶芸家、バーナード・リーチも参加。米のサンディエゴには、「Mingei International Museum」という、世界の民芸品を集めた博物館がある。　※ 21 近代以前の手仕事に立ち返り、生活と芸術を一致させようとする運動。

←

own characteristics. High-fired Bizen stoneware, which dates back a thousand years, uses no glazes and gives pride of place to the rustic beauty of its red-brown clay.

Vocabulary

dyeing ｜染め物	become associated with ... ｜…と結び付けられるようになる
sheen ｜艶	
preservative ｜防腐剤	boast ... ｜…をもっている、誇る
sublime ｜卓越した、崇高な	glaze ｜釉薬
resurgence ｜復活、再生	give pride of place to ... ｜…を優先する

08 Mingei

The Mingei movement of the 1920s sought to showcase the "beauty of use" found in everyday utilitarian objects handmade by ordinary people. *Mingei*, meaning "folk arts," was a word coined to describe such works.

Philosopher Yanagi Soetsu and his colleagues called for a reappraisal of **handicrafts** that were not made by artists purely for appreciation, and that were on the verge of being rendered obsolete and replaced by mass-produced industrial goods. They actively promoted new uses and designs for these objects.

The Mingei movement resonates with other traditions ranging from the **sado** practice of putting everyday utensils to novel uses in the tea ceremony, to the Arts and Crafts movement led by William Morris and others in 19th-century England.

Over time the term "mingei" has come to conjure up images of unsophisticated craft items sold in regional souvenir shops, but recent years have seen a renewed interest in the philosophical underpinnings of the original movement.

Vocabulary

seek to *do* ｜…しようとする［過去形 sought］	resonate with ... ｜…と共鳴する
showcase ... ｜…を紹介する、展示する	conjure up ... ｜…を思い起こさせる
utilitarian ｜実用的な	underpinnings ｜（物事の）基礎、土台［通例複数形］
on the verge of ... ｜…の寸前で	

09 藤田嗣治（レオナール・フジタ）

藤田嗣治（1886〜1968）[22] は、20世紀前半のパリ[23] で大きな人気を集めた画家です。油絵を描くのに日本の細い面相筆や墨を使い、猫と女性が得意なモチーフ。裸婦像にみられる「乳白色の肌」が、人々を魅了しました。第二次世界大戦時は日本に戻り、陸軍から要請された戦争画の仕事に打ち込みました。パリでの優美な画風からは想像できないような、生々しい戦闘場面を描いた『アッツ島玉砕』などの大作が残されています。そして敗戦後には一転して、戦争協力の責任を問われることになります。

晩年は第二の故郷であるパリに向かい、フランスに帰化して、カトリックの洗礼を受けました。

Notes

※22 初期には Tsuguji のサインもあったが、後期は Tsuguharu。洗礼名はレオナール。
※23 当時のパリには世界各地から画家が集まり、エコール・ド・パリ（パリ派）と呼ばれた。

Comment

嗣治の戦争画は、戦意高揚を目的に描かれたはずですが、多様な受け止め方をされています。有名なアッツ島の絵には小花が描きこまれていて、「戦場の悲惨さを伝える反戦画ではないか？」という人さえいるようです。

Fujita's battle paintings were ostensibly intended to promote Japan's war effort, but they have provoked diverse reactions. Some people have even suggested that *Final Fighting on Attu*, in which tiny flowers appear here and there, is really an antiwar work through which Fujita tried to convey the horrors of the battlefield.

10 岡本太郎「芸術は爆発だ！」

絵画や彫刻、文筆など、多方面で活躍した岡本太郎（1911〜96）は、戦後日本における芸術家のアイコンでした。80年代のテレビCMで、カメラに向かって発した「芸術は爆発だ！」という宣言が、そのまま彼のキャッチフレーズになっています。テレビというメディアにいち早く馴染んだことで、晩年はむしろ軽薄に見られていましたが、没後にその先見性などが見直され、岡本太郎ブームが再燃しました。

19歳でパリに留学し、最先端のフランス思想や芸術運動のただ中で青年時代を過ごした彼は、戦後、兵役から戻ると、「右に倣

→

09 Fujita Tsuguharu (Léonard Foujita)

Fujita Tsuguharu (1886-1968) was a Japanese painter who made a name for himself in early 20th-century Paris. An innovator who painted oils using Japanese materials such as sumi ink and extremely fine brushes, he had a penchant for portraying cats and women. Many art aficionados were captivated by the "milk-white skin" of his nudes.

Fujita returned to Japan as World War II was starting, and spent the war years painting battle pictures commissioned by the army. Several large works survive—the most notable being *Final Fighting on Attu*—that graphically depict combat at its cruelest. It is hard to believe they are by the same person who produced such genteel art in Paris.

After Japan's defeat, Fujita's fortunes underwent a reversal when he was accused of active complicity in the war effort. In his later years he moved permanently back to France, took French citizenship, converted to Catholicism, and adopted the name Léonard.

Vocabulary

have a penchant for …	…しがちである	complicity	共犯の
aficionado	ファン、愛好者［スペイン語］	convert to …	…に改宗する
commissioned by …	…に依頼された	adopt …	…を選ぶ
genteel	上品な、優雅な	ostensibly	表向きは、見かけは

10 Okamoto Taro: "Art Is an Explosion!"

An artistic icon of postwar Japan, Okamoto Taro (1911-96) was a genre-straddling personality—a painter, sculptor, writer, and more. In the 1980s, "Art is an explosion!" became an enduring catchphrase associated with his name after he uttered it on-camera in a TV commercial. His comfort with television as an expressive medium earned him a reputation for flippancy later in life, but his foresight won praise after his death, when a "Taro boom" triggered a reevaluation of his thought and character.

Okamoto traveled to Paris as a student at age 19, and spent much of his twenties in the vortex of France's avant-garde philosophical and artistic movements. Upon being discharged from the army after World War II he became a provocateur against conformism in Japanese society. Having studied with Marcel Mauss, the "father" of modern French ethnology, he did field research on indigenous cultures in different regions of Japan—notably Okinawa and Tohoku—and came to be regarded as the earliest champion of the aesthetics of ancient **Jomon pottery**.

At Expo '70, a world's fair held in Osaka, he unveiled *Tower of the Sun* (image at left), a 70-meter-tall sculpture whose primitive appearance seemed

→

え」式の日本社会に挑みかかるような芸術・言論活動を展開しました。また、「フランス近代民族学の父」といわれるマルセル・モースに学んだ造詣を生かして、沖縄、東北など列島各地の土着文化をフィールドワーク。**縄文土器**の美を提唱した功績も特筆されます。

1970年の大阪万博では、「人類の進歩と調和」という万博のテーマに対抗するかのように、原始的にも見える高さ70メートルの『太陽の塔』（写真 P. 46）を登場させました。

11 縄文土器と土偶

縄文土器は、世界最古の土器のひとつで、約1万6000年〜2800年前に作られていました。表面に縄を押しつけたり、ころがしたりして付けた文様があることから、その名が付きました。「火焔型（かえん）」という炎が燃えさかるような、ダイナミックな形のものもあります。

かつて縄文土器は、野蛮でグロテスクなイメージが持たれていて、考古学の世界で発見されていても、美術品としては扱われていませんでした。しかし**岡本太郎**がその魅力を語ったのをきっかけに、今では日本美術史の最初のページを飾るようになりました。

その後の日本美術は、中国や西洋の影響を受けたものとなりましたが、この原初の土器は、世界中どこにもない形をしています。

縄文時代にはまた、土偶といわれる、極端にデフォルメされた土の人体像[24]も作られました。巨大な尻や、ゴーグルのような目をした像が有名で、モダンな抽象彫刻のようにもみえます。

土偶が作られた目的には諸説あって、神像や護符[25]、豊穣や多産を祈るためのもの、あるいは地球にやってきた宇宙人の像だという人もいます。

Notes

[24] 同じく土の人体像の「埴輪」は、強大な権力者が現れた古墳時代（3世紀後半〜7世紀頃）のもので、おもに筒状のシンプルな形をしている。古墳（大きな墓）の上に並べられた。　[25] 厄除けやお守り等。

Comment

前から思っている説だけど、火焔型土器の形は、火山の噴火や溶岩流を表しているんじゃないかな。当時は火山噴火がひんぱんに起こっていたそうだから、天地を揺るがす一大事として、表現したかったと思う。

I have my own pet theory about the "flames" on *kaen* Jomon ware: I'll bet they represent volcanic eruptions and lava flows. The Jomon was a period of intense volcanic activity, so it makes sense that people back then would want to depict these dramatic, truly earth-shaking events.

Photos courtesy of Institute of Esthetic Research (pp. 46, 49)

←

a rebuttal to the fair's slogan of "Progress and Harmony for Mankind."

Vocabulary

genre-straddling｜ジャンルを超えた	provocateur｜挑発者、工作員［フランス語］
flippancy｜軽薄、ふまじめ	conformism｜順応主義、画一主義
the vortex of ...｜(大きな出来事など) …の渦	unveil ...｜…を披露する
be discharged from the army｜除隊になる	rebuttal｜反論、反ばく

¹¹ Jomon Pottery and Dogu

Dating back anywhere from 2,800 to 16,000 years ago, Jomon-era earthenware is counted among the oldest pottery in the world. The name *Jomon*, meaning "cord-patterned," refers to the patterns typically inscribed on the surface by pressing or rolling rope into the clay. But the most memorable Jomon ware is the *kaen* type, with what appear to be roaring flames erupting from the vessels.

Jomon pottery was once thought to look primitive and even grotesque; though an object of archeological interest, it was not appreciated for its artistic value. Thanks in no small part to **Okamoto Taro**'s paeans to their beauty, however, Jomon works now grace the opening pages of any history of Japanese art. While the art of subsequent eras reflected the influence of China or the West, these earliest ceramics bear designs not found anywhere else in the world.

岡本太郎の撮影による縄文土器
Jomon pottery photo by Okamoto

Another hallmark of the Jomon era is the *dogu*. These extremely deformed human figures, made of clay, are known for their exaggerated hips and goggle-like eyes. Indeed, they bear an uncanny resemblance to modern abstract sculpture.

Theories abound as to the original function of the dogu. They may have been images of gods, or talismans to ward off evil or illness, or figurines used in rituals to ensure good harvests or fertility. And then there are those who believe they are effigies of visiting space aliens.

Vocabulary

inscribed on ...｜…に刻みつけられた	uncanny｜不可思議な
erupting from ...｜…から噴出している	theories abound as to ...｜…については諸説ある
paean｜賛辞	talisman｜お守り
exaggerated｜強調された	ward off ...｜…を避ける、かわす
bear a resemblance to ...｜…と似ている	effigy｜肖像

12 裸の大将・山下清

山下清（1922～71）は、知的障害児として入園した養護施設で、貼り絵（ちぎり絵）を習いました。彼の作品が放つ異彩は、やがて大人たちを驚かせるようになります。

18歳から日本各地を放浪し、施設や実家に戻っては、旅先の風景を貼り絵にしました。なかでも『長岡の花火』をはじめとする、大好きな花火を描いた作品群が有名です。

いがぐり頭にランニングシャツ、半ズボンといういでたちがトレードマークで、「裸の大将」の愛称で親しまれました。彼の旅行記をもとにして、虚像をまじえた「裸の大将放浪記」というテレビドラマが、80年代から17年にわたって放送されていました。

13 前衛から現代アートへ

日本の前衛美術は、西洋のダダイズムなどの影響から1910年代に始まり、第二次世界大戦後の50～70年代[26]に盛り上がりをみせます。

身体を使った実験的なパフォーマンスや、空間全体を作品とするインスタレーションなど、新しい美術の形態が登場。思想的には反近代志向が生まれ、そこから仏教などの、東洋回帰に向かうアーティストも少なからずいました。またこの時期、いけばなや書などの伝統的な芸術も、前衛美術と共鳴しました。当時から活躍しているアーティストには、オノ・ヨーコ、草間彌生、横尾忠則などがいます（2014年に亡くなった赤瀬川原平も、特筆すべき存在です）。

70年代以降、最先端の美術活動は多様化していき、「前衛」に代わって、「現代美術」と呼ばれるようになりました。90年代頃からは、より軽く柔軟なイメージのある「現代アート」という言葉も使われています。また、地域おこしとアートを結び付けたプロジェクトが、各地で開催されるようになりました。

現在、評価の高いアーティストは、村上隆、奈良美智、会田誠など。また、若手ユニットの「Chim↑Pom」は、社会問題とゲリラ的にかかわる、体を張ったアート活動で物議を醸しています。

Notes

[26] 「具体」や「もの派」の活動は、海外の美術界でも知られている。

¹² Yamashita Kiyoshi, the Naked General

As a child, Yamashita Kiyoshi (1922-71) was placed in an institution for the mentally handicapped, where he learned to make *hari-e*—pictures made of torn, multicolored bits of paper. Strikingly original and bursting with life, Yamashita's work astonished the adults who saw it. When he turned 18 he began wandering around Japan on his own, periodically returning to the institution or his home, where he would create hari-e from memories of the scenes he encountered during his travels. Many of his best-known pictures, typified by *Fireworks in Nagaoka*, testify to his love of firework displays.

An instantly recognizable figure with his close-cropped head and trademark attire of a running shirt and shorts, Yamashita acquired the affectionate nickname "The Naked General." A dramatic TV series by that title, based on his travel diaries but partially fictionalized, ran for 17 years in the 1980s and 1990s.

Vocabulary

bursting with life	非常に生き生きとした	close-cropped head	坊主頭

¹³ From Avant-Garde to Contemporary Art

Inspired by such Western movements as Dadaism, avant-garde art first emerged in Japan in the 1910s. It reached its pinnacle in the postwar decades of the 1950s through the 1970s, when new art forms—experimental performances, installations filling entire exhibit spaces, and so forth—came into vogue.

Not a few artists during this period adopted an anti-modernist stance that drew them to **Buddhism** and other elements of an Eastern-oriented revival. Traditional arts like **ikebana** and **calligraphy** also resonated with the avant-garde impulse. Some avant-gardists who remain active to this day are **Ono Yoko**, Kusama Yayoi, and Yokoo Tadanori (also deserving special mention is Akasegawa Genpei, who passed away in 2014).

From the 1970s on, cutting-edge art began to diversify, and the term "contemporary" came to replace "avant-garde" as a descriptor. By the 1990s the English word "art" (*aato*) had gained cachet as a softer, more flexible-sounding alternative to the Japanese *bijutsu*. Recent years have also witnessed a proliferation of local art projects aligned with efforts to boost regional development outside the major urban centers.

Numbering among the more esteemed artists working today are **Murakami Takashi**, Nara Yoshitomo, and Aida Makoto. Also making a name for itself is Chim↑Pom, a group of young artists that has stirred controversy with outrageous guerrilla-style performances that confront social issues head-on.

Vocabulary

gain cachet	流行する	esteemed	評価の高い
witness a proliferation of …	…の増加を目にする	stir controversy	議論を呼ぶ

¹⁴ オノ・ヨーコ

小野洋子（ヨーコ・オノ・レノン／1933〜）は、ニューヨークを拠点とするアーティストです。50年代の終わり頃から前衛芸術運動を開始。また音楽、詩、マスメディアなどを通して、平和やフェミニズムのメッセージを発信し続けています。そして、三度目の夫ジョン・レノン[27]との活動によって、「もっとも有名な日本人」といわれるようになりました。

ザ・ビートルズの解散を、ヨーコのせいだったと考える人が、今でも多くいます。ヨーコが彼らの作品制作に加わるようになって、メンバーの反感を買ったといわれているのです。一方でジョンにとってヨーコは、インスピレーションの源でもありました。たとえばジョンの代表曲『イマジン』は、ヨーコの詩集『グレープフルーツ』に着想を得たものでした。

Notes

[27] イギリス出身のミュージシャン（1940〜80）。60年代にロックバンド「ザ・ビートルズ」のメンバーとしてヴォーカル／ギター／作詞作曲を担当。70年代からはソロとして活動するも、80年に殺害された。

WORLD CAFÉ **ジョンとヨーコ（John and Yoko）**

二人が出会ったのは、1966年にロンドンの画廊で行われた、ヨーコの個展会場でした。脚立を上って、天井にあるキャンバスの点を虫眼鏡でのぞくと、「YES」と書いてある作品『天井の絵（Ceiling Painting）』を、ジョンが気に入ったといわれています。

1968年、ジョンとヨーコはレコード『未完成作品第一番 トゥー・ヴァージンズ（Unfinished Music No. 1: Two Virgins）』を発表。二人並んだヌード写真がジャケットに使われて、話題を呼びました。

ベトナム戦争の最中に当たる1969年に結婚した彼らは、ハネムーンで『ベット・イン（Bed-In）』というパフォーマンスを行います。これは、アムステルダムとモントリオールのホテルで、パジャマ姿の二人がダブルベッドに横たわったまま、何日も記者たちと対話し、「暴力なんかに関わる代わりに、ベッドにこもるか髪を伸ばそう」（ジョン）と訴えるというものでした。

¹⁴ Ono Yoko

Also known as Yoko Ono Lennon, Ono Yoko (1933-) has long made New York City the base for her artistic endeavors. She began creating avant-garde art in the late 1950s, and continues to broadcast messages on such themes as peace and feminism through music, poetry, and the mass media. Thanks to her collaborations with her third husband, John Lennon (1940-80), she was once dubbed the "world's most famous Japanese."

There are still many people who believe Ono was responsible for the breakup of the Beatles. She is said to have earned the enmity of band members by involving herself in the production of their music; on the other hand, she served as a source of inspiration for Lennon. His hit song *Imagine*, for example, had its beginnings in Ono's poetry book *Grapefruit*.

Vocabulary

artistic endeavor｜芸術的な試み
be dubbed ...｜…と呼ばれる

enmity｜敵意、憎しみ

アムステルダム（オランダ）にて、『ベッド・イン』初日のジョンとヨーコ
John Lennon and Ono Yoko on the first day of *Bed-In for Peace* at the Amsterdam Hilton Hotel, 1969
Photo: Dutch National Archives, The Hague, ANEFO, 1945-1989, catalog reference number 2.24.01.05, inventory number 922-2302, license CC-BY-SA

¹⁵ 村上隆

現代アート作家・村上隆（1962〜）が、2000年に打ち出した標語「スーパーフラット」は、アート界に大きなインパクトをもたらしました。それは**浮世絵**から**アニメ**にいたるまで、日本の造形表現（や当時の社会構造）が、すべて平面的だととらえる概念でした。以来、「日本人とは何か」は、村上が一貫して提示し続けるテーマです。

自ら設立した有限会社カイカイキキで、大勢のスタッフを率いて作品制作し、アート・ビジネスの戦略を語る彼は、ある種の純粋な作家のイメージと異なる点で、何かと反発を受けやすい存在です。本人もよくネットなどで論争しています。

2003年、フランスの老舗ブランド「ルイ・ヴィトン」の依頼で、カラフルなモノグラムの鞄をデザイン。2008年には、性的要素の強い等身大**フィギュア**のような彫刻作品『My Lonesome Cowboy』が、サザビーズで15万ドル以上の値がついて落札されました。

2011年にはクリスティーズとともに、東日本大震災被災地支援のチャリティオークション「New day」を開催しました。

¹⁶ カメラの国の現代写真

日本にはキヤノンやニコンなど、主要なカメラメーカーがいくつもありますが、近年になって、その写真表現も注目されるようになりました。表現媒体として、特に写真集のクオリティの高さが評価されています。

代表的な写真家の名前を挙げると、砂丘を舞台にした幻想的な作品で知られる植田正治（1913〜2000）や、三島由紀夫（P. 106参照）のヌード写真集『薔薇刑』を撮った細江英公……。スナップ写真では、60年代の「アレ、ブレ、ボケ」写真以来、独特のスタイルを展開している森山大道、生活空間の妻などを活写し、私小説ならぬ「私写真」を提唱している荒木経惟などがいます。

また篠山紀信は、商業分野で大きな成功を収めた写真家です。長年、芸能人の魅力をとらえたポートレイトなどで活躍してきましたが、特に初期作品の芸術性や、作品ジャンルの多彩さなどが見直されつつあります。

90年代以降は、若い女性の写真家が、相次いで登場しました。なかでも蜷川実花は、花や金魚などを撮った極彩色の画面で人気を集めています。

→

¹⁵ Murakami Takashi

"Superflat," a concept first articulated in 2000 by contemporary artist Murakami Takashi (1962-), has made a significant impact on the art world. Murakami says that the word refers to the two-dimensionality of Japanese forms of expression, from **ukiyo-e** to **anime**, as well as of Japanese society at that time. A thematic thread running through Murakami's work since then is the question, "Who are the Japanese?"

At his company Kaikai Kiki, Murakami employs a large staff to produce works and carry out art-business strategies that diverge considerably from conventional notions of "pure art." This has made him a target of criticism from various quarters, which he vigorously rebuts via the Internet.

In 2003, Murakami began designing a series of colorful monogrammed handbags for the venerable French brand Louis Vuitton. In 2008, his full-sized, sexually explicit anime-**figure**-like sculpture *My Lonesome Cowboy* sold at Sotheby's for over 15 million dollars. In 2011, he collaborated with Christie's to produce the New Day charity auction to benefit victims of the East Japan Earthquake.

Vocabulary

articulated｜明確に述べられた	vigorously｜活発に、精力的に
thematic thread｜連続しているテーマ	rebut｜反論する
diverge from ...｜…と異なる	venerable brand｜老舗ブランド
various quarters｜さまざまな人	sexually explicit｜性的描写がきわどい

¹⁶ Contemporary Photography in the "Land of Cameras"

Japan is home to such world-class camera makers as Canon and Nikon, but in recent years it has also garnered attention for its photography. Japanese photo books in particular have earned accolades for their quality.

Among the country's most eminent photographers are Ueda Shoji (1913-2000), associated with surreal compositions shot against sand-dune backgrounds, and Hosoe Eikoh, whose collection *Ba-ra-kei: Ordeal by Roses* featured nude shots of novelist Mishima Yukio (see p. 107). As for snapshot artists, Moriyama Daido has been taking idiosyncratic street photos since the 1960s, when he first captured the public eye with his *are-bure-boke* (grainy, blurry, out-of-focus) style, while Araki Nobuyoshi purveys vivid images of his wife and other scenes from his private life, an approach he dubs "I-photography" after the literary genre of the I-novel.

Shinoyama Kishin made his mark as a commercial photographer, for

→

←

現代アートの分野では、杉本博司がコンセプチュアルな写真作品で有名です。

Comment

石内都さんのハッセルブラッド国際写真賞受賞、おめでたいことですね。日本の女性の写真家としては、初めてだそうですよ。
Congratulations to Miyako Ishiuchi for winning the 2014 Hasselblad Award! I hear she's the first Japanese woman photographer to receive it.

17 仏像

ウィキペディア[28] によると、日本には推定 30 万体以上の仏像[29] があるとのこと。その根拠は不明ですが、数えきれないほど多いことは確かです。近年は寺ではなく美術館で、「仏教彫刻」として仏像を鑑賞する機会が増えました。

日本の仏像の特徴として、木彫が圧倒的に多いことが挙げられます。森林が豊富で（P. 288 参照）、**仏教**伝来より前から霊木が信仰されていた影響のようです（P. 170 参照）。

歴史上、もっとも評価されている仏師といえば、運慶（生年不詳〜1223）でしょう。奈良・東大寺の『金剛力士像』（南大門を守護する二体の神）は、猛々しい忿怒の相で、いかにも武士が政権を取った時代らしい作風だとよくいわれます[30]。

また、江戸時代の僧侶・円空は、日本全国を修行して回り、おそらく人々を救済する祈とうのために、5,000 体以上――通説では 12 万体――の仏像を木から彫り出しました。それは部分的に原木の形を残すなど、シンプルかつ大胆な造形で、現代アートだといわれても違和感がないでしょう。

Notes

※28 誰でも自由に編集に参加できる、インターネット百科事典。ウィキメディア財団が運営し、288 言語（2014 年 12 月）で展開されている。　※29 現在、一般的には「仏」（如来）の像だけでなく、菩薩や天部、明王等、仏教関連の像を総称して仏像という（初期仏教に、仏像はなかった）。　※30 朝廷が差配した、東大寺の再興事業として造られた。運慶を含む 4 人の大仏師が製作を担当したが、各々の役割分担については見解が分かれる。　※31「阿修羅像」734 年／153.4cm ／脱活乾漆像

Comment

このところ、仏像はなぜか、若い人にも人気です。年寄りが手を合わせている脇で、「かっこいい」といって観ているんです。何年か前に興福寺の「阿修羅像」[31] の展覧会があったときには、「美少年みたい」だと騒がれていました。
For some reason, Buddhist statues are a hit with young people these days. You can hear them muttering "Cool!" as they stand in front of one at a temple, next to us older folks bowing in prayer. A few years ago I went to an exhibition of the famed Ashura statue from Kofukuji temple, an image that some fans say looks like a handsome teenage boy. The show caused a buzz usually reserved for pop idols.

←

many years shooting portraits that highlighted the appeal of show-business personalities and the like. His oeuvre is now enjoying critical reappraisal for its thematic diversity as well as its artistry, particularly in his early work.

Since the 1990s young women photographers have increasingly come to the fore. Ninagawa Mika is popular for her color-saturated shots of flowers and goldfish.

In the contemporary art milieu, Sugimoto Hiroshi has established himself as a creator of conceptual photographic art.

Vocabulary

garner ... ｜ …を得る	idiosyncratic ｜ 独特な、特異な
accolade ｜ 称賛、賛美	oeuvre ｜ 作品［フランス語］
eminent ｜ 著名な、有名な	come to the fore ｜ 目立つ、台頭する
sand-dune ｜ 砂丘	milieu ｜ 環境、分野［フランス語］

17 Buddhist Statuary

According to Wikipedia, there are over 300,000 Buddhist statues in Japan. Though the source of that figure isn't clear, we know that the country has a virtually uncountable abundance of Buddhist images. Nowadays there are more opportunities for people to view such statuary in art museums, not only in temples.

Wood is by far the most common material for Japanese Buddhist sculpture. After all, this is a land blessed with forests (see p. 289), where sacred trees were worshiped (see p. 171) long before the arrival of **Buddhism**.

Probably the most venerated Buddhist sculptor in the nation's history is Unkei (??-1223), who directed the carving of the two massive *Kongorikishi* (Vajrapani) statues flanking the Nandaimon gate of Todaiji temple in Nara. With their fierce countenances, these guardian figures are often said to reflect the ascendant political power of the samurai warrior class in Unkei's day.

Later, during the Edo period, the Buddhist monk Enku traveled throughout Japan in the course of his religious training. Perhaps as a form of prayer for people's salvation, he carved wooden Buddhist images wherever he went—over 5,000, it is estimated, but legends place his output at 120,000. Sometimes retaining the shape of the original tree, his work is simple and bold, with a sensibility not far removed from contemporary art.

Vocabulary

virtually ｜ 事実上、実質的に	venerated ｜ 尊敬された
abundance ｜ 豊富さ、大量	fierce countenance ｜ 荒々しい顔つき
be worshiped ｜ 崇拝される	ascendant ｜ 支配的な

WORLD CAFÉ ジャポニスム

19世紀後半、フランスをはじめとするヨーロッパで起こった日本
美術のブームは、当初、「ジャポネズリ」（日本趣味）と呼ばれて
いました。やがてそれは、単なるエキゾチズムを超えて、日本の
美意識や生活様式にまで、関心が持たれるようになります。

そしてゴッホをはじめとするアーティストたちが、浮世絵や琳派
（P. 38参照）などの平面的で色鮮やかな造形原理を、自らの作品
に取り入れました。また、日本で工芸と美術が分かれていないこ
とや、花鳥風月などの自然をモチーフとすることは、当時のヨー
ロッパを中心とした美術運動・アールヌーヴォーとのつながりが
指摘されています。

こうした日本の影響は、欧米各地のグラフィック・デザイン、建
築、演劇、音楽、文学、服飾、料理など広い分野に渡って1920
年頃まで続き、後に「ジャポニスム」と呼ばれるようになりまし
た。現代において、海外で日本のアニメなどが人気を集めている
土壌は、その頃つちかわれたのかもしれません。

なお、関連事項として「シノワズリ」は、17世紀後半～18世紀
を中心に、ヨーロッパで流行した中国趣味を指します（当時は、
日本もよくごっちゃにされていました。現代の中国趣味を指して
いうこともあります）。特に中国の陶磁器が大人気でした。

また、「オリエンタリズム」という要注意の言葉もあります。これ
は従来、中東など広い地域を対象とする、東洋趣味・東洋学を意
味していました。しかし1978年、アメリカの文学評論家エドワ
ード・サイードが、著書『オリエンタリズム』で、「東洋を支配す
るための西洋のスタイル」（植民地主義の表れ）だと定義し直し
て論じ、以来、多くの議論を引き起こしているのです。

葛飾北斎『富嶽三十六景（ふがくさんじゅうろっけい）』のうち、
『神奈川沖浪裏（かながわおきなみうら）』（部分）
The Great Wave off Kanagawa (part), from Katsushika Hokusai's
ukiyo-e series Thirty-six Views of Mount Fuji, c. 1831

03

MANGA

漫画

01 日本の漫画

日本の「漫画」には、英語圏でいうコミックやグラフィック・ノベル、新聞の時事漫画なども含まれています。しかし海外では、日本流の長いストーリーの作品に限って、manga[※1] と呼んでいるようですね。また、日本の漫画は、ほとんどが白黒です。

日本では、年間に発行される出版物全体の販売部数の、じつに3分の1が漫画です。あらゆるジャンルや読者層を網羅しているという意味で、漫画は映画と同じような位置づけの巨大メディアといえるでしょう。そしてアニメはもとより、多くの実写映画やテレビドラマが、漫画を原作としています。

漫画の歴史は、数100年前の戯画[※2] に始まるという声もありますが、コマ割りと吹き出しのある漫画は、近代になって、欧米のコミックの影響で描かれるようになりました。

第二次世界大戦直後、少年向けの漫画本に伝説の漫画家・**手塚治虫**が登場。日本の漫画表現をひらきます。テーマは広く深く、複雑に、そして微妙な人間心理が、漫画ならではの技法で描写されるようになりました。

以来、時代とともに漫画の対象読者が広がり、**少女漫画、青年漫画**……と、新しいジャンルの漫画雑誌が創刊されました。

漫画は映画などにくらべて低コストで、個人作家に制作されてきたことも、斬新な表現に挑戦しやすく、流通しやすい要因でした。400ページを越すものもある分厚い日本の漫画雑誌[※3] には、もっとも安価な再生紙が使われ、何本かの連載漫画が載っています。そこで人気を得た作品は、ソフトカバーの「単行本」にまとめられます。

2000年前後から、漫画は国内外で文化的に高く評価されるようになりました。近年は、漫画雑誌の発行部数が減る一方、『**ONE PIECE**』など人気作品の単行本が記録的に売れています。またウェブ漫画も発達してきました。

Notes

※1 イギリスでは、90年代にアニメを「マンガ」と呼んで売り出した会社がある。　※2 こっけいな絵。風刺の要素をもつものが多い。　※3 米のコミック・ブック（スーパーヒーローもの等）は、ほとんど月刊32ページのカラー印刷、脚本・下絵・ペン入れ・彩色等は分業体制で、一作品だけが連載される。コピーライトは通常、出版社に帰属。

01 Comics in Japan

The word *manga* includes everything from cartoons to comic books to newspaper comic strips to graphic novels. Though the word has caught on overseas, it typically refers to long stories of the sort that appear in manga magazines in Japan. Unlike comics in many other countries, Japanese manga are almost entirely in black and white.

Of all the books and magazines sold in Japan each year, one third are manga. A major entertainment medium that rivals the movies, manga appeal to all kinds of readers and span every imaginable style or subject. Many live-action films and TV dramas—not to mention anime, of course—are based on manga.

Scholars like to trace the history of manga back to the centuries-old caricatures called *giga* ("funny pictures"). But manga with cartoon panels and speech balloons are a modern invention that was inspired by Western comics.

Tezuka Osamu, the celebrated "god of manga," published his first comic book, aimed at a readership of schoolboys, just after World War II. His works pioneered the style that came to be associated with manga, with innovative drawing techniques and stories of breadth, depth, and complexity that explore the subtleties of human psychology.

In the postwar years, manga steadily expanded their audience with magazines that offered a variety of new genres—**girls' manga**, **young-adult manga**, and more.

Thanks to their low cost compared to such media as film, and to the fact that they were created by individual artists, manga turned out to be an ideal platform for experimenting with, and popularizing, daring new forms of expression. Manga magazines, which could run to over 400 pages, used cheap recycled paper and featured several serialized stories in every issue. Publishers could then make extra money by bundling the more popular series into softcover books, known as *tankobon*.

Over the past couple of decades, manga have gained increased respect both in Japan and overseas as a cultural phenomenon. Today, though the print runs of manga magazines are on the decline, popular titles in book format like ***One Piece*** are enjoying record-setting sales, and web manga are attracting readers as well.

Vocabulary

cartoon｜漫画的な絵や作品全体。アニメも	speech balloon｜吹き出し
graphic novel｜（おもに）大人向けの長編漫画	subtlety｜繊細さ、微妙さ

02 少年漫画

「少年漫画」とは、おもに 10〜15 歳前後の男の子を対象にした、「少年漫画誌」に掲載される漫画を指します[4]。ヒーローは同年代の少年で、冒険や戦いと成長をテーマにした作品が典型です。『DRAGON BALL』や『SLAM DUNK』、『ONE PIECE』など、海外で知られている日本アニメには、少年漫画を原作にしたものが多いですね。人気が高いのと同時に、子ども向けにしてはエロティックで暴力的、刺激的な描写に走りやすいという批判[5]が、集中してきたジャンルです（P. 144 参照）。

『週刊少年ジャンプ』(集英社)
Weekly Shonen Jump　©Shueisha

先ほど挙げた作品はすべて、1994 年に週刊誌の最多発行部数 653 万部を記録した、『週刊少年ジャンプ』に連載されていた／あるいは連載中の作品です。同誌の作品テーマは、「友情・努力・勝利」が三大要素だといいます。また、「チームワークの重視」も指摘できます。日本のこうした作品に描かれる価値観が、現在ではアニメや漫画を通して、世界の子どもたちになんらかの影響を与えているのかもしれません。

ほかの雑誌から生まれた作品をいくつか挙げると、70 年代以来ずっと、第一線で活躍している漫画家・高橋留美子の『うる星やつら』や『犬夜叉』は、『少年サンデー』に連載されていました。また、『少年ガンガン』掲載の『鋼の錬金術師』は、2000 年代を代表する作品のひとつ。最近では、『少年マガジン』の『進撃の巨人』がヒットしていますね。

近年は読者層が広がり、作品によっては大人や女性も少年漫画を読んでいます。

Notes

※4　小学校低学年向けの漫画は「幼年漫画」といわれる。　※5　米でも 50 年代に、有害図書としてコミック・ブックの撲滅運動があった。

Comment

少年漫画は、人気次第で突然、連載が打ち切りになったり、逆にだらだら話が引き伸ばされたりすることがあって、時々しらけてしまうよ。好きな漫画に限って、そうなんだ。
Depending on their popularity, shonen manga are notorious for suddenly disappearing from the pages of the magazine that was serializing them. Others keep going on and on, long after they've gotten boring. For some reason these things always seem to happen to the manga you like the best!

02 Manga for Boys

Shonen manga ("boys' manga"), probably the most prevalent of all manga genres, are stories geared to a readership of boys around 10 to 15 years old. They appear in serial form in weekly or monthly magazines dedicated to shonen manga. A typical story features a young hero, about the same age as his readers, who grows up in the course of some sort of adventure or struggle. Many of the best-known anime, like *Dragon Ball*, *Slam Dunk*, and **One Piece**, are based on shonen manga. However, the genre has also been a target of criticism that, despite being supposedly for school-age boys, it often includes erotic, violent, or otherwise inappropriate content (see p. 145).

03

All of the aforementioned titles have appeared as serials in one particular shonen manga magazine: *Weekly Shonen Jump*, which set the all-time record for Japanese weeklies with a print run of 6.53 million in 1994. The magazine makes a point of emphasizing the "three big themes" of friendship, effort, and victory, as well as the importance of teamwork. With the spread of manga and anime, there have been suggestions that the values embedded in shonen manga could have an unforeseen impact on children elsewhere in the world.

Of course there are hit manga from other magazines too. One of the most popular manga artists since the 1970s has been Takahashi Rumiko, creator of *Urusei Yatsura* and *InuYasha*, which appeared in *Shonen Sunday*. *Fullmetal Alchemist* (in *Comic Gangan*) was a major hit of the 2000s, while *Attack on Titan* (in *Shonen Magazine*) has made a splash more recently.

Lately shonen manga have expanded their audience with stories that appeal not just to young boys but to girls and adults as well.

Vocabulary

prevalent ｜流行している、普及している	**supposedly** ｜おそらく、建前としては
geared to ... ｜…向けの	**values embedded in** ... ｜…に散りばめられた価値観
readership ｜読者層	
in serial form ｜連載の形で	**make a splash** ｜大評判をとる
feature ... ｜…を主役にする	

03 漫画の記号表現

日本の漫画には、特有の記号がたくさん出てきます。たとえば、キャラクターの額などに、垂れるような縦線が何本か引かれるのは、内心の落ち込みや恐怖を表しています。由来はおそらく、心に暗い影が差すイメージでしょう。また、まじめな話のときはリアルに描かれていたキャラクターが、ギャグシーンになると、いきなり小さくコミカルに描かれるときがあります。「これは冗談ですよ」といった意味です。

私たちは、こうした漫画の表現に慣れていて、意識もせずに読んでいますが、初めて見る方には、わかりにくいようですね。近年は海外でも、日本の漫画の影響を受けた manga やグラフィック・ノベルがみられます。

04 漫画の神様・手塚治虫

手塚治虫（1928〜89）は、第二次世界大戦後の日本文化に多大な影響を及ぼした漫画家／アニメーターで、「漫画の神様」と呼ばれていました[※6]。

第一の功績として、手塚は漫画に「映画的手法」を持ち込んだことで知られます。映画のカメラワークのように描かれた漫画は、手塚以前にもみられましたが、彼はクローズアップを多用し、**記号表現**を工夫して、臨場感あふれる画面を構成。こうした技術をもとに、それまで漫画が扱わなかった、シリアスで複雑なテーマが表現されるようになりました。

もともとはアニメーター志望で、60年代にアニメのプロダクションを設立。『鉄腕アトム』[※7]などの自作漫画を原作とした、テレビアニメ制作に乗り出します（P. 138 参照）。また、大人向けの劇場版アニメや、実験アニメーションにも意欲的に取り組みました。

生涯で発表した漫画は 600 作以上。アニメは 70 作以上。代表作には、アトムや『ジャングル大帝』（図版 P. 85）のほか、**少女漫画**の『リボンの騎士』、壮大な歴史ドラマの『火の鳥』や『ブッダ』、医学漫画の金字塔『ブラック・ジャック』――手塚は医師免許をもっていました――などがあります。

Notes

※6 対して石ノ森章太郎が、「漫画の王様」と呼ばれていた。　※7 今日においては違和感が大きいが、「アトム」の名は原子力を想起させる（atom/ 原子、atomic power/ 原子力）。1950 年代当時、手塚は、原子力が安全に利用できる未来の技術開発を夢見ていたようだ。ただし、原子力発電には反対の立場だった。

03 Symbols in Manga

Japanese comics have their own unique vocabulary of symbols. One example is the use of parallel vertical lines drawn on a character's forehead or face to indicate depression or fear. The image probably comes from the idea of a dark shadow hovering over the character's state of mind.

Another manga device is to have a character that was illustrated in realistic fashion suddenly appear as a miniaturized caricature. This indicates that the situation has morphed into a gag—basically telling the reader "this is a joke!"

Japanese readers are used to these conventions, but a first-time reader may wonder just what is going on. Still, as Japanese manga have begun to influence the styles of cartoons and graphic novels overseas in recent years, many of these distinctive symbols are becoming a part of comics everywhere.

Vocabulary

depression｜落ち込み、憂うつ
hover over ...｜…の上に浮かぶ

morph into ...｜…に変形する
convention｜慣習、取り決め

04 Tezuka Osamu

Such was his influence on postwar Japanese culture that even today, cartoonist and animator Tezuka Osamu (1925-89) is revered throughout Japan as the "god of manga."

First and foremost, Tezuka is hailed for having introduced cinematic effects to manga. Previous manga artists had used camera angles and other film-like techniques, but Tezuka was master of the close-up and of **symbolic representation**, infusing his pages with dynamic realism and motion. His pioneering style made it possible for manga to address serious, complex themes in a way they had never done before.

Tezuka originally wanted to be an animator, and in the 1960s he launched a production company creating animated TV series based on his own manga, such as *Astro Boy* (see p. 139). He went on to produce animated films for theatrical release targeted at an adult audience, as well as experimental animation.

Tezuka created over 600 manga and over 70 anime titles. In addition to such hits as *Astro Boy* and *Kimba, the White Lion*, he authored **girls' manga** like *Princess Knight*, grand historical epics like *Phoenix* and *Buddha*, and the iconic "medical manga" *Black Jack* (Tezuka himself was a licensed physician).

Vocabulary

be revered as ...｜…として尊敬されている
first and foremost｜何よりもまず
be hailed for ...｜…のために認められる、称賛される
infuse A with B｜A に B を注ぐ、吹き込む

address ...｜…に取り組む
launch ...｜…を始める、…に乗り出す
historical epic｜歴史大作

コラム **手塚治虫とディズニー**

ディズニー映画『ライオン・キング』が 94 年に公開されたときには、60 年代にアメリカでも放送された**手塚**のテレビアニメ『ジャングル大帝』[8]と似ていて、盗作に当たるのではないかと、日米で話題になりました。『ジャングル大帝』の主人公は、白いライオンのレオですが、アメリカ版では、キンバという名前でした。『ライオン・キング』の主人公は、シンバというライオンです。

もともと手塚治虫は、ウォルト・ディズニーの大ファンでした。ディズニー映画『バンビ』を 100 回ほども観て、劇場の暗がりの中でスケッチしたといいます。1950 年代には、『バンビ』や『ピノキオ』などのディズニー作品を、手塚流にアレンジして漫画化したことがあります（後者は無許可でしたが、後にディズニー社の許可を得て復刻されました）。そして、ついにはディズニーと面会した思い出を、手塚は大事に語っていました。

結局この騒動のとき、手塚プロダクションは、「二つの物語を別のものと考えているが、もし手塚が、ディズニーに影響を与えたというのなら光栄だ」という声明を出して、法的な闘争などには至りませんでした。

Notes

※8　日本初のカラー・テレビアニメで、50 年代の手塚漫画が原作。66 年の劇場版は、ヴェネツィア国際映画祭サンマルコ銀獅子賞受賞。

05 漫画の起源をたどる

日本に『鳥獣人物戯画』という、12〜13 世紀の墨絵のユーモラスな絵巻物が遺されていて、最古の漫画に当たるのではないかと議論されています。カエルやウサギなどを擬人化した箇所（図版 左・下）が有名で、とても生き生きと描かれた略画です。鳥羽僧正という高僧をはじめ、複数の作者の筆によるものといわれています。

時代は下って、江戸時代の**浮世絵**のなかでも、面白おかしい略　→

COLUMN **Tezuka and Disney**

When the Walt Disney film *The Lion King* came out in 1994, fans in both the U.S. and Japan noticed the striking similarity to **Tezuka**'s animation series *Kimba, the White Lion*, which had appeared on American TV in the 1960s. Critics on both sides of the Pacific accused Walt Disney Pictures of plagiarism. The hero of the original Japanese anime was a white lion named Leo. This was changed to Kimba for the American version; the hero of *The Lion King* was named Simba.

Tezuka himself was a huge fan of Walt Disney. He said that he saw the Disney film *Bambi* a hundred times and would sit in the dark theater sketching away. In the 1950s Tezuka even made manga versions, in his own style, of such Disney films as *Bambi* and *Pinocchio* (the latter was done without consent from Disney, but was later republished with the company's permission). Tezuka often spoke of his eventual meeting with Walt Disney as one of his most cherished memories.

In the end, the controversy over *The Lion King* did not result in any legal action. Tezuka Productions issued a statement that they were "honored if Tezuka had been an influence on Disney."

Vocabulary

accuse *A* of *B*｜A を B の理由で非難する	eventual｜最終的な
plagiarism｜盗作、盗用	controversy over ...｜…に関する論争

⁰⁵ The Origins of Manga

The "oldest manga" is often said to be the *Choju Jinbutsu Giga* ("Caricatures of Animals and Humans"), a set of scrolls of humorous sketches, drawn in black **sumi** ink, that dates back to the 12th or 13th century. The most famous of the scrolls vividly depicts frogs and rabbits frolicking in very human ways (images at left). Though traditionally attributed to a Buddhist priest, Bishop Toba, they are now thought to be the creation of several artists.

The bishop's name remained associated with funny pictures down through the centuries. Among the *ukiyo-e* of the Edo period (1603-1868) were a genre of amusing sketches known as *toba-e*. During the same era,

➔

← 画は、鳥羽僧正にちなんで、「鳥羽絵」と呼ばれていました。また当時の
「黄表紙」という一種の絵本にも、吹き出しに近いものなど、現在の漫画に
通じる表現がみられました。

一方、浮世絵師の葛飾北斎（P.36参照）は、1814年に出版した「絵手本」
（絵を描くための見本となるスケッチ集）に、『北斎漫画』というタイトルを
付けています。その頃、すでに漫画という言葉はありましたが、現在と異な
り「気ままに描く絵」といった意味で使われていました。

06 少女漫画

少女向けの漫画は、一目でわかるほど、**少年漫画**と異なります。線が細く、
80年代くらいまでは、登場する少女たちの眼に、星のように光るキャッチ
ライト[9]が入っていました。また見せ場のシーンでは、バックに花が描き
込まれます。作家はほとんど女性で、内容は大半がラブストーリー。登場
人物の心情が丹念に描かれて、読者の共感を呼びます。

歴史に残るヒット作には、アニメ化で世界的な人気となった『キャンディ・
キャンディ』、革命期のフランスを舞台にした『ベルサイ
ユのばら』、演劇をテーマに40年近く連載が続いている
『ガラスの仮面』（図版 右／美内すずえ・作／白泉社）
などがあります。

『ガラスの仮面』1巻
Glass Mask vol. 1

70年代には、萩尾望都、大島弓子、竹宮惠子など、革
新的な漫画家たちが現れます。それまでのロマンティッ
クな少女漫画の定型を越えて、壮大なSF、ファンタジ
ーや少年の同性愛など、深みのあるテーマと表現を、こ
のジャンルにもたらしました。彼女らの作品はよく評論の対象になり、漫画
だけでなく文学などにも影響を与えています。

その後、クールな筆致の吉田秋生、現代女性を描く岡崎京子などが登場し、
大人の女性や男性にも読まれる作品が増えました。現在では、大人の女性
向け漫画ジャンル[10]が、新たに形成されています。

近年のヒット作には、『NANA』や『君に届け』などがあります。

Notes

※9 人物の撮影技法で、瞳に映り込ませる光。　※10 20代前後向けは「ヤング・レディース」、20代以
上向けは「女性漫画」や「レディースコミック」と呼ばれる。後者は女性向けポルノ漫画を指すこともある。

kibyoshi ("yellow cover") picture books appeared in a format suggestive of modern manga with text balloons.

In 1814 the renowned ukiyo-e artist Katsushika Hokusai (see p. 37) published *Hokusai Manga*, a collection of drawings intended to serve as an art instruction manual. Thus the word *manga* was already in use two centuries ago, though at the time it meant something like "casual sketches."

Vocabulary

frolicking｜はしゃいでいる、遊び騒いでいる
attributed to ...｜…の作品だとされた

suggestive of ...｜…を連想させる
renowned｜有名な、高名な

06 Manga for Girls

A brief look at stories of the *shojo manga* ("girls' manga") genre will make it clear that they are different from **shonen manga**. The lines are more delicately drawn, and, at least till the 1980s, the young heroines' eyes sparkled with reflected light. For climactic scenes, flowers are often drawn into the background. Most of the writers are women, and most of the plots are love stories. The characters' emotions are described in painstaking detail and appeal to the sympathies of the reader.

Among the greatest shojo manga hits are *Candy Candy*, the animated version of which won fans all over the world; *The Rose of Versailles*, a historical epic about the French Revolution; and *Glass Mask* (image at left), which takes place in the world of theater and has been serialized for nearly 40 years and counting.

In the 1970s, shojo manga were transformed by the emergence of such innovative artists as Hagio Moto, Oshima Yumiko, and Takemiya Keiko. They introduced content that went far beyond the standard romances into such realms as science fiction, fantasy, and love between young men. Their sophisticated styles and subject matter gave girls' comics newfound respect in the eyes of critics, and shojo manga began to influence "serious" literature as well.

With the advent of such talents as Yoshida Akimi, known for her cool touch, and Okazaki Kyoko, who told stories of women in contemporary society, shojo manga earned a following among adult women and even men. Recent hits include *Nana* and *Kimi ni Todoke: From Me to You*. A new category of manga for adult women has also gained ground.

Vocabulary

sparkle with ...｜…で輝く、きらめく
painstaking｜念入りな、徹底した

realm｜分野、領域
gain ground｜支持を得る、人気が出る

⁰⁷ 劇画と青年漫画

日本では、戦後の**少年漫画**になじんだ読者が成長するにつれて、1950 年代くらいから大人向けにシリアスなストーリーの漫画が描かれるようになりました。漫画家の辰巳ヨシヒロ^{※11} らは、そうした自作を「劇画」と呼んで、従来の漫画と差別化しました。60〜70 年代には、ハードボイルドな『ゴルゴ 13』や『子連れ狼』^{※12} などの、リアルで荒々しい絵が、劇画調といわれるようになりました。『ルパン三世』も、この頃生まれた名作です。

80 年代には、フランスのバンド・デシネ^{※13} 作家・メビウスの影響を受けた、大友克洋の『**AKIRA**』^{※14} が登場。世界に日本の大人向け漫画のクオリティを印象付けました。

こうした大人の男性向け漫画は、現在、総称して「青年漫画」と呼ばれています。「青年」とは若者という意味ですが、40 代以上も読んでいます。表現規制が比較的ゆるく、作家にとっては創造性を発揮しやすいジャンルといえるでしょう。会社生活をモチーフにした「サラリーマン漫画」も、サブジャンルを形成しています。

青年漫画を描いて、評価の高い現役作家には、『MONSTER』、『20 世紀少年』の浦沢直樹、『バガボンド』の井上雄彦などがいます。アニメで有名な『クレヨンしんちゃん』も、もともと子ども向けではなく、青年漫画誌に連載されていました。最近の話題作はというと、たくさんありますが、『宇宙兄弟』と『テルマエ・ロマエ』を挙げましょうか。

なお、ポルノ漫画を「成年漫画」ということがありますが、発音は同じでも字（P. 94 参照）が違います。

Notes

※11 2010 年、『劇画漂流』がアイズナー賞最優秀アジア作品／最優秀実話作品受賞。同年、シンガポールで辰巳漫画数作を原作としたアニメーション映画『TATSUMI』が制作された（監督：エリック・クー）。
※12 87 年という早い時期に米で翻訳出版された。映画・ドラマ化も（P. 208 参照）。　※13 バンド・デシネは仏やベルギーの漫画で、おもにカラー印刷。メビウスは仏を代表するバンド・デシネ作家。ジャン・ジローのペンネームもある。　※14 海外では彩色版が最初に発売されたが、オリジナルは単色。

『ルパン三世』1 巻
モンキー・パンチ・作（中央公論新社）
Lupin the Third vol. 1 by Monkey Punch
© モンキー・パンチ／中公文庫コミック版

⁰⁷ Gekiga and Young-Adult Manga

As the postwar generation of **shonen manga** readers grew up, a new style of serious cartoon stories for adult readers emerged in the 1950s. Manga artist Tatsumi Yoshihiro and his colleagues coined the term *gekiga* ("dramatic pictures") to distinguish their own work from the "funny pictures" of manga. In the sixties and seventies, the realistic, sometimes harsh images in such works as the hardboiled *Golgo 13* and *Lone Wolf and Cub* came to typify the "gekiga style." Another popular work for adults during this period was *Lupin the Third*.

In the 1980s, Otomo Katsuhiro's *Akira*, which showed the influence of the French *bande dessinée* artist Moebius, earned widespread fame as a masterpiece of adult-oriented manga.

Today, manga for an adult male audience are generally referred to as *seinen manga*; though *seinen* means "youth," men in their forties are known to read them. As a genre, seinen manga are relatively free of expressive conventions, giving artists a chance to experiment in creative ways. One sub-genre is the salaryman manga, which portrays the lives of company employees.

Among the most acclaimed seinen manga authors are Urasawa Naoki (*Monster* and *20th Century Boys*) and Inoue Takehiko (*Vagabond*). Even *Crayon Shin-chan*, which became a big anime hit, is not really a comic for kids, but a series that appeared in a seinen manga magazine. Two of the more popular seinen manga these days are *Space Brothers* and *Thermae Romae*.

The genre should not be confused with another category of *seinen manga*, pronounced the same but spelled with a different kanji character (see p. 95), that refers to "adult," i.e. pornographic, manga.

Vocabulary

distinguish *A* from *B*｜A を B と区別する	experiment in ...｜…の実験をする
widespread｜広範囲の、普及した	acclaimed｜評価された

『バガボンド』1 巻　井上雄彦・作（講談社）
Vagabond vol. 1 by Inoue Takehiko
© I.T. Planning, Inc.

03

MANGA / Gekiga and Young-Adult Manga

08 ボーイズラブとやおい

和製英語の「ボーイズラブ」とは、女性の読者に向けて、美男子どうしの同性愛を描く、漫画や小説のジャンルのことです。こうした趣味は海外でもみられますが、ジャンルとして確立しているのは、おそらく日本だけでしょう。古くは 70 年代、**少女漫画**誌に竹宮恵子（P. 70 参照）が描いた『風と木の詩』が、この路線のさきがけでした。耽美的で、芸術的評価の高い作品です。

また、漫画**同人誌**の世界では、「やおい」といって、メジャーな漫画に出てくる男性キャラクターを、勝手に同性愛関係に飛躍させる一種のパロディ作品（**二次創作**）が、さかんに描かれています。やおいは、「ヤマなし、オチなし、イミなし」から採ったスラング。最初は性描写に主眼が置かれたパロディを指したそうですが、現在はプラトニックなストーリーのやおいもあります。

さて、こうした男性による恋愛物語が、どうして女性に人気なのでしょう？ある同人作家[15] は、女性が肉体的・社会的なリスクから解き放たれて、ファンタジーのなかで性差によらない純愛をコントロールできるからだと説明します。

「ボーイズラブ」と「やおい」の使い分けはあいまいで、海外のファンには、やおいという言葉のほうが通っているようです。

Notes

※ 15 野火ノビタ（榎本ナリコ）『大人は判ってくれない―野火ノビタ批評集成』（日本評論社、2003）より

09 スポーツ漫画

国民的スポーツの野球をはじめとする、スポーツが題材の漫画は、**少年漫画**を中心に数えきれないほどあります。東京オリンピックが開催された 60 年代から 70 年代には、とりわけ「スポ根」といわれるジャンルが流行しました。スポ根は「スポーツ」と「根性」を合わせた造語で、主人公が過酷な練習に耐え続けて、勝利をつかむまでの過程を描いたもの。野球の『巨人の星』やボクシングの『あしたのジョー』は、あまりにも有名です。**少女漫画**にも、テニスの『エースをねらえ！』などのスポ根漫画があります。

その後、才能や楽しさ、練習効率よりも、努力自体を美徳とするスポ根の価値観は、衰退していきます。野球漫画だけれど恋愛を物語の主軸に据えた『タッチ』は、日本経済がピークに向かいつつあった 80 年代前半に登場しました。

→

08 "Boys' Love" and Yaoi

"Boys' love" is an English term coined in Japan to describe manga and other literary works, targeting a female readership, that portray love between attractive young men. Works of this sort may appear in various media overseas, but Japan is probably the only country where it is an established genre.

The title that set the stage for the "boys' love" phenomenon was *Song of the Wind and Trees*, a **shojo manga** by Takemiya Keiko (see p. 71) that came out in the 1970s and earned critical praise for its artistry and aestheticism.

In the world of *doujinshi* manga fanzines, the popular sub-genre known as *yaoi* features homages or parodies (known as "**derivative works**") of major manga that depict the male characters engaging in homosexual relationships. (Yaoi was originally an acronym for "no climax, no punchline, no meaning.") Although yaoi manga have had a reputation for focusing on sex scenes, nowadays many of the stories are about platonic relationships.

Why are stories of male-male love such a hit with young women? One doujinshi writer explains that they enable girls to fantasize about a pure love that doesn't involve sex differences or the physical and social risks associated with male-female love.

While there is no clear distinction between the yaoi and boys' love genres, yaoi appears to be the more popular term of the two among manga fans overseas.

Vocabulary

coined｜新たに作られた
aestheticism｜耽美主義
derivative｜派生した［derivative works で「二次創作物、二次的著作物（法律用語）」］

acronym for …｜…を意味する頭字語
punchline｜オチ
fantasize about …｜…について空想にふける

09 Sports Manga

A very high percentage of **shonen manga** are about sports, and especially about baseball, arguably Japan's national sport. From around the time of the 1964 Tokyo Olympics and well into the 1970s, the *spokon* genre of manga ruled the market.

Short for *sports konjo*, or "sports spirit," spokon is a term for stories showcasing heroes who endure harsh training conditions and other ordeals on their way to eventual victory. Two of the biggest titles in this category are *Kyojin no Hoshi* (Star of the Giants), about baseball, and *Ashita no Joe* (Tomorrow's Joe), about boxing. Spokon for girls also exist, a major hit being the **shojo manga** *Aim for the Ace!*, which is about tennis.

After this golden age there was a decline in spokon-type sports manga that glorified sheer effort over talent or fun. The baseball manga *Touch*, which

→

海外で知られているスポーツ漫画といえば、なんといってもサッカーの『キャプテン翼』でしょう。1981年に初登場し、現在も新たなシリーズが描かれています。報道によると、元フランス代表ジネディーヌ・ジダンや元イタリア代表フランチェスコ・トッティなど、何人ものワールドカップ出場選手が、同作のアニメ版を観てサッカーを始めたそうです。また、90年代の『SLAM DUNK』（バスケットボール）も、一時代を築くヒットとなりました。最近の作品では、雑誌連載中の『GIANT KILLING』（サッカー）が人気ですね。

10 忍者漫画とNARUTO

忍者とは、武士（P. 296 参照）が政権を握っていた時代、集団でスパイ活動や暗殺などの隠密行動をしていた者のことです。彼らは実際に特殊な技術をもっていましたが、小説や映画、漫画などの忍者は、人間ばなれした架空の技を使っています[16]。

それらの作品では、服部半蔵という実在の忍者（二代目以降は武士）や、伝統的な忍者ヒーローのキャラクター・猿飛佐助[17]にちなんだ名前が、よく使われています。たとえば、『忍者ハットリくん』や『サスケ』という漫画がありますね。

忍者漫画のなかでも、**劇画**『カムイ伝』は、60年代に登場して、未だシリーズが完結していない大作です。封建時代を舞台にした「権力との戦い」というテーマは、当時の学生運動家たちに圧倒的に支持されました。

ところで本当の忍者は、平凡で目立たない紺や茶系の服装をしていたそうですが、フィクションでは陰の存在というイメージのせいか、よく黒装束の忍者が出てきます。若い世代に大人気の**少年漫画**『NARUTO ─ナルト─』をごぞんじでしょうか？　架空世界の忍者・うずまきナルトは、オレンジの服に黄髪のパンクヘア。これまでにない忍者像でしたね。

Notes

[16] 80年代、米で流行った忍者映画では、ヌンチャク等、忍者の使わない武器がよく出てくる。

[17] 講談等で人気のヒーロー。実在説もある。

Comment

ナルトを見ると、80〜90年代に大ヒットした『DRAGON BALL』の孫悟空を思い出すなあ。やっぱりオレンジ色の格好をしていた。孫悟空は忍者じゃなくて、中国の『西遊記』っていう伝奇小説から採ったキャラクターだけどね。
Naruto reminds me of Son Goku, the hero of the big 1980s-90s hit *Dragon Ball*. Goku wore orange clothes, too. On the other hand, he wasn't a ninja, but a character from the Chinese fantasy classic *Journey to the West*.

centered around a love story, typified the early 1980s, when Japan was approaching the peak of its economic prosperity.

Without a doubt the best-known sports manga outside Japan is *Captain Tsubasa* (also titled *Flash Kicker* overseas), still ongoing since its launch in 1981. The anime version reportedly inspired such World Cuppers as Zinedine Zidane of France and Francesco Totti of Italy to take up soccer in their youth. A big 1990s hit was the basketball manga *Slam Dunk*. Currently another soccer manga, *Giant Killing*, continues to draw readers in serialization.

Vocabulary

arguably｜ほぼ間違いなく、おそらく	sheer effort｜純粋な努力
endure ...｜…に耐える	typify ...｜…の典型となる、…を代表する
harsh｜厳しい、過酷な	ongoing｜継続している
ordeal｜試練、苦しい体験	inspire *someone* to *do*｜人を刺激して…させる

10 Ninja Manga and *Naruto*

Ninja were secret agents who formed groups to engage in covert operations, such as spying and assassination, during the period when the samurai (see p. 296) ruled Japan. The original ninja did indeed employ a number of special techniques, but the characters in ninja novels, movies, and manga use tricks, some of them completely imaginary or supernatural, that were never available to real ninja.

Ninja stories often feature characters named after Hattori Hanzo, a historical ninja (his descendants by the same name were samurai), or the mythical ninja hero Sarutobi Sasuke. Some examples are the manga *Ninja Hattori-kun* and *Sasuke*.

The ninja **gekiga** *The Legend of Kamui* first appeared in the 1960s, and the long-running series continues to this day. Among its biggest fans were the student activists of the sixties who identified with its theme of battling against the authorities of feudal Japan.

Actual ninjas wore normal clothing in subdued colors like brown or dark blue, but in fiction they usually wear black, perhaps because of their shadowy reputation. If you've seen the recent super-hit **shonen manga** *Naruto*, you may think that ninja wear orange clothes and blond punk-style hair, like the story's fictional hero Uzumaki Naruto. He definitely does not look like any ninja we've seen before.

Vocabulary

covert operation｜秘密工作、隠密活動	identify with ...｜…と（自分を）一体と考える
descendant｜子孫	feudal｜封建時代の
long-running｜長く続いている	subdued｜地味な、控えめな
student activist｜学生運動家	definitely｜[否定文で] 決して、絶対に

コラム **妖怪**

日本には古くから、「妖怪」という化け物のようなものの存在が、伝えられてきました。

水中に棲む河童や、長鼻の天狗……。「幽霊」が死んだ人の霊なのに対して、妖怪は不可思議な自然現象、長く生きた動物や古道具などの化身です。各地の民間信仰（P. 168 参照）に根ざしていて、人間の怖れが生み出した存在と考えられています。

もとをたどれば、インドや中国が起源の妖怪も多いのですが、日本の文化のなかで育まれてきた妖怪は、もはや中国語の妖怪とも、また英語のフェアリーやモンスターとも同じではありません。

現代では、妖怪の実在を信じる人は、減ってしまいました。一方で、その奇怪なキャラクターと、信仰の背後にある、自然への敬意などを描いたフィクションは、繰り返し作られています。

11 水木しげると『ゲゲゲの鬼太郎』

日本の**妖怪**がたくさん出てくる『ゲゲゲの鬼太郎』は、これまでに 5 回アニメ化されている古典的な漫画です。主人公の妖怪・鬼太郎は、味方の妖怪たちとともに、人間に悪をする妖怪と戦います。伝承上の妖怪だけでなく、少年の姿をした鬼太郎をはじめ、作者・水木しげるが創作したユニークな妖怪も登場します。

水木は 1922 年生まれ。子どもの頃の思い出を描いた『のんのんばあとオレ』は、2007年にフランスのアングレーム国際バンド・デシネ・フェスティバルで、最優秀作品賞（最高賞）を受賞しました。

水木は第二次世界大戦時に、ニューブリテン島で爆撃にあって左腕を亡くし、片手で漫画を描いてきました。その時、出合ったトライ族の人たちと、生涯の親交を深めた話も有名です。

『水木しげる　妖怪まんが鬼太郎』
水木しげる・作（小学館）
Mizuki Shigeru Yokai-Manga Kitaro

COLUMN **Yokai**

Since ancient times, Japan has abounded with stories of the super-natural creatures called *yokai*. Among the most popular examples are the long-nosed goblins known as *tengu* and the water imps known as *kappa*. Unlike ghosts, yokai are not spirits of the dead, but include apparitions of mysterious natural phenomena, long-lived animals, and even inanimate objects. They are thought to originate in local folk beliefs (see p. 169) and people's everyday fears and superstitions.

Many yokai can be traced back to India or China, but over the centuries Japanese yokai have acquired their own unique identities, quite unlike the *yaoguai* of China or the fairies and monsters of the English-speaking world.

Nowadays few Japanese believe that yokai actually exist. But yokai characters, and stories that treat nature with the same reverence that sustained traditional beliefs in yokai, remain as popular as ever.

Vocabulary

abound with ... │ …で満ちている	apparition │ 幻影
long-nosed goblin │ 鼻の長い化け物	reverence │ 畏敬の念
water imp │ 水中に住む子鬼	sustain ... │ …を支える、維持する

¹¹ Mizuki Shigeru and *GeGeGe no Kitaro*

GeGeGe no Kitaro is a manga classic that features many Japanese **yokai**. It has been made into an animated TV series five times. The hero is Kitaro, a yokai who looks like a young schoolboy. Together with a variety of spooky friends, he fights other yokai who try to do bad things to humans. Mizuki Shigeru, the author, mixes traditional yokai with some unique ones of his own invention, like Kitaro himself.

Born in 1922, Mizuki won the Prize for Best Album at the Angoulême International Comics Festival in 2007 for *NonNonBa*, a story based on his childhood memories.

Mizuki lost his left arm in an air raid on New Britain Island during World War II, and pursued his manga career literally single-handedly. He is also famous for his lifelong friendship with the Tolai people of New Britain, whom he met during his time on the island.

Vocabulary

spooky │ 不気味な、化け物のような	air raid │ 空襲
invention │ 創造物	pursue ... │ …を続ける、…に従事する

国民的漫画ピックアップ

天才バカボン (赤塚不二夫 作)	60年代のナンセンスなギャグ漫画。少年バカボンと、浮世離れしたバカボンのパパが、町内を騒がせる。パパの決めゼリフは「これでいいのだ」。
ドラえもん (藤子・F・不二雄 作)	ドラえもんは、未来から来たネコ型ロボット――ただし、耳がない――で、どこでも行ける「どこでもドア」など、便利な道具を出してくれる。ダメ少年ののび太は、ドラえもんの道具に頼りすぎては失敗する。東/東南アジア各国でも大人気。
ONE PIECE (尾田栄一郎 作)	2000年代少年漫画の金字塔で、単行本発行部数の記録を更新しながら連載中。海賊王をめざす少年ルフィとその仲間たちが、「ひとつなぎの大秘宝（ワンピース）」をめぐって、冒険と戦いの旅を続ける。

12 同人誌と二次創作

「同人誌」とは、個人やサークルが漫画や小説などを自費出版する冊子[18] のことで、漫画の同人誌は、趣味の域を超えた規模の市場を形成しています。東京で年2回開催されている「コミックマーケット」[19] などの同人誌即売会では、人気サークルのブース前に、同人誌を買い求める長蛇の列が出来ますし、大きめの街には同人誌を扱う書店もあります。

同人誌の作品は玉石混合で、じつのところポルノが目に付きますが、同人出身の漫画家は多く、自由な表現ができるので、商業誌と合わせて同人活動を続けるプロもいます。

同人誌の世界では、人気作品のキャラクターを勝手に使って、新しい作品を創る「二次創作」（P.74参照）がさかんに行われています。著作権上の問題はあるものの、ほとんどの場合は、原作の人気を盛り上げるファン活動として、作者や出版社に黙認[20]、あるいは歓迎されているのです。

最近は同人誌だけでなく、ウェブサイトを作品発表の場とする人も増えました。

Notes

※18 定期刊行する雑誌もある。 ※19 3日間の会期中に出展者・来場者合わせて50万人以上が参加する。 ※20 原作のイメージを損ねる場合など、厳しい法的措置が取られたケースもある。

A Few of Japan's Favorite Manga

Tensai Bakabon **(Genius Bakabon)** by Akatsuka Fujio	A nonsensical gag manga from the sixties. The young boy Bakabon and his wild and crazy Papa cause all kinds of trouble in their neighborhood. Papa's catchphrase is "Everything's fine!"
Doraemon by Fujiko F. Fujio	A blue, earless robot-cat from the future, Doraemon has a bunch of useful gadgets like the Anywhere Door. Nobita, a hapless schoolboy, gets in trouble when he depends on Doraemon's bag of tricks too much. A big hit throughout East and Southeast Asia.
One Piece by Oda Eiichiro	The runaway **shonen-manga** bestseller of the 2000s, still in serialization and setting new print-run records in book format. The hero is a boy named Luffy who wants to be a pirate king. He and his friends embark on one adventure after another in search of the One Piece, "the world's ultimate treasure."

¹² Doujinshi and Derivative Works

Doujinshi are small booklets or magazines containing manga or fiction self-published by individuals or fan clubs. Manga doujinshi have grown into an entire market far beyond the scale of a mere hobby. At events like Comiket, the vast comic market held in Tokyo twice a year, long lines of fans wait to purchase doujinshi at the booths of popular clubs, and bookstores carrying such publications can be found in the larger cities.

Doujinshi vary widely in quality, and in fact many are simply pornographic. But quite a few established manga artists got their start in these alternative publications, and some professionals continue to publish in doujinshi as well as commercial magazines, thanks to the freedom of expression allowed by the former.

Parodies and other derivative works that use characters from hit manga to create entirely new stories are common in the doujinshi world. The question of copyright violations notwithstanding, manga artists and publishers tend to tolerate or even welcome these efforts as a fan activity that boosts the popularity of their work (see p. 75).

Recently websites have come to rival doujinshi as a venue for releasing new manga works.

Vocabulary

copyright violation | 著作権侵害
notwithstanding | それにもかかわらず

tolerate ... | …を大目に見る
boost ... | …を高める

¹³ 日本漫画の多様性

60年代に創刊された伝説のアンダーグラウンド漫画雑誌『ガロ』は、カルト的な漫画家を幾人も輩出しました。暗くシュールな作風のつげ義春は、その筆頭に挙げられます。

一方、日本では一般的な漫画雑誌にも、バトルものなどの主流作品とともに、個性的な作品が掲載されてきました。たとえば、ホラー漫画の巨匠・楳図かずおもユニークな作風で、サイバーパンクかつ「愛」がテーマの『わたしは真悟』には、熱い信奉者がいます。

70年代に登場した『はだしのゲン』は、原爆投下時の広島の惨状などが描き出された、中沢啓治の自伝的ストーリー。数カ国のボランティアによって英訳され[21]、初めてアメリカで出版された日本漫画でもあります。こうの史代の『夕凪の街 桜の国』も、広島をテーマにした名作で、戦後を生きる女性たちの心象を淡々と描きました。

80年代には「不条理ギャグ」といって、意味不明な展開で意表を突くギャグ漫画が流行りました。近年のギャグ漫画では、しりあがり寿や西原理恵子が、それぞれ「シュールで深い」、「破天荒でどこか切ない」といった独特の世界を展開しています。

最近、注目されている中村光の『聖☆おにいさん』は、仏陀とイエスが日本で仲よく休暇を過ごす、という大胆な設定のコメディ[22]です。

海外で描かれる漫画も増えました（P. 84参照）。2001年にはフランスの漫画家フレデリック・ボアレらが、日仏を中心とした作家性の強い漫画（あるいはバンド・デシネ）を「ヌーベルまんが」と呼んで、活動の場を広げる運動を展開しています。

漫画の形式を超えた、絵本や現代アートなどの分野で評価される作品もあります。長新太のナンセンスな漫画、タイガー立石のサイレント漫画[23]や、横山裕一の「ネオ漫画」（図版 P. 85）などです。

Notes

※21 近年、プロがボランティアで参加して、翻訳見直しが行われた。　※22 日本におけるギャグ漫画とコメディ漫画にはっきりとした線引きはないが、後者はおもにストーリー漫画（長編のストーリーがある漫画等）を指す。　※23 言葉を排し、ビジュアルだけで表現した漫画。

¹³ The Diversity of Manga

The legendary underground manga magazine *Garo*, founded in the 1960s, produced a number of artists who enjoyed cult followings. One of the most noteworthy was Tsuge Yoshiharu, celebrated for his dark and surrealistic style.

Even commercial manga magazines have been known to include more idiosyncratic work alongside their typical action-oriented fare. Umezu Kazuo, the "king" of horror manga, attracted a devoted readership to *My Name Is Shingo*, a serial in which Umezu brings his unique touch to a tale of cyberpunk love.

Barefoot Gen, which appeared in the 1970s, is a semi-autobiographical story in which Nakazawa Keiji depicts the horrors of the atomic bombing of Hiroshima. Translated into English by an international group of volunteers, it was the first manga to be published in the United States. Another Hiroshima-themed manga, Kono Fumiyo's *Town of Evening Calm, Country of Cherry Blossoms*, is a gentle portrayal of the emotions of girls growing up after the war.

The 1980s saw the rise of "*fujori* (absurd) gag" manga, given to off-the-wall humor and nonsensical plot twists and surprises. Lately, gag manga have come to embrace authors with highly original styles like Shiriagari Kotobuki, known for tales of surreal profundity, and Saibara Rieko, whose work is wild and daring, yet with a touch of melancholy.

A recent hit series that belongs to the comedy-manga category is Nakamura Hikaru's *Saint Young Men*, which hilariously imagines Buddha and Jesus as friends taking a vacation together in Japan.

Another trend of late is manga created overseas. In 2001 the French cartoonist Frédéric Boilet and his colleagues coined the term *nouvelle manga* for a sophisticated genre of manga (or manga-inspired *bande dessinée*) drawn and promoted primarily by Japanese and French artists.

Manga have also broken out of their conventional format to appear in critically acclaimed picture books and contemporary artworks. Some examples are Cho Shinta's nonsense manga, Tiger Tateishi's "silent" manga, and Yokoyama Yuichi's "neo-manga" (image on p. 85).

Vocabulary

noteworthy ｜注目すべき	off-the-wall ｜とっぴな、奇妙な
idiosyncratic ｜特異な、独特な	hilariously ｜陽気に、愉快に
portrayal ｜描写	break out of ... ｜…から抜けだす

WORLD CAFÉ **世界の Manga**

海外の漫画ファンは、日本のアニメから入って原作の漫画を読み始める人が多いようです。日本では漫画が先に世に出ますから、順番が逆ですね。

アメリカでは 80 年代に、本格的に日本漫画の翻訳出版が始まりました。日本の本は右開きですが、英語版は当初、一般的な英語の本に合わせて、原稿を反転させて左開きにしていたため、「日本には左利きが多いの？」といった誤解を生んだそうです。現在では、オリジナルに合わせた右開きで出版されるようになりました。

フランスは日本漫画の売上げが、世界有数の国です。同国のアングレーム国際バンド・デシネ・フェスティバルでは、水木しげる、谷口ジロー、浦澤直樹などの漫画が受賞しています。

アジア各地では、60〜80 年代頃に海賊版が多く出回ったせいで、日本漫画の普及がうながされました。現在、台湾、香港、タイなどでは、正式に許可を得た漫画が翻訳出版されています。

また、『少年ジャンプ』などの少年漫画誌や、少女漫画をいくつか集めた雑誌が発行されている／あるいは過去に発行されていた地域も、アジア各地やアメリカ、ドイツ、ポーランドなど、かなりあります。中国では日本の講談社が、現地出版社と共同で中国の漫画家を起用した漫画雑誌を発行しています。

漫画家同士の国際交流の場に、日本の漫画家たちの発起で始まった「国際マンガサミット」（前身は東アジアマンガサミット）があります。年に一度、世界中から何百人もの漫画家が、毎回異なる開催国に集まるのです。

現在では、日本スタイルの影響を受けた漫画が、世界各地で描かれるようになりました。英語で書かれた漫画は OEL manga（original English-language manga）と呼ばれています。ほかに world manga や global manga といういい方もあります。

『ジャングル大帝』（手塚治虫・作）の主人公・レオとその父パンジャ
The hero Leo and his father Panja, from *Jungle Emperor Leo* (*Kimba, the White Lion* overseas)
by Tezuka Osamu 　 © Tezuka Productions

横山裕一のネオ漫画『トラベル』（イースト・プレス）Yokoyama Yuichi's neo-manga *Travel*, 2006

04

LITERATURE

文学

01 日本文学の概要

日本文学の特徴※1として、季節感や微妙な人間心理を、主観的な視点で描くのが得意だとよくいわれます。

それには背景があって、古代から19世紀にいたるまで、日本の正式な文章は、おもに中国の文語で書かれていました。文字の読み書き自体が、ごく限られた階級のものだった時代、日本語※2は私的な文章で使われていたのです。日本には、和歌（短歌）という31音節の短い定型詩がありますが、平安時代の貴族たちは、手紙などで日常的にやりとりする短歌のなかで、季節を話題にし、気持ちを伝え合っていました。

また、10〜14世紀に、閉鎖的な日々を送る貴族の女性たちの間で、体験や心境を回想してつづることが流行り、いくつかは「日記文学」として読まれるようになりました。そうした土壌のなかで、紀元1000年頃、古典文学の最高峰として双璧をなす『源氏物語』と『枕草子』が誕生します。ともに宮仕えの女性が著した、日本の小説と随筆の起源です。

日記文学の流れは、時代を超えて、20世紀の文学ジャンル「私小説」（P. 102参照）にも感じとることができます。しかし、こうしたタイプに収まらない日本文学もあります。

たとえば神話や昔話などには、世界の伝承に通じる空想世界が息づいていますし、僧侶たちは多彩な仏書を書いてきました。また、武家同士の合戦（12世紀）を題材にした、作者不明の『平家物語』は、盲目の旅法師が琵琶で弾き語りをして、日本各地に伝えました。

印刷技術が発達し、識字率が上がった17〜18世紀には、井原西鶴などの流行作家が登場します。俳句（俳諧）という、短歌より短い17音節の定型詩が、発達したのもその頃です。

20世紀に入る頃には、口語の小説や、非定型で近代的なテーマの詩が書かれるようになりました。そして今では、海外にファンをもつ現役作家もいます。特に村上春樹の作品は、「世界文学」と呼ばれるほど、広範な地域で読まれています。

Notes

※1 また、言葉に霊的な力があるとする「言霊（ことだま）信仰」の影響も考えられる。　※2 日本で使用されてきた言語は、日本語以外にアイヌ語、ウィルタ語、ニブフ語等があるが、消滅の危機に瀕している。また、日本では方言とされる八丈、奄美、国頭、沖縄、宮古、八重山、与那国の言葉を、ユネスコは独立した言語としている。アイヌ語の口承文学等も近年、文章化が試みられ、日本語にも訳されている。

Japanese Literature: An Overview

Connoisseurs of Japanese literature often cite such attributes as its sensitivity to the changes of the seasons and the subjective viewpoint from which it explores the intricacies of the human heart.

There are historical reasons for these qualities. From ancient times all the way up to the 19th century, the Japanese wrote formal texts in literary-style Chinese, reserving Japanese for personal communications. For many centuries reading and writing were activities practiced only by certain classes of society. Aristocrats of the Heian period (794-1185) habitually enlivened their everyday correspondence with the short 31-syllable poems known as *tanka*. In these verses they frequently referred to the seasons and expressed their personal feelings for one another.

Between the 10th and 14th centuries it was the fashion among noblewomen, who lived an extremely cloistered life, to write down their thoughts and reminiscences. Several such memoirs gained popularity as what came to be called "diary literature." It was from this culture that two of the greatest works of classical Japanese literature emerged around the year 1000: *The Tale of Genji* and *The Pillow Book*. Both written by women who served in the Imperial Court, they provided the wellspring for an entire tradition of Japanese novels and essays to come.

The influence of diary literature can be seen in the 20th-century genre of the I-novel (see p. 103). But there are other kinds of Japanese literature as well. Old **myths** and folktales tell of imaginary worlds that share much in common with the legends of other cultures, and Buddhist priests wrote a variety of tales to convey religious teachings. *The Tale of the Heike*, an epic account of the samurai conflicts of the 12th century by an unknown author, became known throughout Japan as blind itinerant monks recited it to the accompaniment of the *biwa* lute.

With improvements in printing technology, Japan's literacy rate grew in the 17th and 18th centuries, and popular authors like **Ihara Saikaku** came into vogue. The same era also saw the appearance of a new, shorter poem structure, the 17-syllable **haiku**.

The Meiji period (1868-1912) brought with it novels written in colloquial Japanese and free-verse poetry on modern themes. Today, not a few contemporary Japanese authors boast a following overseas. **Murakami Haruki**, for example, is read around the globe, and might properly be described as a writer of world literature.

Vocabulary

syllable ｜音節（p. 93 参照）　　　　epic account ｜大作、叙事詩

02 源氏物語──世界最古の小説

『源氏物語』は平安時代、紫式部の作とされる全54帖の物語。世界的にみて最古の小説にあたるのではないかと議論されています。「最古にして最高」という人もいます。

主人公・光源氏は、天皇の息子で才色兼備。当時の貴族社会を舞台に、10人以上の女性とラブストーリーを繰り広げます。

相手は、母の面影がある義母の「藤壺（ふじつぼ）」、幼い頃から育てた「紫上（むらさきのうえ）」、嫉妬から生霊になってしまう「六条御息所（ろくじょうのみやすどころ）」など、それぞれ個性豊かに描かれています。

源氏と女性たちとの関係について、この時代は一夫多妻制の通い婚だったと説明されてきましたが、最近出版された本によると、法律上は当時も一夫一婦制だったというので話題になっています。その前提が変わると、話の持ち味が違って読めてくるのです。

文中には、和歌が800首ほども出てきます。また、香を調合して衣装に焚きしめるなどのみやびな趣味も、物語に華を添えています（P.190参照）。

光源氏の人生は途中からかげりが濃くなり、物語は彼の子や孫の代に移行します。

源氏物語に読み取れる仏教的な無常観は、日本文学全体でよく出てくるテーマです。

また、18世紀の学者・本居宣長は、源氏物語に顕著な王朝文学の美意識を、「もののあはれ」という言葉で説明しました。これは、道徳的な分別によらず、物事の本質をあるがままに受けとめて、しみじみと同情するという意味です。

現存最古の『源氏物語絵巻』、「夕霧」の場面（12世紀）
Scene from "Yugiri" on the oldest existing version of the *Illustrated Handscroll of The Tale of Genji* (12th c.)

02 *The Tale of Genji*: World's Oldest Novel

A 54-chapter narrative written during the Heian period, *The Tale of Genji* is attributed to Murasaki Shikibu. Scholars suggest that it is the oldest novel in the world, and some have even called it the "oldest and greatest."

The protagonist is Hikaru Genji, the brilliant and handsome son of an emperor. The tale recounts his romances with over a dozen women against the backdrop of aristocratic society. His lovers are richly drawn characters—among them Genji's stepmother Fujitsubo, who resembles his deceased mother; Murasaki, raised by Genji himself from childhood; and Lady Rokujo, whom jealousy turns into a "living ghost."

Genji's relationships with women have been explained as consistent with the polygynous marital customs of his day. More recently, however, at least one scholar has made the provocative point that even in those days, a man could legally have only one wife. Depending on what we assume about the social mores of this period, the story itself takes on a different flavor.

The Tale of Genji contains some 800 **tanka** verses as well as depictions of elegant pastimes, such as the use of blended incense to perfume clothing (see p. 193), that add further spice to the tale.

In later chapters Genji's life takes on a gloomy aspect, and the narrative shifts to his descendants. The **Buddhist** view of the transience of life that colors the novel is a theme that recurs throughout Japanese literature.

The 18th-century scholar Motoori Norinaga used the term *mono no aware*—an understanding and acceptance of the nature of all things without moral judgment, accompanied by deep empathy—to define the aesthetic that prevails in medieval Japanese court literature and is nowhere more striking than in *The Tale of Genji*.

04

Vocabulary

narrative ｜ 物語	verse ｜ 韻文
recount ... ｜ …を物語る	gloomy ｜ 暗い、陰気な
polygynous marital custom ｜ 一夫多妻制	transience ｜ 無常、はかなさ
provocative ｜ 挑発的な、刺激的な	recur ｜ 繰り返される
social mores ｜ 社会の道徳規範	prevail in ... ｜ …に普及している

⁰³ 和歌 （短歌）

短歌^{※3} は五・七・五・七・七音節の定型詩。ほとんどが抒情詩で、古代から現代まで作られ続けています。

「音節」といいましたが、これは正確には日本で音^{※4} や拍（モーラ）と呼ばれる音声（と文字）の単位で、ほぼすべての音が「ア・イ・ウ・エ・オ」の母音で終わります^{※5}。そして日本では、5 音と 7 音を組み合わせた言葉のリズムが好まれ、古くから歌謡や演劇のセリフにも、よく使われてきました。

現存最古の歌集で 7〜8 世紀の編纂とされる『万葉集』には、すでに廃れた形式の詩歌・歌謡とともに、数多くの短歌が収録されていて、古人のほとばしるような感情を今に伝えています。

平安時代、短歌は貴族のたしなみでした。男女は時に暗示的な表現で想いを歌に託し、贈り合いました。

やがて短歌は、最盛期の王朝文化の象徴として、武家や町人らへと普及していきます。10 世紀に編まれた勅撰 和歌集『古今和歌集』は、その後千年に渡って短歌のお手本となりました。

近代になると世の中の価値観が変わり、新しい感覚が短歌に詠まれるようになります。しかし今でも短歌には、古い文語がよく使われています。短くて字数に収まりやすいのと、擬古的な味わいのためです。

1987 年、俵万智という当時 20 代の女性が、現代的な日常語をちりばめて書いた『サラダ記念日』は、歌集としては異例のベストセラーになりました。

Notes

※3 現代では、「和歌」といえば古典短歌を指し、明治以降に改革された近現代短歌は「短歌」と呼ばれる。
※4 「音」は日本人が通常、音声の最小単位と認識しているもの（専門用語では拍／モーラ）で、カナ 1 文字で表記される。日本語の 1 音＝英語の 1 音節に相当することが多いが、例外もある。例えば「にっぽん」は 4 音節だが、英語では 2 音節 (nip-pon)。　※5 撥音（ん）、促音（っ）、引く音（ー／長母音の後半）は例外で、単独では現れず、独立する拍の後にくる。

Comment

私が子どもの頃は、正月に「（小倉）百人一首」といって、歌人百人の和歌が一首ずつ載っているカルタで遊びました。一人が歌を読み上げて、他の人は床に並べた札のなかから、対応している下の句が書かれた札を取り合うんです。カルタ取りは競技にもなっていますよ。

When I was a kid, we used to play a card game during the New Year holiday called *Hyakunin Isshu* ("100 Poets, One Poem Each"). The cards display 100 tanka, each by a different poet. One player reads a verse aloud and the other players scramble to find the matching card with the last part of the verse. There are even *Hyakunin Isshu* contests.

⁰³ Tanka

The tanka ("short poem") has a fixed form with phrases of five, seven, five, seven, and seven syllables. Most tanka are lyric verses. People have been composing them since ancient times and continue to do so today.

A Japanese "syllable" is, to be more precise, what linguists call a mora, generally recognized by Japanese speakers as the minimum unit of verbal sound as well as of their **writing system**. In the Japanese language nearly every such unit ends with a vowel. The rhythm of words combined in sets of five or seven syllables has always found favor in Japan, and the pattern has been used for many centuries in songs and dramatic dialogue.

The oldest extant collection of Japanese poetry is the *Man'yoshu* (Collection of a Myriad Leaves), compiled in the seventh and eighth centuries. In addition to poems and songs in long-outdated forms, it includes a great number of tanka that eloquently convey the joys and sorrows of people of that era to contemporary readers.

During the Heian period, writing tanka was an accomplishment expected of members of the nobility. Men and women would exchange poems that hinted at their feelings for one another, sometimes through evocative metaphors.

The tanka came to symbolize Heian court culture at its height, and eventually spread to the samurai (see p. 296) and commoner classes as well. The anthology *Kokin Wakashu* (Collection of Ancient and Modern Japanese Poems), compiled by imperial command in the 10th century, set the standard for tanka for the next millennium.

Amid the changing values of the modern age, tanka have served as a medium for expressing new sensibilities and points of view. But even today, composers of tanka employ a lot of archaic literary terms. Besides adding a classical air to the verses, these words tend to be shorter and take up fewer syllables than more modern equivalents.

In 1987 Tawara Machi, then in her twenties, made a splash with *Salad Anniversary*, a collection of tanka sprinkled with current expressions. It became a bestseller, a rarity for poetry books.

Vocabulary

vowel｜母音	convey ...｜…を伝える
extant｜現存している	commoner｜庶民
compiled｜編纂された	archaic｜古語の
eloquently｜雄弁に、表情豊かに	equivalent｜（価値などが）同等のもの

コラム 文字

現代日本語[※6] では、同じ文章のなかで、ひらがな、カタカナ、漢字の3種類の文字が使われています[※7]。

日本で作られたひらがなとカタカナは、1字が1音（拍／P.92参照）に対応する表音文字[※8]。画数が少なく、50字ほどしかないので、書くのが簡単です。

すべてひらがなでも文章を書くことはできます。小さな子どもはそうしています。どの言葉にカタカナや漢字をあてるかは、基準や慣例はあるものの、書き手の意図によります。

カタカナは、擬音語・擬態語や外来語など、何らかの理由でほかと区別したい場合によく使います。英語のイタリックに相当するでしょうか。

漢字は中国から来た文字で、一つひとつが絵のように意味を表します。たとえば tree は「木」、123 は「一二三」。そして組み合わせて、別の言葉を作ることができます。漢字は使われる言葉によって、読み方が変わります。日本の「常用漢字」は、現在2,000字あまりです[※9]。

見た目の印象としては、漢字は力強く、ひらがなは柔らかく、カタカナは無機質でしょうか。また、ローマ字などアルファベットも普及しているので、日本語にまじえて使うことがあります。

日本文学の作者は、これらのうち、どの文字を選ぶかという視覚的な要素にも、心をくだいて執筆しているのです。

Notes

※6 日本で使用される、日本語以外の言語については、P. 88 参照。　※7 日本には、漢字伝来以前にも文字があったという説がある。　※8 「きゃ」、「きゅ」、「きょ」等の拗音（ようおん）は例外。日本語の音数は約 120（諸説あり）。　※9 漢字の総数は数万字（どれを正式な漢字とするか等、諸説あり）。日本で作られた漢字もある（峠、畑、辻、働 等）。

あいうえお　　hiragana
アイウエオ　　katakana
a　i　u　e　o

Japanese Writing Systems

Modern Japanese text is a mix of three different types of character: *hiragana*, *katakana*, and *kanji*. Hiragana and katakana are phonetic characters, each representing a single sound or syllable (see p. 93). With only a few strokes required to write them and about 50 characters in each set, both hiragana and katakana are easy to learn.

It is possible to write Japanese using nothing but hiragana, so young children learn these characters first. Which words to write in hiragana, and which to write in katakana or kanji, is a choice determined to some extent by criteria and conventions, but is ultimately up to the writer.

Katakana typically represent words that for one reason or another are meant to stand out from the rest of the text. They may be used for onomatopoetic or mimetic words, or loanwords from other languages—much as italics are used in English.

Kanji, which originated in China, are ideographs—characters that, like pictures, convey a meaning. For example, the kanji for "tree" is 木 and the kanji for the numbers 1, 2, and 3 are 一二三 . Kanji also combine together to form different words, and their pronunciation can vary with the word they belong to. The standard list of "kanji in common use" today comes to a bit over 2,000 characters.

To Japanese readers, the solid-looking kanji give an impression of strength, while the gently curving hiragana seem softer, and the sharp-angled katakana rather cold and impersonal. Japanese also learn the Roman alphabet, so these letters, called *romaji*, frequently appear in Japanese text too.

Japanese writers carefully choose the types of characters they use in order to evoke a certain visual image in their prose.

Vocabulary

phonetic｜表音の	mimetic word｜擬態語
onomatopoetic word｜擬音語	ideograph｜表意文字

人 **person**
[*hito*]

二人 **two people**
[*futari*]

04 枕草子──随筆のはじまり

日本文学の一大ジャンル・随筆とは、種々のテーマについて著者の体験や見聞、思うところなどを自由につづった短い散文を指します。英語でよくエッセイと訳されていますが、アメリカの essay に多くみられるように、自分の意見を論理的に説明するものではありません。実体験と、文章表現の味わい深さが随筆のポイントで、結論がないこともあります。

千年ほど前に書かれた『枕草子』は、随筆の起源であり、最高傑作といわれています。作者は天皇の妻に女房※10 として仕えた清少納言と伝えられ、自然の美しさや宮廷生活などを記した、300 ほどの短いエピソードから成っています。題名の「枕」が何を意味するかはわかっていませんが、枕元に置く備忘録だという説があります。

「春はあけぼの」で始まる有名な一段目では、四季それぞれに、清少納言の一番お気に入りの時間が描写されています。

Notes

※ 10　貴族の邸宅で、乳母や家庭教師、秘書等の役割をして仕えた女性。女房も通常貴族で、個室が与えられた。

05 神話と歴史

古代ギリシャの『イリアス』や古代インドの『ラーマーヤナ』にあたるような書物※11 というと、日本では 8 世紀初頭に書かれた『古事記』※12 や『日本書紀』などが挙げられます※13。日本の「現存する最古の歴史書」と「初の正式な歴史書」です。ただし散文なので、叙事詩（出来事を記した長編の韻文※14）ではありません。

そこには、「八百万の神」と例えられるほど、数多くの神々が登場します（P. 168、170 参照）。そして、アマテラスという太陽神が、現在まで続く天皇家の祖先とされています。

これらが書かれた時代は、日本という国名※15 が出来て間もない頃でしたから、民間に伝わる神話を、新しい国の政治的意図に合わせてアレンジしたという見方ができます。

『古事記』と『日本書紀』に対して、日本人の間には、少々交錯した感情があります。日本では、明治時代から第二次世界大戦が終わるまでの数十年、天皇崇拝がいわば国教化していたので、終戦とともに天皇が「人間宣言」をすると、そのことと矛盾する両書に対して、拒絶反応が起こったのです。

→

04 *The Pillow Book*: Birth of the Zuihitsu Tradition

One of the pillars of Japanese literature is the genre known as *zuihitsu*, literally "following the brush," in which the writer jots down recollections, views, or impressions on all manner of topics. They are usually short prose pieces written in a free style.

Zuihitsu frequently gets translated into English as "essay," but unlike many Western-style essays, these are not writings that advance a logical argument or a clearcut opinion. The point of zuihitsu is the author's personal experience and the flavor of the prose. Often there is no conclusion.

Written a thousand years ago, *The Pillow Book* is regarded as the original zuihitsu, and indeed a masterpiece of the genre. Attributed to Sei Shonagon, a lady in waiting to an empress, it consists of some 300 brief episodes that touch on the beauties of nature and the everyday details of court life. The meaning of "pillow" in the title is not clear, but some scholars believe it refers to a compilation of private notes.

The famous opening line of *The Pillow Book*, "In spring it is the dawn," begins a chapter in which Sei Shonagon writes about her favorite time of day for each season.

Vocabulary

jot down ... │ …を書きとめる、メモする	clearcut │ 明快な、はっきりした
recollection │ 回想、思い出	lady in waiting │ 女官
prose │ 散文	dawn │ あけぼの［反意語は dusk（たそがれ）］

05 Mythology and History

Like the *Iliad* of ancient Greece and the *Ramayana* of India, Japan has its epic narratives, notably the *Kojiki* (Record of Ancient Matters) and *Nihon Shoki* (Chronicles of Japan), both written in the early eighth century. The *Kojiki* is Japan's oldest surviving historical account, and the *Nihon Shoki* is its first official history. Unlike the *Iliad* or the *Ramayana*, they are written in prose, not verse.

Both the *Kojiki* and *Nihon Shoki* feature a huge cast of ancient deities, typically referred to as the "eight million gods" (see pp. 169, 171). Among the most prominent is Amaterasu, the sun goddess and legendary ancestor of Japan's imperial line, which continues to the present day.

These chronicles were written shortly after the country adopted its formal name of *Nippon* (often pronounced *Nihon* today), so the myths they relate may well have been compiled and published to legitimize the political structure of the new nation.

←
しかし最近は、特に『古事記』の文学性や、民俗学的価値が見直されてき
ています。

Notes

※ 11 これらは民族に伝わる神話や英雄伝などを物語った民族叙事詩。　※ 12 『古事記』は数世紀後に書かれたとする偽書説や、序文だけ偽書とする説がある。　※ 13 『平家物語』も民族叙事詩に似た性格をもつ。その他、各地方の神話も日本に残っている。　※ 14 韻文とは一定のリズムをもつ文。日本語の短歌等では、拍（モーラ）を同数反復するが、言語によっては、音節の長短やアクセント等にパターンがある。西洋では押韻（rhyme）も重要な要素。反意語は散文。　※ 15 中国の『新唐書』の記述等から、天武期（673 ～ 686）に「日本」の号が成立したと考えられている。

⁰⁶ 井原西鶴

1682 年、井原西鶴（1642～93）の『好色一代男』が出版されると、初めて巷の風俗や、男たちのリアルな夢を謳い上げたフィクションとして、町人の間で大きな反響を呼びます。

主人公の世之介は、諸国を巡りながら色道修行に明け暮れ、やがて莫大な遺産を譲り受けて、名妓たちを相手にする粋人となります。封建時代の道徳観などまったく無視した、アンチヒーローの登場でした。

それだけだと、ポルノと呼ばれるような内容ですが、西鶴の文体※ 16 は絶妙でした。

西鶴は俳諧師（P. 100 参照）でもあり、しかも一昼夜の興行で 2 万 3,500 句詠んだと伝えられる早詠み名人でしたから、小説※ 17 でもリズムよく鋭い描写を繰り出すなかに、掛け言葉や現実味のある数字——例えば日付や値段——を盛り込むなど、しかけ満載で読者を引き込み、また笑わせました。

最初期の流行作家として登場した西鶴は、現代では世界の偉人に数えられています。

Notes

※ 16 挿絵も西鶴の自筆という説がある。　※ 17 西鶴の散文は、江戸時代には「浮世草子」と呼ばれた。

東京の古書店
A second-hand bookstore in Tokyo
Photo: Kawasaki Satoko (The Japan Times)

←

Some Japanese have mixed feelings about the *Kojiki* and *Nihon Shoki*. For several decades, from the Meiji period to the end of the Second World War, emperor worship was a state religion of sorts. When the emperor made his "declaration of humanity" at the war's end, many people rejected these ancient texts because of the role they had played in justifying the now-discredited creed.

Nowadays, however, the two epics—particularly the *Kojiki*—are enjoying renewed appreciation for their literary and ethnological value.

Vocabulary

mythology｜神話	adopt ...｜…を選ぶ、採用する
chronicle｜年代記、(壮大な) 物語	legitimize ...｜…を正当化する
account｜報告、記述	discredited creed｜疑惑に満ちた教義
prominent｜卓越した、有名な	ethnological｜民俗学的な

04

LITERATURE / Mythology and History / Ihara Saikaku

06 Ihara Saikaku

As the first work of fiction to celebrate the lives of common people, and the dreams of men in particular, *The Life of an Amorous Man*, a novel by Ihara Saikaku (1642-93), created a sensation with Japan's city-dwellers when it was published in 1682.

Yonosuke, the amorous man of the title, travels from place to place in pursuit of erotic pleasure, eventually—after he inherits a huge sum of money—becoming a stylish man about town who consorts with famous courtesans. Someone who pays no heed to the conventional morality of feudal Japan, he represents a new kind of protagonist, the antihero.

If that was all it offered, the book might have been dismissed as little more than pornography, but its prose is exquisite. Ihara was also a composer of *haikai* linked verse (see p. 101) and was known for his compositional speed. Legend has it that he once came up with 23,500 stanzas at an event lasting a single day and night. His novels, too, are rhythmic and packed with sharp-eyed observations, wordplay, realistic figures for dates and prices, and other devices that hooked readers in his day and made them laugh.

Initially viewed as a commercial writer, today Saikaku is counted among the great novelists of the world.

Vocabulary

city-dweller｜町の住人	conventional｜月並みな、因習的な
in pursuit of ...｜…を追い求めて	be dismissed｜退けられる
courtesan｜高級娼婦 [フランス語]	hook ...｜…を引きつける、夢中にさせる
pay heed to ...｜…に注意を払う	

俳句──世界最短の定型詩

俳句は、五・七・五音から成る定型詩です。たとえば 17 世紀に松尾芭蕉（1644〜94）が詠んだ、蛙の句は有名です。ためしに直訳してみると：

> 古池や（Old pond）
>
> 蛙飛び込む（A frog jumps in）
>
> 水の音（The sound of water）

この句にはたくさんの英訳があって、日本語では蛙が複数か単数かわからないため、1 匹の蛙が立てた小さな水音が、かえって場の静けさを際立たせた、という解釈もありますし、frogs と訳しているものもあります。

松尾芭蕉は「漂泊の俳人」として知られ、それまで軽いものだった文学形式・俳諧[18] の発句（冒頭の句）を、独立した芸術として開花させました。それが俳句と呼ばれるようになったのは、近代以降です。禅味を感じさせる芭蕉の句は、今ではさびの体現ととらえられるようになりました。

海外でも英語などで haiku を作る人が増えていますが、音数にこだわらず、短い 3 行詩として作られることが多いようです。

日本では、定型より字数＝音数（P. 92、94 参照）が多くなったり少なくなったりすることを、「字余り」、「字足らず」といって、多少は許されています。また俳句には、季語という季節を表す言葉を入れる決まりがあります。先ほどの芭蕉の句では、蛙が晩春の季語です。もうひとつ重要な手法として、途中で一カ所、「切れ字」[19] という語を入れて、文を切ります。「古池や」の「や」が切れ字にあたり、そこで一呼吸置く合間に、人は状況などを思い浮かべるのです。

自由律といって、定型や季語にとらわれない俳句や**短歌**もあります[20]。

Notes

※ 18 俳諧は連歌の遊戯性を高めた文学形式。　※ 19 強く言い切ったり、曲折を持たせたりする助詞や助動詞。音調を整える役割もある。「や」は詠嘆（exclamation）や呼びかけ（call）等の意味がある。他の切れ字には「かな」、「けり」等がある。　※ 20 俳句と同じく俳諧を源流とする五・七・五の定型詩「川柳」は、季語や切れ字がなく、風刺や軽さ、ユーモアを旨とする。

Comment

芭蕉は**忍者**だったという説があるんですよ。忍者の里の出身ですし、彼の『おくのほそ道』という旅行記の行程をみると、ものすごく速いペースで移動していて、スパイ活動をしていたんじゃないかという話です。

Some people theorize that Basho was a **ninja**! He was born in Iga, a region famed as the birthplace of the ninja, and if you look at his itinerary in the travel diary *Narrow Road to the Deep North*, he moved around at a remarkable pace, prompting speculation that he might have been working as a spy.

⁰⁷ Haiku: World's Shortest Verse Form

The haiku is a fixed form of poetry in three phrases of five, seven, and five syllables (or mora). A celebrated example is the 17th-century haiku by Matsuo Basho (1644-94) about a frog:

> *furuike ya / kawazu tobikomu / mizu no oto*
> Old pond / A frog jumps in / The sound of water

There are many English translations of this verse. It is impossible to tell from the original Japanese how many frogs Basho is talking about, so while most translators believe that the tiny sound made by one frog leaping into a pond is meant to highlight the quietness of the setting, others have translated the word into the plural "frogs."

Basho is revered as the wandering poet who took the opening stanza (*hokku*) of the humorous linked-verse format known as haikai and transformed it into a work of art. It was not until the modern era that this new verse form acquired the name haiku. With their **Zen**-like sensibility, Basho's poems came to define the essence of *sabi*, a quality embodying elements of age and serenity.

Writing haiku in English and other languages has become a popular pastime with people around the world. Many such efforts consist of short poems of three lines, without a fixed number of syllables. Some leeway is accepted in Japan as well, and haiku are occasionally written with more or fewer characters—i.e., syllables (see pp. 93, 95)—than the standard number.

One convention in haiku is the use of "season words" that indicate the time of year. In the aforementioned Basho haiku, the frog is a season word that suggests late spring. Another important aspect is the division of the verse with a "cutting word." In Basho's frog haiku the *ya* at the end of the first phrase is a cutting word that produces a pause, giving the reader a chance to take a breath and envision the scene of the old pond.

You can also find free-verse haiku and **tanka** that ignore the standard structures or leave out traditionally mandatory elements like season words.

Vocabulary

leaping into ... | …に飛び込んでいる
opening stanza | 冒頭の節、連 [ここでは発句のこと]
quality embodying elements of ... | …の要素を具体化するもの
leeway | 余地
i.e. | すなわち、言い換えれば [id est (ラテン語) の略]
mandatory | 義務的な、強制的な

⁰⁸ 日本の近代文学

19世紀末に始まる明治時代、日本文学は大転換期を迎えます。

西洋の文学概念が輸入され、文学の首座は、個人がやりとりする和歌から、読み手の限定されない小説に代わりました。そして数世紀ぶりに、女性作家^{※21}の活躍が目立つようになりました。また、それまでの日本語は文語と口語がかけ離れていましたが、言文一致運動が起こります。

次々と伝わる欧米発の文学潮流は、日本独特のかたちで展開しました。たとえばフランスの自然主義文学は、科学的な客観描写をめざすものでしたが、日本では主観をありのままに描くものと解釈され、その流れから、実体験を素材にした「私小説」というジャンルが生まれました。私小説作家たちは、暴露趣味や無理想といった批判を受けながらも、告白を文学における誠実な態度としたのです。

一方、近代日本の二大文豪といわれる夏目漱石と森鷗外は、自然主義と一線を画す理知的な作風で、高踏派^{※22}などと呼ばれました。

漱石に影響を受けた芥川龍之介は、『今昔物語集』などの古典に題材を取った作品で知られています。黒澤明の映画『羅生門』は、この芥川の短編『羅生門』（1915）と『藪の中』（1922）を合わせた内容です。

文学者としてほとんど無名のまま亡くなった宮沢賢治は、今では日本でもっとも愛されている詩人のひとりです。生前は北国で農業指導に力を尽くし、「農民芸術」を説きました。彼の心に映る郷土^{※23}「イーハトーヴ」などの造語や、異時空を感じさせる童話も、広く親しまれています。

Notes

※21 樋口一葉、与謝野晶子 等。　※22 元は19世紀フランス詩の一文学様式をいう。　※23 岩手県

夏目漱石　Natsume Soseki
（1867〜1916）

与謝野晶子　Yosano Akiko
（1878〜1942）

宮沢賢治　Miyazawa Kenji
（1896〜1933）

⁰⁸ Modern Literature

The Meiji era, which began in the latter half of the 19th century, was a major turning point for Japanese literature. It was during this period that Western literary concepts flooded into Japan. The novel, written for an unspecified audience, replaced the **tanka**, primarily a vehicle for personal communication, as the dominant literary form. Another change was that female writers came to the fore again, for the first time in centuries. And whereas spoken and written Japanese had traditionally occupied separate worlds, a movement began to unify the two styles.

As one Western literary trend after another reached the country, writers put a distinctive Japanese spin on them. French naturalism, for example, was an attempt to describe the world in a scientific, objective manner. In Japan, however, it was interpreted as an invitation to write from a natural, subjective viewpoint. From this current emerged a new genre, the I-novel, that took its inspiration from the author's personal experiences. I-novelists were accused of being exhibitionists or anti-idealists, but their belief in confession as a legitimate literary device was sincere.

Meanwhile, two towering figures of modern Japanese literature, **Natsume Soseki** and Mori Ogai, distinguished themselves from the naturalists with a coolly intellectual style that acquired such labels as "Parnassian."

A Soseki-influenced writer named Akutagawa Ryunosuke became known for works based on old stories such as those found in the *Konjaku Monogatarishu* (Anthology of Tales from the Past). The late filmmaker **Kurosawa Akira** created the scenario for his famous film *Rashomon* by combining two Akutagawa short stories, *Rashomon* (1915) and *In a Grove* (1922).

Miyazawa Kenji died a virtual unknown as a writer, but today he is one of Japan's most beloved poets. He devoted his life to improving agricultural conditions in northern Japan, and promoted the virtues of "peasant art." Countless readers are familiar with his children's tales, which draw us into a different time and space, as well as names he invented like Ihatov, the imaginary land that represented Miyazawa's home prefecture of Iwate.

Vocabulary

flood into … ｜ …にどっと押し寄せる	legitimate ｜まっとうな
vehicle ｜（伝達）手段	sincere ｜誠実な
dominant ｜支配的な、優勢な	late … ｜故…
put a Japanese spin on … ｜ …に日本的な味付けをほどこす	virtual ｜実質上の
	devote *A* to *B* ｜ A を B に捧げる
distinctive ｜独特の	virtue ｜長所、美徳
invitation ｜誘因	

09 文豪・夏目漱石

夏目漱石は 100 年ほど前に活躍した作家で、日本では巨匠中の巨匠とされています。台湾や中国、韓国にも、漱石ファンがわりと多いらしいですね。しかし、欧米での知名度が比較的低いのはなぜか、と話題になることがあります。私小説や耽美的といった、日本的な作家のイメージに当てはまらないせいか、はたまた作風の変化が大きくて、全体像がつかみにくいからか──初期の『吾輩は猫である』（1905〜06）は軽妙で、後期の『こゝろ』（1914）などは、暗く重い作品です。

では日本で漱石が、絶大な評価を得ているのはなぜでしょう。彼はまず、近代の文化変動のなかで、口語による新時代の文体を洗練させました。ロンドンで英文学を研究し、漢詩も書いた漱石ですが、誰もが読みやすくて、品のある日本語を書いたのです。

そして彼が提示した、近代人としての問題提起や思想は、現代の私たちにも響くものがあります。また作品の解釈が一筋縄でいかず、奥の深さを感じさせる作家かもしれません。

Comment

いや、最近漱石は、わりといろいろな国の人に読まれていますよ。村上春樹が漱石を、好きな作家だと言っている影響じゃないでしょうか。
Hey, seems like people in all sorts of countries are reading Soseki these days. Maybe it's because Murakami Haruki said Soseki is one of his favorite authors?

10 芥川賞と直木賞

日本の文学賞では、近代作家（P. 102 参照）の名を冠した「芥川龍之介賞」と「直木三十五賞」が特に有名で、年 2 回の授賞式に注目が集まります。前者は「純文学」、後者は娯楽性の高い「大衆文学」を対象としています。この分類には、曖昧なところがありますが……。元々は両方とも新人のための賞でしたが、直木賞は特に、キャリアを積んだ作家も受賞するようになりました。

09 Natsume Soseki

A writer who was active a century ago, Natsume Soseki is still acclaimed as the greatest of Japan's modern novelists. There are apparently a lot of Soseki fans in China, Taiwan, and Korea as well. Yet he remains relatively unknown in the West, an oversight that puzzles many. A number of explanations have been advanced—the fact that he doesn't fit the popular image of Japanese authors as I-novelists or aesthetes, or the fact that his style went through dramatic changes over time, making it hard to get a definitive sense of his work. Whereas his debut novel, *I Am a Cat* (1905-06), was light and witty, one of his last masterpieces, *Kokoro* (1914), was heavy and somber.

Why, then, do Soseki's countrymen hold him in such high regard? First of all, he developed and refined a new style of writing in colloquial Japanese at a time when the nation was undergoing the cultural upheavals of modernization. A scholar of English literature who studied in London, as well as a writer of Chinese poetry, Soseki penned Japanese that was at once elegant and accessible.

Moreover, Soseki's views and concerns as a child of the modern age resonate with readers today. Another reason for his reputation may be that his works have a philosophical depth and do not lend themselves to easy interpretation.

Vocabulary

puzzle ... ｜…を困惑させる	colloquial ｜口語の
whereas ｜…である一方、…であるのに	upheaval ｜激動、大変動
somber ｜暗い、陰気な	lend *oneself* to ... ｜（ものが）…に向いている

10 The Akutagawa and Naoki Prizes

Named after two different modern writers (see p. 103), the Akutagawa Ryunosuke Prize and the Naoki Sanjugo Prize are Japan's most prestigious literary awards. The twice-annual announcements of the prizewinners garner considerable media attention.

The Akutagawa Prize is given to works of "serious" literary fiction, and the Naoki Prize to "popular" fiction judged to have high entertainment value, although this distinction can often seem ambiguous. Originally, both prizes were meant to be for newly published writers, but nowadays the Naoki Prize in particular goes to established authors as well.

Vocabulary

named after ... ｜…にちなんで名づけられた	distinction ｜区別、違い
prestigious ｜名声のある、一流の	ambiguous ｜あいまいな

¹¹ 太宰治

太宰治（1909〜48）について、多くの日本人は、破滅型作家の典型という
イメージを持っています。自殺未遂を繰り返して心中した本人像と、代表
作『人間失格』（1948）などの、自己憐憫とも受けとめられる陰鬱な内容が、
重ねてとらえられているのです。

一方、清らかな友情を謳った短編『走れメロス』（1940）は、まるで別人が
書いたような作風で、学校の教科書に載っています。また太宰に詳しい人
は、多くの作家が国策文学^{※24}を書いた第二次世界大戦中にも、彼はマイペ
ースを貫いて、質の高い作品を執筆し続けたと評価します。

ともあれ、いつまでも若者たちに読み継がれ、信奉者が絶えない作家です^{※25}。

Notes

※ 24 国策の宣伝となる文学。太宰はそれを否定したわけではないが、距離を置いていたと評価される。
※ 25 戦後の作風から、坂口安吾らとともに、無頼派（outlaw）の作家と呼ばれている。

¹² 日本の現代文学

現代では日本の文学が、同時代のうちに多くの言語に翻訳されて、海外で
も読まれるようになりました。

1968 年に川端康成、1994 年には大江健三郎がノーベル文学賞を受賞しま
す。ほかに谷崎潤一郎や三島由紀夫なども、候補に挙がっていたそうです。
三島由紀夫は端正かつ絢爛な文体で読者を魅了していましたが、なにより人々
の記憶に大きく刻まれたのは、その衝撃的な最期です。1970 年、彼は自衛
隊にクーデターをよびかけ、直後に、古式に則った割腹自殺をしたのです
（P. 180 参照）。

現在活動している作家では、**村上春樹**をはじめ、村上龍、よしもとばなな
などが海外でも人気ですね。

近年、楊逸^{ヤン・イー}やシリン・ネザマフィ、アーサー・ビナード（詩人）など、日本
語を母語としない作家による「日本語文学」が、日本語へのいい刺激にな
っています。視点や言語感覚が、新鮮なのです。

ノンフィクションというジャンルは、60〜70 年代に日本に定着しました。
随筆が身近な出来事を扱うのに対し、社会問題などの取材活動に重きを置
くものをおもに指します。作家の沢木耕太郎^{※26}は、取材対象と積極的に関
わって、その体験をつづる「私ノンフィクション」などの、新しい試みを提
示しています。

→

[11] Dazai Osamu

Most Japanese think of Dazai Osamu (1909-48) as the archetypal self-destructive writer. Both his life and his work reinforce this impression: he attempted to kill himself several times before finally succeeding in a double suicide with a lover, and such representative works as *No Longer Human* (1948) are relentlessly gloomy—one might even say self-pitying.

On the other hand, his short story *Run, Melos!* (1940), which extols the purity of friendship, seems as if a different person wrote it, and appears in school textbooks. Dazai aficionados also praise him for having persisted in turning out high-quality work on his own terms throughout World War II, at a time when many writers were producing pro-war literature at the behest of the government.

For whatever reasons, Dazai has always been a favorite of youthful readers, and retains a devoted following today.

Vocabulary

archetypal｜典型的な	extol ...｜…をほめそやす
reinforce ...｜…を強固にする	aficionado｜ファン、愛好者
double suicide｜心中	at the behest of ...｜…の強い要請で

[12] Contemporary Literature

Recent years have seen more instances of Japanese literature translated into multiple languages shortly after publication, affording it a growing readership outside of Japan.

Two Japanese authors have received the Nobel Prize for Literature to date: Kawabata Yasunari in 1968 and Oe Kenzaburo in 1994. Several others, including Tanizaki Jun'ichiro and Mishima Yukio, were also listed as candidates for the prize.

Mishima Yukio captivated readers with his chiseled, glittering style, but it was his shocking demise that etched him indelibly in the public memory. In 1970, immediately after an abortive attempt to exhort Japan's Self-Defense Forces to launch a coup d'etat, Mishima committed ritual suicide by hara-kiri (see p. 181).

A number of Japanese writers working today enjoy large fan bases abroad, among them **Murakami Haruki**, Murakami Ryu, and Yoshimoto Banana.

Conversely, works written in Japanese by non-native authors like the Chinese novelist Yang Yi, the Iranian fiction writer Shirin Nezammafi,

→

←

日本のノンフィクション（ルポルタージュ）は、小説に比べて英訳される機会が少ないのですが、たとえば映画化された山崎朋子の『サンダカン八番娼館』（1972）は、英語版が出ています。

詩は現代において、マイナーな文学ジャンルになりましたが、谷川俊太郎や白石和子は英語でも読まれていますね。また、90年代から始まった「詩のボクシング」という自作詩の朗読を競うイベントは、現代詩の世界に新風をもたらしました。

Notes

※26 初期には、ニュー・ジャーナリズム（米）の影響が強かった。

左：『1Q84 BOOK 1』村上春樹・著（新潮社）
Left: *1Q84 Book 1* by Murakami Haruki
右：『キャッチャー・イン・ザ・ライ』J.D. サリンジャー・著　村上春樹・訳（白水社）
Right: Japanese edition of *The Catcher in the Rye* written by J.D. Salinger, translated by Murakami Haruki, 2003

¹³ 村上春樹

村上春樹（1949〜）は1979年、『風の歌を聴け』で小説家デビュー。当初は世間とのかかわりが希薄な若者を描いて、どちらかというとポップ・カルチャーの旗手として受け止められていました。それから30年あまり、多数の言語に翻訳された村上作品は、世界各地で都市生活者の共感を呼び、文化のグローバリゼーションの一現象として語られるようになっています。

日本での彼は、サリンジャーやフィッツジェラルドなど、アメリカ文学の日本語への翻訳者としても知られています（日本は「翻訳文学」の文化的評価が高いのです）。自身の小説も原語の日本語で読むと、まるで翻訳文体のようで、それがまた地域性を限定しない効果を生んでいるのかもしれません。

1997年、地下鉄サリン事件（P. 176参照）被害者へのインタビューを重ねたノンフィクション『アンダーグラウンド』は、初めて社会問題に正面から取り組んだ作品でした。

代表作は、『ノルウェイの森』（1987）、『海辺のカフカ』（2002）、『1Q84』

→

and the American poet Arthur Binard have introduced fresh perspectives and linguistic sensibilities to the Japanese literary world.

Nonfiction also came into its own as a category of literature in the 1960s and 1970s. Unlike **zuihitsu** pieces that focus on events familiar to the author, works labeled "nonfiction" tend to highlight the actual information-gathering process, particularly in the context of examining social issues. Sawaki Kotaro is one such writer who actively engages with his subjects and chronicles those experiences in such innovative formats as what has been called "I-nonfiction." English translations of Japanese reportage are rare, but one outstanding example is Yamazaki Tomoko's 1972 book *Sandakan Brothel No. 8*, which was also made into a film.

Although poetry is something of a minor literary genre these days, Shiraishi Kazuko and Tanikawa Shuntaro have earned recognition for their verses in English translation. Since the 1990s competitive poetry readings referred to as "Poetry Boxing" have blown a breath of fresh air into the contemporary poetry scene.

Vocabulary

chiseled｜彫りの深い、端正な	abortive attempt｜失敗した試み
glittering｜光り輝く	exhort *someone* to *do*｜（人に）…するよう促す
demise｜死亡、逝去［death の遠回しな表現］	commit suicide｜自殺する
etch ...｜…を刻みつける	conversely｜逆にいえば
indelibly｜永久に、消えないように	novelist｜（fiction writer の中でも）長編小説の作家

[13] Murakami Haruki

Murakami Haruki (1949-) made his debut as a novelist in 1979 with *Hear the Wind Sing*. His early works, which featured young protagonists with a tenuous relationship to the world at large, were generally regarded as a form of pop literature. After three decades during which they have been translated into numerous languages, Murakami's novels are heralded today as the embodiment of cultural globalization, resonating as they do with members of urban society in every part of the world.

At home Murakami is also known as the translator of Salinger, Fitzgerald, and other American writers (translated literature is held in high esteem in Japan). Indeed, the Japanese in his own work strikes many readers as sounding as if it were translated from another language, a characteristic that may well contribute to the pan-regional effect of his prose.

→

← (2009〜10) ほか。フランツ・カフカ賞（2006）などの国際的な文学賞を
数々受賞していて、受賞式での社会批判——戦争犯罪や原子力政策などに
対して——をふくんだコメントが話題になっています。

¹⁴ ライトノベルとケータイ小説

10 代の若者を中心に読まれている、比較的新しい形態の小説に「ライトノ
ベル（ラノベ）」と「ケータイ小説」があります。

ラノベは要所に漫画のようなイラストがはさみ込まれていて、80 年代頃の
黎明期には、俗に「字マンガ」とも呼ばれていました。内容は SF、ファン
タジー、ミステリー、ホラーなど、おもに非日常を扱います。近年では「涼
宮ハルヒ」シリーズが、アニメ化されて人気を呼びました。

ケータイ小説は、文字通り、携帯電話で読む（書く場合もある）小説で、
読み手はおもに女性です。一時期、投稿サイトに素人が、実話を元にした
という「リアル系ケータイ小説」を投稿するのがブームになり、『恋空』な
どのヒット作が生まれました。

しかし、ほんとうに実話なのか首をひねるほど、悲惨な事件が頻発し、最
後には真実の愛に出合うというパターンでした。それをリアルだと感じさせ
るのは、一人称で、文が短く、記号が混じるなど、まるで友人からの携帯
メールのような表現形式のせいです。

最近は、スマートフォンの「スマホ小説」に移行して、読者年齢や内容の
幅が広がっているようです。

『涼宮ハルヒの憂鬱』
谷川流・著（角川書店）
The Melancholy of Haruhi Suzumiya
by Tanigawa Nagaru, 2003

04

文学／村上春樹／ライトノベルとケータイ小説

←

His 1997 nonfiction book *Underground*, which contains interviews with victims of the 1995 Tokyo subway sarin gas attack (see p. 177), was the first work in which Murakami directly addressed social issues.

Among his best-known novels are *Norwegian Wood* (1987), *Kafka on the Shore* (2002), and *1Q84* (2009-10). The winner of many international literary awards, including the 2006 Franz Kafka Prize, Murakami has attracted controversy for his critical remarks at award ceremonies on such issues as war crimes and nuclear power.

Vocabulary

tenuous ｜希薄な、薄い	resonate ｜共鳴する、反響する
embodiment ｜具体化、体現	remark ｜意見、発言

LITERATURE / Murakami Haruki / Light Novels, Cell Phone Novels

¹⁴ Light Novels, Cell Phone Novels

Two relatively new literary formats are the light novel and the cell phone novel. Both are read primarily by young people in their teens.

Light novels often contain manga-like illustrations inserted at strategic points in the plot. When these works first made their appearance in the 1980s they were sometimes dubbed "text manga." Most light novels are about extraordinary events in such categories as science fiction, fantasy, mystery, and horror. A recent light-novel series, *Suzumiya Haruhi*, has become a big hit in anime form.

As the name indicates, the cell phone novel is read, and sometimes written, on a mobile phone. Most readers are women. For a time there was a boom in "reality" cell phone novels, ostensibly based on true stories, which amateur authors posted to a site set up for that purpose. One such hit was *Koizora* ("Love Sky").

Whether stories of this sort are in fact reality-based or not, however, is open to question. A typical plot involves a series of tragic events culminating in the discovery of true love. What makes the tales seem "real" is their use of first-person narrative, brief sentences, and symbols—elements you might find in a text mail from a friend.

Recently the genre has seen a shift to the "smartphone novel," and with it an expansion of both target readership and range of content.

Vocabulary

be dubbed ... ｜…と呼ばれる	be open to question ｜議論の余地がある
ostensibly ｜表面上は	culminate in ... ｜結果的に…になる

05

PERFORMING ARTS
舞台・パフォーマンス

日本の舞台・パフォーマンス事情

日本には、約千年から数百年前にひとつの完成形をみた舞台芸能[※1]が、かたちを変えながらもたくさん残っています。歌舞劇の一種である**能**や**歌舞伎**、人形劇の**文楽**などはその代表格です。

そうした芝居に共通する特徴として、舞台に上がるのは男性だけで[※2]――例外はありますが――女性の役も男性が演じます。

それらは使われている言葉が古くて、日本人でも予備知識なく観ると、何がなんだかわかりません[※3]。しかしほとんどの演目が定番ですから、あらかじめ筋や解説、台本の訳[※4]などに目を通しておけば、独特の表現様式を味わうことができるでしょう。

一方、西洋の近代劇にならった演劇（P. 120 参照）は、明治時代から発展し、現在では多彩な舞台が観られます。現代日本を描いた脚本だけでなく、シェイクスピアやブロードウェイの演目も、日本の役者でさかんに演じられていますし、サムライ（P. 296 参照）などの出る**時代劇**は、現代語まじりでわかりやすくなっています。

80 年代からは、蜷川幸雄や野田秀樹といった演出家が、イギリスなど海外でも活躍するようになりました。

ダンスに目を移すと、前衛的な**舞踏**が、国内よりも海外で大きく評価されていますね。

また日本には、人を笑わせるショーにも、**落語**をはじめ多くのジャンルがあります。

テレビでは、現在**お笑い**と総称される種々の芸を交えた番組が人気です。お笑い芸人たちがおもしろいフレーズなどを流行らせると、一時期みんなが真似するようになりますよ。

Notes

※1 例として、舞楽（雅楽と踊り）は、7〜9 世紀に伝来して日本化した。　※2 近代以前は、西洋でも男性だけの演劇がめずらしくなかった（例えば、シェイクスピア劇では少年俳優が女性を演じていた）。
※3 歌舞伎の世話物は、現代語に近くわかりやすい。　※4 能では、謡曲が台本にあたる。

01 Drama and Dance in Japan

Though their styles may have undergone changes over time, many of Japan's performing arts retain classic forms perfected anywhere from several hundred to a thousand years ago. The best known are the **Noh** and **Kabuki** dance-dramas and the **Bunraku** puppet theater. One characteristic shared by all of these traditional forms is that—with rare exceptions—only men appear on the stage. Female roles are played by male actors.

The language used in the performances tends to be archaic as well. In many cases, even Japanese viewers have a hard time understanding what is going on without a little advance preparation. However, most of the current repertoire consists of famous pieces for which scripts or summaries are available. If you look them over beforehand, such texts will help you enjoy the unique modes of expression used in these dramas.

Modern plays (see p. 121) in the style of Western theater came into vogue in the Meiji era (1868-1912); nowadays theatergoers can choose from a wide variety of stage performances. They range from contemporary Japanese dramas to Shakespeare to Broadway musicals, mostly performed by Japanese actors. *Jidaigeki*—period pieces about samurai (see p. 296) and the like—use a mixture of traditional and contemporary language that makes them easy for audiences to follow.

Since the 1980s, playwrights like Ninagawa Yukio and Noda Hideki have had their works performed in the U.K. and elsewhere overseas. In the world of dance, the avant-garde genre of **Butoh** earns even more praise abroad than it does at home.

Comedy, too, is a diverse field in Japan, with traditional **Rakugo** storytellers still attracting devotees. *Owarai* TV shows, which feature a variety of comic acts, are immensely popular. When an owarai performer coins an amusing new phrase, you may hear people repeating it all over the country.

Vocabulary

retain ... ｜ …を保つ	period piece ｜ 時代劇 [日本だけでなく海外が舞台でも、過去の時代を想定したセットで演じられる劇。period drama ともいう]
with rare exceptions ｜ ほとんど例外なく	
repertoire ｜ (演劇などで上演可能な) レパートリー	
come into vogue ｜ 人気になる、台頭する	devotee ｜ ファン、愛好者
	immensely ｜ 非常に、とても

02 歌舞伎

カブキ（傾き）という言葉のもともとの意味は「奇抜なもの」。今では文化遺産の歌舞伎ですが、17世紀に異様な格好の艶っぽい踊りとして登場し、大衆の人気に支えられながら、歌舞劇として発展していったのが成り立ちです。より歴史の古い能との違いを挙げると、歌舞伎では面を付けず、くっきりした化粧で、善人悪人などの役柄※5 を表します。強いヒーローや超人的な役などのときに描く顔の模様・隈取（くまどり）は、中国の京劇（あるいはロックバンドのKISS）の化粧と似ていますね。感情が激変した場面でも、隈取を変えることがあります。

三味線、唄（P. 14参照）、鳴り物（P. 18参照）に合わせた踊りは、様式にのっとりながらも伸びやかで、女形は女性らしさ、勇者などの役では猛々しさを強調します。そしてクライマックスなどで、ポーズを決めて静止します（見得（みえ））。常連客が一斉にかけ声をかける場面です。

歌舞伎の舞台には、ファッションショーのように客席を縦断する「花道」が付いていて、観客の背後から、役者が花道を通って登場することもあります。また中央には、円形の「廻り舞台」※6 があり、客の目の前で場面転換が出来ます。おもしろいのが「黒衣（くろご、くろこ）」という黒ずくめのアシスタント。舞台上にいながら「いない」というお約束で、小道具を動かしたりするのです。

歌舞伎役者は世襲が多く、誰でも養成所に入れますが、幼い時から舞台に立つ役者の子がスターに育ちやすいようです。また、弟子が養子になるケースもあります。

こうした歌舞伎は、今では江戸時代を疑似体験する場として、楽しまれているように思います。また、一度すたれた宙乗りなど、派手な演出の復元や、現代的な演出の新作を打ち出す「スーパー歌舞伎」などの新しい試みも、歌舞伎を大いに盛り上げています。

Notes

※5 例えば赤く塗った顔は、大悪人の手下等の敵役。　※6 廻り舞台を本格的に舞台に取り入れたのは、歌舞伎が世界初。

Comment

芝居通たちのかけ声、威勢がいいでしょう？　だけど初心者の私には、どう声をかけていいかわかりません。決まったかけ声に、役者が答えるセリフが入っている演目もあるそうですよ。
You hear those shouts by the audience regulars, cheering on a Kabuki actor? I love it! But a beginner like me doesn't know what to yell! I've heard that some plays include lines for the actors to shout back in response to specific calls from the seats.

⁰² Kabuki

Originally, the word *kabuki* meant something eccentric or bizarre. Kabuki is now designated an Intangible Cultural Heritage by UNESCO, but it has its origins in suggestive dances performed in outlandish costumes during the 17th century. Sustained by its popularity with the general public, this early form of Kabuki evolved into the drama with song and dance that we know today.

One noticeable difference between Kabuki and the older **Noh** theater is that Kabuki actors do not wear masks; instead, makeup is used to clearly identify heroes and villains. The gaudy *kumadori* makeup worn by strong characters or those with superhuman powers may remind you of the Peking Opera, or even the rock band Kiss! Sometimes the kumadori gets changed between scenes to indicate a dramatic shift in the emotions of the character.

Kabuki dances, accompanied by singing (see p. 15), **shamisen**, percussion (see p. 19), and other instruments, follow prescribed patterns but are relatively unconstrained and relaxed. A dance by a female character will accentuate her femininity, while that of a hero will emphasize power and ferocity. At the climax, the actor often strikes a pose and holds it, to cheers from the audience.

The Kabuki stage has a runway, much like that of a fashion show, extending to the back of the theater. Actors will occasionally make their entrance from behind the audience and proceed along this *hanamichi* or "flower way" to the stage. A revolving platform in the center of the stage makes it possible to switch scenes before the audience's eyes. Another interesting aspect of Kabuki is its use of *kurogo*, black-clad stage assistants who move props and perform other "invisible" tasks.

Hereditary relationships are the norm among Kabuki actors. Although the training schools are open to anyone, it is no doubt easier to make a star out of an actor's son who has trod the stage since childhood. Sometimes an actor will formally adopt a pupil as his son.

Retaining these traditions as it does, Kabuki may well appeal to present-day fans as a way of experiencing a little bit of the Edo period (1603-1868). Kabuki continues to thrive with the revival of midair stunts and other showy practices that had fallen into disuse, as well as attempts to add a contemporary flair through new works like "Super Kabuki."

Vocabulary

outlandish costume ｜風変わりな衣装	prop ｜小道具
accentuate ... ｜…を強調する、目立たせる	hereditary ｜世襲の
revolving platform ｜廻り舞台	thrive with ... ｜…で成功している、栄える

03 文楽（人形浄瑠璃）

文楽（人形浄瑠璃）は芸を極めた人形芝居で、子ども向けでなく大人が鑑賞します（写真 P. 131）。舞台の上手には、**三味線**と太夫（語り）※7 が、通常一人ずつ座っています。太夫は声色を変えて、登場人物すべてのセリフを語り、ナレーションの部分は時に節をつけた唄になります。

人形は全長 120〜150 センチメートルほど。一体三人がかり※8 で、まるで人形が生きているかのように、細かく操るのです。

文楽は江戸時代の大阪で発展し、一時は**歌舞伎**をしのぐ人気を誇っていました。近松門左衛門（1653〜1725）をはじめとする劇作家たちが耳目を集め※9、その脚本の多くは歌舞伎に翻案されています。

文楽のストーリーは概して湿っぽく、当時の事件を元にした男女の心中や、武士の敵討ちなどの、痛ましいエピソードがよく出てくるのですが、人形で演じられると生々しさが消えて、美しい物語として観られるのでしょう。

文楽の世界は、世襲制ではなく実力主義で、現在もっとも人気があるのは、円熟した芸をみせる 80 歳台の演者たちです。

Notes

※7 三味線と太夫だけの芸能は浄瑠璃という。義太夫節が代表的な流派。　※8 主遣い（首と右手担当）は顔を出すことがある。　※9 人形の機能が劇的に改良され、三人遣いが始まるのは近松の死後。

04 能

能※10 は、きらびやかな装束をまとった役者が、**邦楽**※11 の生演奏に合わせて舞い、謡う仮面劇です。シテ（主役）は亡霊や神、ものの精など「この世ならぬ者」が多く、そうした役では必ず面を付けます。

能の舞は、細部まで神経を張りつめて、スローモーションのようにゆっくりと舞うのが典型的。膝を曲げて重心を低く保ち、すり足で移動するのも特徴です。リアリスティックな演技は目指さず、動作や心情も象徴的な型によって表現します。たとえば、悲しいときには涙を押さえるポーズなど。海外の人には、ミニマリズム※12 と受け止められていますね。

能舞台のかたちや使い方も、わずかな要素で異空間を思わせるしくみになっていますよ。そのあたりは、実際にご覧になってみてください。

能は、現存する世界最古の職業的演劇といわれ、8 世紀頃までにアジア大陸から伝わった芸能の影響を残しています。

現在につながる能のスタイルは、14〜15 世紀に能役者兼作家の親子、観阿

→

03 Bunraku

A highly artistic form of puppet theater, Bunraku (image on p. 131) is geared to adult audiences, not children. At the side of the stage sit a **shamisen** player and a chanter, the *tayu*, who recites the lines of every part, altering his voice for each role. Some of the narration is sung to a melody.

The puppets are anywhere from 120 to 150 centimeters long. Three puppeteers work together to handle a single puppet, expertly manipulating it in an astonishingly lifelike manner.

Bunraku began in Osaka during the Edo period, and at one time was even more popular than **Kabuki**. Playwrights like Chikamatsu Monzaemon (1653-1725) entranced fans with their scenarios, many of which were adapted to the Kabuki stage as well.

Bunraku stories tend toward pathos and tragedy. Episodes based on actual incidents, involving lovers' double suicides or warriors wreaking revenge, are common. The use of puppets instead of human actors somehow takes the edge off the vivid, sometimes gruesome scenes and raw emotions on display, turning these harrowing tales into works of beauty.

Unlike Kabuki, Bunraku is not a hereditary system but is merit-based. These days, the top-drawing stars are performers in their eighties who display the consummate skills that come with maturity.

Vocabulary

recite ... ｜…を演じる、朗唱する	pathos ｜哀愁、ペーソス
expertly ｜うまく、たくみに	wreak revenge ｜復讐する
manipulate ... ｜…を操る	gruesome ｜陰惨な、ぞっとするような
entrance *A* with *B* ｜ A を B で魅了する	consummate skill ｜円熟した芸、至芸

04 Noh

Noh is a masked drama in which actors in resplendent costumes dance and chant to the accompaniment of a chorus and an ensemble of **traditional Japanese instruments** (flute and percussion). The main actor or *shite* often plays the part of a ghost, god, or other supernatural being; such characters are always masked.

The Noh dance is typically very slow and intense, with every movement carefully controlled. The actors move in a distinctive manner, maintaining a low center of gravity, bending their knees and sliding their feet across the floor. The acting is not meant to be realistic, but to express actions and emotions through symbolic *kata* or stylized gestures. To express sorrow, for example, the actor will raise his hand to his eyes as if to suppress tears. In this respect, overseas audiences may view Noh as a kind of minimalist theater.

The Noh stage, too, represents an effort to conjure up an otherworldly space

→

← 弥と世阿弥が大成し、長い間、将軍などの権力者がスポンサーでした。世阿弥が秘伝として残した『風姿花伝』などの演劇論は、今日では誰もが読めるようになっています（P. 186 参照）。

Notes

※ 10 能、式三番（『翁』等）、狂言を合わせて能楽ということもある。
※ 11 大鼓、小鼓、笛、太鼓、地謡（役柄が特定されていないコーラス／ナレーション）。
※ 12 芸術等において、無駄をそぎ落とし、要素を最小限まで突き詰める主義。

宮島・厳島神社にて『春日龍神』より
シテ：大江広祐（観世流）
From *The Kasuga Dragon God* at the Itsukushima Shrine's Noh stage on the water, Miyajima, 2012
Shite: Oe Kosuke, Kanze School
Photo: Miura Fumiko

05 狂言

狂言は、おもに能の上演の合間に演じられるセリフ劇で、多くは召使に対する主人などのたわいもない失敗を描いた喜劇です。役者は素顔で表情を豊かに表し、音楽も大がかりな道具もほとんど使いません。

深淵とされる能に対して、わかりやすいけれど軽視されがちだった狂言ですが、最近は野村萬斎などのスターが出て、その魅力や可能性が見直されています。独特の型による身体表現が、現代のパフォーマンスとして応用されやすいのです。たとえば海外公演では、誰もが知っているシェイクスピアや喜劇オペラを狂言仕立てにすると、新鮮にとらえられるようです。

06 新派から現代演劇まで

日本が国を挙げて西洋化を志向した明治時代、「新派」や「新劇」といった新しい演劇が起こりました。このとき「旧派」、「旧劇」と呼ばれたのは歌舞伎です。

→

←

with a minimum of elements. To truly appreciate how this is done, you will just have to go see a Noh play yourself.

Said to be the oldest surviving form of professional theater in the world, Noh retains vestiges of performing arts brought to Japan from the Asian continent in the eighth century or even earlier. The style of Noh performed today was first perfected in the 14th and 15th centuries by the father-and-son actors and playwrights Kan'ami and Zeami. Noh enjoyed the patronage of shoguns and other powerful figures for a long time. Zeami's treatises on Noh, including the legendary *Fuushi-kaden* ("The Transmission of the Flower of Acting Style"), were originally secret teachings, but now anyone can read them (see p. 187).

Vocabulary

resplendent｜きらびやかな、まばゆい	otherworldly｜異世界の
conjure up ...｜...を呼び起こす	patronage｜援助

⁰⁵ Kyogen

A spoken-dialogue drama usually performed between Noh plays, Kyogen typically consists of comedies about human folly, particularly by people in positions of authority. The actors normally wear no makeup and use exaggerated facial expressions, while music and stage props are sparse.

In the past, Kyogen has been given short shrift compared to the "deeper" (and more difficult to understand) Noh. Recently, however, such stars as Nomura Mansai have helped spark a reappreciation of Kyogen's appeal and potential. The physical expressions of Kyogen's unique kata readily lend themselves to contemporary performances. In fact, the adaptation of Kyogen to such divergent genres as Shakespeare and comic opera has won over theatergoers abroad for the fresh twist it gives to old favorites.

Vocabulary

human folly｜人間らしい愚かさ	readily｜すぐに、容易に
sparse｜少ない、わずかな	lend *oneself* to ...｜...に役立つ
be given short shrift｜軽んじられる	divergent｜異なる

⁰⁶ From Shinpa to Contemporary Theater

The Meiji era, during which Japan embarked on a nationwide effort to westernize itself, saw the birth of new forms of theater called *Shinpa* (New School) and *Shingeki* (New Drama). These terms contrasted the emergent movements with **Kabuki**, which became known during this period as "old school" or "old drama."

Though its style was rooted in Kabuki, Shinpa took up contemporary themes and came to make its mark as a type of melodrama. Shingeki, on the other hand, imported realistic modern theater from the West. In turn, Shinpa and Shingeki appear to have had a significant influence on drama in neighboring East Asian

→

新派は、歌舞伎の演技をもとにしながら、同時代的なテーマを扱い、やがてメロドラマで一時代を築きました。新劇のほうは、欧米のリアリスティックな近代劇を移入した演劇です。近隣の東アジアの国々にも、新派や新劇の影響は大きかったようです。

一方、江戸時代から続く旅芝居の流れは、「大衆演劇」として、時代劇やレヴューを中心とした舞台が、現代まで受け継がれています。

戦後には新劇が娯楽として定着し、三島由紀夫（P. 106 参照）や安部公房なども、優れた戯曲を書いています。

1960 年代には寺山修司など、反体制的な若い世代がテントや小さい空間で上演する、「アングラ（アンダーグラウンド）演劇」が盛り上がります。80 年代には、ポップでスピーディな舞台が流行し、小空間の実験的な演劇のムーブメントは、「小劇場ブーム」と呼ばれました。バブル全盛期には、各地に新しい劇場が建ちました。

現在の先鋭的な舞台は、メディア・アートやダンス、パフォーマンスなどとの境界がなくなりつつあります。また、海外の演劇人たちとのコラボレーションの機会が増え、多言語の舞台も出てきたようです。

07 男装の麗人と「宝塚歌劇団」

宝塚歌劇団は、未婚の女性だけでレヴューやミュージカルを演じる劇団です。大きなつけまつ毛と太いアイラインがトレードマーク。男性と女性のどちらを演じるかは、団員によって固定していて、男役のトップ・スターを中心に舞台が構成されます。このような芸能は 20 世紀に興隆し、「少女歌劇」と呼ばれて、一時は日本各地に多数の歌劇団がありました。

こうした「男装の麗人」[13] は、日本の芸能史においてめずらしくありません。12 世紀頃にはすでに、女性の男舞（白拍子）が流行った時代[14] がありましたし、歌舞伎もじつは、17 世紀に女性が男性を演じたのが始まりでした。遊女の参加で風紀が乱れるといって禁止令が出たため、男性の歌舞伎に変わったのです。

時代は下って人気漫画の『ベルサイユのばら』（P. 70 参照）にも、男装の麗人が登場します。この作品は、宝塚のミュージカルになって大ヒットしました。

Notes

※ 13 キリスト教等で異性装はタブーと考えられる（現在は重視されない地域が多い）。
※ 14 12 世紀以前に成立した『とりかへばや物語』は、男児と女児が性別を替えて育てられる話。

←

countries.

Meanwhile, the tradition of the traveling troupes that flourished during the Edo period endures to this day through *taishu-engeki* (literally, "theater of the masses"), which consists mainly of period dramas and revues.

Shingeki solidified its position as an established category of entertainment after World War II, attracting the talents of such writers as Mishima Yukio (see p. 107) and Abe Kobo, who wrote some acclaimed plays in the genre.

With the 1960s came the rise of the *angura* (from "underground") theater, which staged works by young, anti-establishment playwrights like Terayama Shuji in tents and other cramped spaces. In the 1980s, poppish, fast-paced plays drew an audience to the experimental movement known as the *shogekijo* (little theater) boom, which also favored small venues. During the economic bubble of the late 1980s, new theater facilities sprang up throughout Japan.

Nowadays, cutting-edge stage performances increasingly ignore traditional boundaries between the media arts, dance, and drama. Collaborations with non-Japanese dramatists, including multilingual performances, are another growing trend.

Vocabulary

embark on ...	···に乗り出す	endure	存続する、持ちこたえる
in turn	今度は	solidify ...	···を固める

07 Takarazuka: Beautiful Women Dressed as Men

The Takarazuka Revue Company is a theater troupe that performs musicals and revues with a cast consisting exclusively of unmarried women. Among their trademarks are large false eyelashes and thick eyeliner. The actors are divided into specialists in male roles and female roles, with the *otokoyaku* male-role stars receiving top billing. This form of theater, known as *shojo kageki* or "girls' opera," had its heyday during the 20th century, and for a time such companies could be found all over the country.

Spectacles featuring "fair ladies in male garb" are not rare in the history of stage performance in Japan. As far back as the 12th century, *shirabyoshi* dances featuring women dressed as men were popular. In fact, **Kabuki** originated with a 17th-century dance style in which women played the male parts. Only when this was banned because the participation of prostitutes was deemed a threat to public morals did Kabuki switch to its all-male format.

One of Takarazuka's most popular musicals is an adaption of the hit manga *The Rose of Versailles* (also known by the anime title *Lady Oscar*), which features a heroine disguised as a man (see p. 71).

Vocabulary

billing	序列	be deemed a threat to ...	···への脅威とされる
male garb	男性の服装、男装	disguised as ...	···の変装をした

123

日本の伝統的なダンスは、近代になって「日本舞踊」と総称されるようになりました。狭義には、歌舞伎から派生した舞踊をこう呼びます。

一方、「盆踊り」など、各地の祭りで楽しまれる民俗的な踊りは、たいてい大勢が振りを合わせて、かざした手の平を翻（ひるがえ）しながら踊ります。こうしたスタイルの流れは、少し前に流行った「パラパラ」にも受け継がれています。クラブでギャルたちが、ユーロビートやJ-ポップに合わせて、手の振りをそろえて踊るのです。

「暗黒舞踏（舞踏）」は、1960年代に舞踏家・土方巽（1928〜1986）を中心に生み出された前衛芸術です。体をあやしくくねらせ、こわばりを解きほぐすような動きに特徴があります。基本的に拍子に合わせた振り付けはせず、舞踏家自身が言葉やイマジネーションから想起して踊ります。そして、観念を表現するのでなく、「肉体の質感」を提示するという概念が、ダンスの新領域を拓きました。土方と影響を受け合い、100歳を超えて最晩年まで踊り続けた大野一雄（1906〜2010）は、世界の舞踏家たちから尊敬を集める存在です。また、パリをはじめ世界各地で公演を重ねる「山海塾」という舞踏カンパニーも有名になりましたね。

海外発のダンスもさかんです。クラシックバレエではイギリスから帰国した熊川哲也ほか、世界的なダンサーが何人もいます。

コンテンポラリーダンスは、バレエや舞踏の系統のものもありますし、映像やコンピューターを使うなど、いろいろな試みがみられます。

若い世代には、観るのも踊るのもストリートダンスがかなり普及しています。ヒップ・ホップは最近、政府の方針で学校教育に取り入れられました。

⁰⁸ Buyo and Butoh

In modern times, Nihon Buyo ("Japanese dance") has become the general term for classical Japanese dance. More narrowly, Nihon Buyo refers to dances derived from **Kabuki**.

Japan also has plenty of folkdances, like the Bon-odori, that people perform at local festivals, typically in large groups with coordinated gestures, such as waving your hands over your head. The influence of this style could be seen in the Para-Para dance craze not too long ago, which had young *gyaru*-fashioned women waving in synchronized motion to Eurobeat and **J-Pop** music.

Ankoku Butoh is an avant-garde dance form (the name means "dance of darkness") that emerged in the 1960s from the work of Hijikata Tatsumi (1928-86). Butoh, as it is usually called, is known for grotesque but captivating contortions of the body and movements that suggest extreme tension and cathartic release. The dancers do not rely on count-based choreography, but take their inspiration from certain words or their own imagination. Butoh pioneered a new approach to dance that has been described as actualizing the "inner landscape" of the body. Another figure in the Butoh world who both influenced and was influenced by Hijikata is Ohno Kazuo (1906-2010), who continued dancing past the age of 100 and remains a legend among dancers around the globe. Sankai Juku, which frequently performs in Paris and elsewhere, has also made a name for itself.

Non-Japanese dance forms are popular too. Japan has produced a number of world-class ballet dancers, among them Kumakawa Tetsuya, who studied and worked in England before returning to start his own company in Japan. Recent developments in dance range from works inspired by ballet or Butoh to multimedia experiments with video and computers.

Street dance has gained a following with young Japanese, both as something to do and something to watch. In recent years the government has even mandated the inclusion of hip-hop as an option in school dance programs.

PERFORMING ARTS / Buyo and Butoh

Vocabulary

craze｜流行	count-based choreography｜拍子に合わせた振
captivating｜魅了的な、心奪われる	り付け
contortion｜ゆがみ、ねじれ	mandate ...｜…を命じる
cathartic release｜カタルシスを伴うような解放	

左：コンポラリーダンス・カンパニー「珍しいキノコ舞踊団」の
公演『ホントの時間』より
Left: From *Quality Time* by Strange Kinoko Dance Company,
a contemporary dance troupe with an original flair, 2012
Photo: Kataoka Yohta

⁰⁹ 落語

落語とは、「着物を着たコメディアンによる一人芝居」だと説明できます。ただし高座（寄席の舞台）の落語家は、客のほうを向いて座布団の上に正座したまま立ちません。声と上半身の身振りだけで、一人何役も演じ分けるのです。時には、扇子や手ぬぐいを小道具にします。特に扇子は、箸や筆、刀など、いろいろなものに見立てられます。

落語は江戸時代からの歴史があり、師匠から弟子へ口伝された古典落語と、現代の新作落語※15 があります。古典といっても、100年ほど前の話し言葉がベースで、今の日本人が聞いてもわかります。また同じ演目でも、落語家によって演じ方が異なるものです。

演目の種類には、最後に急展開して笑わせる「落とし噺」や、おかしいだけでなくしみじみとした感動を呼ぶ「人情噺」などがあります。

Notes

※15 古典と新作をどこで区分けするかは難しいが、第二次世界大戦後につくられたものを指すことが多い。

高座で噺をする落語家・柳家権太楼
Yanagiya Gontaro performing Rakugo on the stage, 2013
Photo: Muto Naomi

¹⁰ お笑い

日本のテレビでは、お笑いを交えた番組が大人気です。もともと寄席で演じられてきた演芸──「コント」と呼ばれる寸劇や、「漫才」という大阪発祥の話芸などを、観客の笑い声とともに収録した番組もあります。

漫才とは、通常「ボケ」と「ツッコミ」に役割分担された二人組※16 が客の前に立ち、ボケのほうがおかしなことを言うと、ツッコミが「なにいうてんねん」などと批判して、客の笑いを誘うものです。

→

⁰⁹ Rakugo

The comic monologue known as Rakugo could be described as a one-man play by a kimono-wearing comedian. But unlike a stand-up comic, a Rakugo storyteller kneels on a cushion in the formal *seiza* position the whole time, facing the audience from a raised stage. Using only his voice and his upper body, he plays the parts of all the characters in his stories. Sometimes he uses a facecloth and a **folding fan** as props. The fan may serve as a pair of chopsticks, a writing brush, or a sword, to name just a few possibilities.

The Rakugo tradition extends back to the Edo period. In addition to "classical" Rakugo tales orally handed down from master to pupil, there are also contemporary "New Rakugo" stories. Even the classical pieces use language from no more than about a century ago, so they are comprehensible to present-day Japanese listeners. Different practitioners will tell the same story in different ways.

The Rakugo repertoire includes several types of monologue, ranging from *otoshi-banashi* ("punchline stories") that suddenly end with a funny twist, to *ninjo-banashi* ("sentimental stories") that may have humorous moments but ultimately aim to move audiences emotionally.

Vocabulary

monologue	独白劇、一人芝居、長談義	comprehensible	理解できる
orally handed down	口頭で伝えられた	practitioner	演者

¹⁰ Owarai

Owarai (literally "laughter") shows are a ubiquitous presence on Japanese television. Some programs broadcast comedy acts (and the audience's response to them) in styles that date back to the *engei* vaudeville stages of an earlier generation. Examples include *konto* (from the French *conte*) skits and the *manzai* comic duo routines that originated in Osaka.

Manzai normally consists of a two-person dialogue between a straight man (the *tsukkomi*) and a funny man or fool (the *boke*). The boke typically makes some off-the wall comment, to which the tsukkomi retorts with something like "What are you saying, you idiot?"—drawing guffaws from the audience.

Some comedy programs made especially for TV involve audience participation, such as the wildly popular "Takeshi's Castle."

The most common form of owarai involves an entertainer overdramatizing his or her own foibles or mishaps. But every era sees the emergence of new approaches. In the 1980s, a duo called The Two Beats (Beat Takeshi—better known today as the filmmaker **Kitano Takeshi**—and his partner Beat Kiyoshi) earned notoriety with their *dokuzetsu* ("poison-tongue") mode of viciously insulting manzai. In the 1990s, the duo Downtown became stars with a more

→

←

また、視聴者参加型の『痛快なりゆき番組　風雲！ たけし城』※17 のように、テレビ向けに作られたお笑い番組もあります。

笑いのタイプとして、芸人が自分の欠点や失敗を強調するのは一般的ですが、80 年代ツービート（現在、映画監督・北野武として活躍するビートたけしとビートきよしのコンビ）の毒舌漫才や、90 年代ダウンタウンのシュールな漫才など、時代によって新しいスタイルの笑いが開拓されています。

彼らは笑いの力で、タブーを突き抜けた発言がしやすく、また人々の願望を代弁するところもあり、お笑いで人気を得た人が、政治や、映画・小説など別の文化ジャンルに進出するケースもめずらしくありません。

最近は知識量や、ルックスのよさを売りにする若手もいます。浮き沈みの激しい世界で、テレビで見る顔がめまぐるしく変わります。

Notes

※16　3 人以上のときもある。　※17　80 年代 TBS の番組で、159 以上の国／地域で放送される。現地版が作られたケースもある。

11　芸者（芸妓）

大きく結い上げた髪（P. 254 参照）、白塗りの化粧、着物の襟を下げた艶っぽい着こなし──まるで江戸時代のような芸者の佇まいは、今日の日本でも異彩を放っています。

古都・京都では、芸者を「芸妓」、見習いを「舞妓」※18 といい、花街で道を行く彼女たちが、観光資源のひとつになっています。その仕事は、料亭（P. 230 参照）などの客室で、日本舞踊※19 や三味線、唄などを客に披露し、客と座敷遊びと呼ばれる種々のパーティーゲームをしたり、お酌をしながら話し相手になったりして、酒席を楽しませることです。伝統芸能の担い手として、彼女たちは時代劇の遊女と混同されることを嫌います。

芸者遊びができる店は、少し前までは「一見さんお断り」とする敷居の高いところが多く、政財界や芸能界などの有力な男性が出入りしていました。しかし最近は、初心者や女性でも座敷の雰囲気を味わえるコースができています。また年に何度か、芸者の舞踊の舞台公演があります。

ちなみに、時代劇などに出てくる「花魁」※20 とは、当時の高級遊女のこと。着物の帯を前に結んでいます。

Notes

※18　関東では「半玉（はんぎょく）」。　※19　現在の日本舞踊は、東京中心の歌舞伎舞踊と、京阪の上方舞（地唄舞ともいう）に大別される。　※20　元は吉原での呼び方。関西では最高位の遊女を太夫といった。

←

surreal type of dialogue.

Thanks to the power of laughter, owarai comedians find it relatively easy to defy cultural taboos or articulate people's unspoken desires. It is not unusual to see performers who have made their mark in the owarai world venture into other fields, including politics, film, and literature.

These days, some young owarai talents sell themselves through their knowledgability or their looks. It is an extremely competitive world, and the faces that appear on TV comedy shows get replaced with dizzying frequency.

Vocabulary

ubiquitous ｜よくある、おなじみの	foible ｜欠点、弱み
off-the wall ｜めちゃくちゃな	earn notoriety ｜評判を得る［悪い意味も含む］
retort ｜応じる、やり返す	defy ... ｜…に反抗する、無視する
draw guffaws from ... ｜…から大笑いを引き出す	articulate ... ｜…をはっきりと話す

[11] Geisha

With their elaborately coiffed hair (see p. 255), white makeup, and **kimono** that alluringly reveal the nape of the neck, geisha (also known as *geigi*) who look as if they had stepped right out of the Edo period still cut a conspicuous figure in Japan.

In the traditional nightlife districts of Kyoto, where they are called *geiko* and young apprentices *maiko*, glimpses of passing geisha rank as one of the old capital's top tourist attractions. Their work consists mainly of entertaining customers at the Japanese-style luxury restaurants known as *ryotei* (see p. 231) by performing traditional dances, plucking the **shamisen**, singing, playing party games, pouring drinks, chatting, and generally adding to the festive air of such gatherings. As serious practitioners of traditional performing arts, they resent being confused with the prostitutes who often appear as characters in **jidaigeki**.

Until very recently, many of the establishments where one could fraternize with geisha refused admittance to first-time customers without an introduction. Their clientele were often limited to powerful politicians and wealthy members of the business and entertainment worlds. These days, however, there are dinner courses that give first-timers and women the opportunity to experience the atmosphere of one of these geisha-attended banquets. Several times a year you can also see geisha perform traditional Nihon **Buyo** dances on stage.

Incidentally, the high-class courtesans in the period dramas who get mistaken for geisha were actually called *oiran*. They can be identified by their *obi* sashes, which are tied prominently in front.

Vocabulary

elaborately coiffed ｜念入りにセットした	conspicuous ｜目立つ
alluringly ｜魅惑的に	fraternize with ... ｜…と親しくする

129

芸者とムスメとジャポニスム

日本の芸者はいつ頃、世界中で知られるようになったのでしょう？
19世紀末には、すでに欧米に渡った芸者たちが少なからずいて、
ジャポニスムの流行に一役買っていたようです。たとえば1867
年のパリ万博では、3人の芸者が日本パビリオン内に設置された
座敷で接客し、大きな反響を呼びました。

また1899年から貞奴という元芸者が、最初期の新派女優として、
日本の劇団とともにシカゴやパリなど欧米各地で公演を重ね、旋
風を巻き起こしました。「ヤッコ」香水やドレスの「キモノ・サ
ダ・ヤッコ」が発売され、ピカソの彼女を描いたスケッチが、ス
ペイン・バルセロナのピカソ美術館に残されています。

この頃から、芸者や日本女性をモデルにした小説が目立ち始めま
す。ピエール・ロティの『お菊さん』（1887年）は、フランスの
軍人の目から見た、不可思議で小さな「人形」のような女性像を
描いてベストセラーとなり、ムスメという言葉がフランス語に加
わりました。その後、ロングの小説『蝶々夫人』をもとに、プッ
チーニが有名なオペラ（1904年初演）を作曲します。

そこで描かれているのは、男性に対して一途で献身的な女性像。
当時から2005年の映画『SAYURI』にいたるまで、こうしたい
じらしいゲイシャあるいはムスメ像は、世界の創作物のなかに繰
り返し立ち現れてくるのです。

Comment

『SAYURI』のチャン・ツィイーはかわいかったけれど、あの踊りは日本舞踊とはまったく違いますよ。
Zhang Ziyi, the Chinese actress who played the title role in the movie *Memoirs of a Geisha*, was cute enough, but her dancing style sure didn't look anything like Nihon **Buyo**!

文楽の演目『曽根崎心中』より、ヒロイン・お初。人形遣いは吉田
簑助。1703年、実際の心中事件を題材に書かれた悲恋物語。
Puppet heroine Ohatsu from the famous **Bunraku** play *The Love Suicides at Sonezaki*, performed by Yoshida Minosuke, 2012. A tragic love story based on an actual incident in 1703.
Photo: Watanabe Hajime
Cooperation: Ningyo Joruri Bunrakuza Mutsumikai

06

ANIME, GAMES, CHARACTERS
アニメ、ゲーム、キャラクター

01 アニメからボーカロイドまで

アニメ——アニメーション[1] の略語——は今や、日本のポップカルチャーの代表格です。十数年ほど前まで、アニメの文化的価値を顧みる大人はあまりいませんでした。ところが、日本のアニメを観て育ったという人たちが世界中に増えて、影響力が無視できなくなったのです。

日本でテレビアニメが、子どもの娯楽として普及し始めたのは 1960 年代。おもに漫画を原作にした、週 1 回 30 分のアニメシリーズが放送されるようになり、キャラクター商品との複合ビジネスがさかんになりました。

やがて漫画と同様、10 代や大人まで熱中する作品が登場し、70 年代の『宇宙戦艦ヤマト』、80 年代の『機動戦士ガンダム』、90 年代の『新世紀エヴァンゲリオン』（P. 140 参照）などが、一大ブームを巻き起こします。

また劇場映画では、宮崎駿作品や、『AKIRA』をはじめとする近未来 SF が、芸術作品として高く評価されるようになりました。

一方、80 年代以降、二次元の娯楽はテレビゲームへと比重が移り、「スーパーマリオブラザーズ」や「ポケットモンスター（ポケモン）」が世界を席巻します。

現在では同じキャラクターの作品が、アニメ、ゲーム、漫画、ライトノベル、ボーカロイド[2]……と、さまざまなメディアで展開されているので、若い世代はどれが最初だったのか、あまり気にしないようです。

これらを極端に好む人はオタクと呼ばれています。2000 年代頃からは、海外の日本文化ファンにも、オタクを自称する人たちが出てきましたね。

最近は、「初音ミク」という仮想アイドル歌手をめぐる、ネット文化の日本事情が注目されています。

Notes

※1 商業用セルアニメ以外の作品、芸術性が認められる作品等は、アニメではなくアニメーションと呼ばれる傾向がある。　※2 音声を合成するソフトウェア、またその製品のキャラクター（P. 162 参照）。

⁰¹ From Anime to Vocaloid

Anime (an abbreviation of "animation") ranks as one of the leading genres of Japanese pop culture today. Less than two decades ago, few grown-ups attributed any cultural value to the medium. But as the number of people reared on Japanese anime has grown around the globe, its impact is no longer so easily dismissed.

Animated programs began to appear on Japanese television in the 1960s as entertainment for children. Most were based on manga and broadcast in weekly 30-minute installments. The anime character merchandising business also flourished.

As with manga, anime that appealed to teens and even adults eventually followed. In what evolved into a sustained anime boom, one hit followed another—*Space Battleship Yamato* in the 1970s, *Mobile Suit Gundam* in the 1980s, and *Neon Genesis Evangelion* in the 1990s, to name three (see p. 141). Feature-length anime films, led by the works of **Miyazaki Hayao** and near-future sci-fi epics like *Akira*, garnered critical praise for their artistry.

From the 1980s on, the market in screen-based entertainment shifted heavily toward **video games**, and *Super Mario Bros.* and *Pokémon* proceeded to conquer the world.

Today works featuring the same cast of characters quickly diversify into anime, games, manga, **light novels**, Vocaloids (see p. 163), and more. Younger fans do not seem to care which medium appears first.

Meanwhile, *otaku* has caught on as a term for people infatuated with these media. Since around the turn of the millennium, fans of Japanese culture in other countries have also begun referring to themselves as otaku.

The latest phenomenon of Japan's Internet culture to capture the public eye is the virtual pop-music idol **Hatsune Miku**.

(see p. 141). (see p. 163),

06

ANIME, GAMES, CHARACTERS / From Anime to Vocaloid

Vocabulary

attribute *A* to *B* | A（の性質）が B にあると考える
be dismissed | 片付けられる、はねつけられる
30-minute installment | 30 分のシリーズ番組
[installment は（連続するものの「1 回分」]
evolve into ... | …に発展する

feature-length | 長編の
garner ... | …を獲得する
diversify into ... | …に分野を広げる、多角化する
infatuated with ... | …に夢中になった
capture the public eye | 人々の注目を集める

⁰² 宮崎駿とスタジオジブリ

日本のアニメーション作家といえば、筆頭に挙げられるのは宮崎駿（1941
〜）^{※3}でしょう。彼自身、立ち上げに関わった「スタジオジブリ」の制作
による、『となりのトトロ』（1988）、『千と千尋の神隠し』（2001）^{※4}など、
おもに子どもを主人公にした長編映画の数々は、家族三世代がそろって鑑
賞できる、質の高い作品として、世界中で親しまれています。2005年には、
ヴェネツィア国際映画祭で、宮崎に栄誉金獅子賞が授与されました^{※5}。

ダイナミックな空中飛行シーンは、「宮崎アニメ」の得意技です。たとえば
『魔女の宅急便』（1989）では、ほうきに乗った少女の魔女が空を飛びました。
初期の代表作『風の谷のナウシカ』（1984）^{※6}や、『もののけ姫』（1997）
などの作品は、自然破壊に対する強いメッセージを感じさせます。それで、
よく彼はエコロジーの作家と目されていますが、本人は人間に都合のいいエ
コロジー意識には懐疑的です。彼は漫画家でもあり、ナウシカの漫画版で
は、映画版より複雑なストーリーが展開されています。

2013年、長編アニメーション作家の引退を宣言。同年に発表した『風立ち
ぬ』は、大人を主人公に、人間の矛盾が描かれて、賛否両論を呼びました。
宮崎の友人かつライバルで、同じく「スタジオジブリ」設立メンバーの高
畑勲（1935〜）は、『火垂るの墓』（1988）など、現実へのまなざしを感じ
させる**アニメーション映画**を作ってきました。2013年の『かぐや姫の物語』
は、千年以上前^{※7}に書かれた日本のファンタジーを、現代的な解釈と、独
特の筆致で描いた野心作です。

ジブリには、後進の監督も育っています。巨匠二人と比べられざるを得な
い立場の彼らですが、それぞれ活動や作風の展開が期待されています。

Notes

※3 映画監督デビュー作は79年『ルパン三世 カリオストロの城』。　※4 2002年、ベルリン国際映画祭で
アニメ初の金熊賞を受賞。　※5 2014年には、米アカデミー賞（オスカー）名誉賞を受賞。
※6 ジブリの母体となる「トップクラフト」の制作。　※7 伝承説話を元に、10世紀までに成立したと考
えられている。　※8 1974年、演出：高畑勲、場面設定・画面構成：宮崎駿。ヨーロッパで放送された日
本のアニメ番組の草分け。アフリカ、アジアでも、多くの国で放送された。

Comment

高畑勲はもともと宮崎駿と同じ会社の先輩で、一緒にテレビアニメの仕事も多く手がけていました。
『アルプスの少女ハイジ』^{※8}はごぞんじですか？　日本のアニメとは知らなかった人が多いみたい
ですが、二人はこの作品の制作にも参加していたんですよ。
Takahata Isao was once Miyazaki Hayao's senior colleague at the same company,
and they collaborated on many animated TV series. Have you ever heard of *Heidi,
Girl of the Alps* (1974)? Some viewers might be surprised to learn that it was made
in Japan. Both Takahata and Miyazaki worked on it.

[02] Miyazaki Hayao and Studio Ghibli

No one today boasts higher name recognition among Japanese animators than Miyazaki Hayao (1941-). *My Neighbor Totoro* (1988), *Spirited Away* (2001), and the many other feature-length anime films produced by Studio Ghibli, which he co-founded, have won fans all over the world. Usually featuring children as protagonists, they have a reputation as high-quality works that family members of all generations can enjoy. In 2005 Miyazaki received the Golden Lion for Career Achievement award at the Venice Film Festival.

Thrilling scenes of midair flight are a trademark of Miyazaki films. The heroine of *Kiki's Delivery Service* (1989), for example, is a young witch who flies through the air on a broomstick.

Some of Miyazaki's masterpieces, such as *Nausicaä of the Valley of the Wind* (1984) and *Princess Mononoke* (1997), carry powerful messages about environmental destruction. Though this has earned him a reputation as an "ecological" filmmaker, Miyazaki himself expresses skepticism about the conventional concept of eco-consciousness. Also a cartoonist, he has written a manga version of *Nausicaä* that offers a more complex story than the film.

In 2013 Miyazaki announced his retirement from full-length animation production. His film *The Wind Rises*, released that same year, had an adult protagonist and cast an unsparing eye on human contradictions, to mixed reviews.

Takahata Isao (1935-), also a founding member of Studio Ghibli, is both Miyazaki's friend and rival. *Grave of the Fireflies* (1988) is just one of the **animated films** he has made that deal with the realities of life in a straightforward manner. *The Tale of Princess Kaguya*, released in 2013, is the ambitious contemporary retelling in a distinctive style of a thousand-year-old Japanese tale.

Ghibli has been cultivating a new generation of directors as well. Though comparisons with the studio's two founding giants are inevitable, expectations run high for the output and style of these younger filmmakers.

06

Vocabulary

broomstick｜ほうき（の柄）[witch（魔女）が乗るものとされる]
skepticism｜懐疑的な態度、疑い
conventional｜慣習の、型にはまった
eco-consciousness｜環境への配慮

unsparing｜手厳しい
contradiction｜矛盾
in a straightforward manner｜正面から、はっきりと
inevitable｜避けられない

テレビと日本アニメ

日本では、1963 年の『鉄腕アトム』（P. 66 参照）を皮切りに、週 1 回 30 分という、テレビアニメ・シリーズの枠組みが定着しました。

たとえば『サザエさん』は、69 年から続くホームドラマで、毎週日曜日の夕方に、日常的なエピソードが繰り広げられています。一方、冒険や恋愛などスリルのあるアニメは、毎回ちょうどいいところで終わって、「次週が待ち遠しい」と思わせるのです。

人気のシリーズは映画化されることが多く、『ドラえもん』は長年にわたって春休みに、また『それいけ！　アンパンマン』は夏休みに、毎年、劇場版が公開されています。

90 年代からは、大人向けの深夜アニメが定着。実験的な話題作を次々と打ち出している枠もあります。

こうしたテレビアニメは、かつてはセルという透明なシートに描かれていました（今はほとんどコンピューターで描かれています）。日本のテレビアニメは、長い間、低予算で製作されてきたため、1 秒における絵の枚数が少なく、ディズニー映画のように動きを強調したスタイルが取れませんでした。しかし、代わりに動きを限定した、平面的な映像を効果的にみせる技術が発達し、2000 年代になるとむしろそれが、日本アニメの様式美だという認識が広まってきました。

ところで、最近アメリカで主流の「ピクサー」のような 3DCG アニメは、日本では映画の話題作がいくつか出ているものの、それほど多く作られていません。しかし、ゲームの映画化を中心に、『ファイナルファンタジー』（世界初のフル CG 映画）や『バイオハザード』シリーズなど、リアルな迫力の 3DCG があり（3D 立体視での上映もされています）、また日本的な 2D 調の CG 表現も展開されています。

『それいけ！アンパンマン　アンパンマン誕生』
幼児に大人気のアニメ・シリーズ。原作はやなせたかし。
Sore ike! Anpanman / Anpanman Tanjo
From the *Anpanman* anime series, a favorite with kids, created by Yanase Takashi
© やなせたかし／フレーベル館・TMS・NTV
発売元：バップ

⁰³ Television and Japanese Anime

Launched in 1963, *Astro Boy* (see p. 67) set the template for TV anime to come with a once-a-week, 30-minute format. *Sazae-san*, an animated sitcom that began airing in 1969 and is still going strong, offers a new episode every Sunday evening about a family's everyday ups and downs. There are also animated adventure and romance series that conclude every installment at a cliffhanging moment, enticing viewers to tune in again the following week.

Film adaptations of popular TV cartoons are common. For many years a new **Doraemon** movie has hit theaters every spring, and a new *Anpanman* movie every summer.

Late-night TV anime aimed at an adult audience have established their own niche since the 1990s. This time slot is also fertile ground for experimental and topical works in the anime format.

At one time, TV cartoons were drawn on the transparent sheets known as cels (short for celluloid), but today nearly everything is done with computers. For a long time Japanese TV anime have been low-budget affairs made with few frames per second, and could not compete stylistically with the fluid movements of Disney-type animation. In the new millennium, however, fans have begun to praise the techniques developed to enliven flat, limited-motion productions as the very essence of Japanese anime aesthetics.

While American animation these days is typified by Pixar-style computer graphics, that is not yet the case with Japanese anime, aside from a few hit movies. On the other hand, the photorealistic visuals of full-3D computer-generated anime have become a fixture in film adaptations of **video games**; examples include *Final Fantasy* (the world's first all-CG movie) and the *Resident Evil* series. Computer graphics have also contributed to the development of a Japanese style of anime that incorporates 2D imagery.

06

ANIME, GAMES, CHARACTERS / Television and Japanese Anime

Vocabulary

set the template ｜ひな形を作る、手本となる	film adaptation ｜映画化
sitcom ｜ situation comedy（連続ホームコメディー）の略	fertile ｜たくさん生み出す
everyday ups and downs ｜日々の山あり谷あり	stylistically ｜スタイル的に、様式上
cliffhanging ｜はらはらさせる	enliven ... ｜…を生き生きさせる
entice *someone* to *do* ｜（人を）誘って…させる	incorporate ... ｜…を含んでいる

⁰⁴ ロボットアニメとガンダム現象

ロボットが人間の味方をするアニメは、日本でとても人気があります。その原点といえる『鉄腕アトム』は少年の姿をしたロボットで、空を飛び、10万馬力の腕力を持っています。

また、70年代の『マジンガーZ』以来、主人公が乗り込んで操縦する巨大ロボットのアニメが、一大ジャンルとなっています。続編の『UFOロボ グレンダイザー』は、フランス^{※9}やイラクでも放送され、伝説的なヒットを記録しました。

巨大ロボットアニメのなかでも、79年の『機動戦士ガンダム』をはじめとするガンダム・シリーズは、日本で格別の人気を保っています。**テレビアニメ**から始まって、劇場版もヒットし、これまで小説、**ゲーム**、**フィギュア**など、派生商品を次々と生み出してきました。年間市場規模が2000億円以上というガンダム関連商品を代表するのが「ガンプラ」――ガンダムのプラモデル――で、同作に登場するメカを細かく再現しています。2009年にはガンダム誕生30周年記念に、全長18メートルの実物大ガンダム像が製作され、東京その他の野外で公開されて、話題を呼んでいます。

『新世紀エヴァンゲリオン』シリーズは、95年に登場。極端に線の細い主人公・シンジが操縦するのは、一見巨大ロボットですが、じつは生物工学によって造られた「人造人間」です。謎に満ちたストーリーと、斬新な演出が国内外のファンを引き付けて、これもまたエポックメーキングな作品となりました。

Notes

※9 フランスでのタイトルは『ゴールドラック』。　※10 「W」シリーズは北米向けに本格的に仕かけられた最初のガンダムで、5人の美形少年がヒーロー。

Comment

僕のおじさんが大好きな「ファーストガンダム」の主人公アムロは、兵士になっても戦争を恐れている、内向的な少年だった。だけど、同じガンダムでもシリーズ^{※10}ごとに設定が違って、「G」シリーズは熱血ヒーローが格闘技をする物語なんだ。

Amuro Ray, hero of the first *Gundam* series that my uncle loves so much, is an introverted boy who fears combat, even though he is supposed to be a soldier. But things change from series to series—one of the later ones, *Mobile Fighter G Gundam*, has a hot-blooded hero who engages in martial-arts duels.

06

アニメ、ゲーム、キャラクター／ロボットアニメとガンダム現象

04 Robot Anime and the Gundam Phenomenon

Japanese are extraordinarily fond of anime that portray robots as man's best friends. The precedent for this inclination was *Astro Boy*, whose hero was a robot in the form of a young boy who flew through the air and had 100,000 horsepower of muscle strength.

Giant robots (called *mechas*) piloted by humans emerged as an anime category unto themselves in the 1970s with *Mazinger Z*. One of its sequel series, *UFO Robot Grendizer*, was broadcast overseas and became a legendary hit in countries as diverse as France and Iraq.

Holding a special place in the super-robot anime pantheon is the *Gundam* series, which began with the **TV anime** *Mobile Suit Gundam* in 1979. A hit theatrical version followed, and the franchise has since expanded into books, **games**, **figures**, and other merchandise. Gundam merchandise sells to the tune of over 200 billion yen per year—most notably the plastic models nicknamed *Gun-pla*, which replicate in loving detail the various mechas that appear in the series. To commemorate the 30th anniversary of *Gundam* in 2009, a full-scale 18-meter-tall statue of the original robot was built and displayed at outdoor locations in Tokyo and elsewhere.

The anime series *Neon Genesis Evangelion*, launched in 1995, introduced an exceptionally sensitive hero, Shinji, who operates what at first glance appears to be a giant robot, but is actually a bioengineered "artificial human." A truly epochal series, *Evangelion*'s riddle-filled story lines and innovative productions have earned it fans in Japan and many other countries.

06

ANIME, GAMES, CHARACTERS / Robot Anime

Vocabulary

mecha ｜巨大ロボット、またそのジャンル［日本の アニメ等の用語から、英語他にとり入れられた］	commemorate ... ｜…を記念する
sequel series ｜続編シリーズ	exceptionally ｜特別に、非常に
pantheon ｜（偉大なものを祭る）殿堂	epochal ｜画期的な
replicate ... ｜…を再現する	riddle-filled ｜謎に満ちた

コラム **日本のロボット工学**

日本ではフィクションだけでなく、現実の世界でもロボット工学がさかんで、人型ロボットも実際に開発されています。

たとえばホンダの「ASIMO」は二本足でスムーズに歩き、ダンスしたり、人と握手したりします。こうしたロボットの開発者が、鉄腕アトムをはじめとする**ロボットアニメ**の影響を公言することはめずらしくありません。

大阪大学の石黒浩博士は、皮膚の感じまで人間そっくりのアンドロイドを研究開発しています。それら（彼らというべきか）が舞台で演じる、「アンドロイド演劇」というプロジェクトがあって、平田オリザが演出しています。

また、このほど（2014 年）ソフトバンク（携帯電話通信事業で知られる IT 企業）が発表した「pepper」は、同社によると「世界初の感情認識パーソナルロボット」。人の気持ちをよみとり、出来事を覚えたり、ネットから情報を取り出したりして[11]、友人同士のように会話ができるそうです。

Notes

※ 11 ロボットの状態の、遠隔モニタリングもされるという。

05 **美少女キャラクターと萌え**

日本のアニメや漫画には、瞳が極端に大きい美少女がよく出てきます。典型的なのはあどけない少女、素直になれずにツンとすました少女などもいます。『美少女戦士セーラームーン』や『新世紀エヴァンゲリオン』（P. 140 参照）など、戦士としての宿命を負わされた少女が多いのも、日本のコンテンツの特徴といえるでしょう。ほかには、のんびりした学園生活を描く『けいおん！』なども人気です。

そうした少女のキャラクターや**アイドル**などに魅了されることを、**オタク**の俗語で「萌え」といいます。詳しくいうと、「距離を保ったまま、対象への想いが高揚すること」といった意味合いでしょうか。だけど、定義はあいまいです。

COLUMN **Japan's Robot Technology**

Japan is a hotbed of robot technology not only in fiction, but in the real world too, where it is a leader in the development of actual humanoid robots. Honda's ASIMO, for example, has two legs capable of smooth walking and dancing motions, and can shake people's hands. It should come as no surprise that the robot's developers have publicly acknowledged **anime robots** like Astro Boy as a source of inspiration.

Professor Ishiguro Hiroshi of Osaka University is engaged in R&D on androids that resemble humans right down to the texture of their skin. He has even teamed up with director Hirata Oriza to produce an "Android-Human Theater" featuring robot-actors on stage.

In 2014 SoftBank, the IT and telecommunications company, introduced Pepper, "the world's first emotion-sensitive personal robot," which it claims can read people's moods, remember events, access information on the Internet, and converse like a friend.

Vocabulary

humanoid robot｜人型ロボット	claim ...｜…だと主張する
acknowledge *A* as *B*｜（行為など）A を B だと認める	converse｜会話をする

⁰⁵ **Bishojo and Moé**

The beautiful young girl (*bishojo*) with huge eyes is an ubiquitous presence in Japanese anime and manga. Though the typical bishojo is childlike and innocent, there are standoffish or stuck-up bishojo characters as well.

One such type that may be unique to Japanese anime is the young girl fated to become a warrior, as in *Pretty Guardian Sailor Moon* and *Neon Genesis Evangelion* (see p. 141). At the other end of the spectrum are the fun-loving schoolgirls of hit anime like *K-On!*

The **otaku** buzzword *moé* (literally "burgeoning," as in spring greenery) refers to an infatuation with characters—or real-life **idols**—in the bishojo mode. More specifically, one might define *moé* as "passionate adoration of the object of your affections from a distance." But the meaning of the word in this context remains vague at best.

Vocabulary

standoffish｜ツンとした	at the other end of the spectrum｜その対極に
stuck-up｜生意気な	burgeoning｜芽を出すこと

コラム 暴力と性表現

日本のアニメや漫画の、暴力やエロティックな表現は、国内外で繰り返し批判の対象になってきました。海外では、それらの問題となるシーンをカットしたり、視聴年齢制限を日本より細かく設定したりすることが多いそうです。

日本では子ども向け[12]アニメでも、ちょっとしたお色気表現が出てきますが（原作が描かれる少年漫画誌の、読者獲得競争が理由のひとつでしょうか）、日本人はたいてい予定調和のように思っていて、あまり驚きません。

また、日本ではアニメや漫画にも、映画などと同じく大人向けのポルノがあって、OVA[13]や、ソフトなものは深夜番組でも流通しています（これを**浮世絵**の春画の伝統という人もいます）。アメリカでは、ヘンタイアニメ／漫画と呼ばれているようですね。「ヘンタイ」とは日本語で、異常なことや性的倒錯を指します。

こうした暴力や性表現は、犯罪を誘発するという説があります。日本は凶悪犯罪が比較的少ないものの、痴漢や学校でのいじめ問題は深刻です。また、80年代の終わり頃から、子どもをねらった連続殺傷事件が一度ならず起こり、容疑者と暴力的なビデオや漫画との接点が報道されて、一時はアニメや漫画、そのマニアが過剰に危険視されました[14]。

表現物が、内容や見せ方によっては、暴力やセクハラ肯定の潜在意識を人に植えつけないかという懸念を、全面的に否定することは難しいでしょう。しかし、時々起こる法規制強化の動きには——たとえば近年の法改正案だと、「児童ポルノに類する漫画等」の定義の難しさなど——さまざまな問題がみられ、法案が出される度に強い反対意見が出ています。

Notes

※12　海外でもグラフィックノベルは大人向けで、暴力や性表現もある。　※13　OVAは和製英語 original video animation の略。テレビ放送や劇場公開のためでなく、レンタル・販売目的で製作されるアニメを指す。　※14　89年、大量のビデオテープを収集していた連続幼女誘拐殺人事件の犯人の異常性が、オタクと結びつけて語られた（P.156参照）。

06

アニメ、ゲーム、キャラクター／暴力と性表現

COLUMN **Violence and Sex in Anime**

Violent or erotic content in Japanese anime and manga is a frequent target of criticism at home and abroad. Many other countries have stricter regulations on viewer age than Japan, and offending scenes are often cut from the material.

In Japan, even anime geared for juvenile audiences may have borderline-erotic content, but this rarely seems to shock the majority of Japanese viewers, who probably see such scenes as obligatory gags, not least because boys' manga habitually include them in an effort to boost readership.

There are also adult-oriented pornographic manga, as well as anime that, like live-action films, get distributed as original video animation (OVA) or (in the case of soft porn) shown on late-night TV. Some critics see erotic manga as part of a tradition dating back to the *shunga* genre of **ukiyo-e**. In the United States these anime and manga have been labeled with the Japanese word *hentai* (which originally refers to sexual perversion and other abnormalities).

There is a hypothesis that violent or sexual content of this sort can encourage criminal behavior. Japan suffers from relatively little violent crime, but bullying in schools and sexual molestation are serious social problems. Since the late 1980s there have also been incidents of indiscriminate attacks on children, accompanied by media reports citing the suspects' contact with violent videos or manga. At one point this prompted a surge in overheated debate about the dangers of anime, manga, and their more obsessive fans.

Depending on the content and the way it is presented, it seems to me that we can't entirely dismiss the concern that media are capable of implanting the notion in our subconscious minds that violence and sexual harassment are acceptable. But the periodic efforts to toughen legal restrictions on such media come with their own problems—the vague definition in a recently proposed legislative amendment to apply obscenity laws to manga "categorizable as" child pornography comes to mind— and are inevitably met with vigorous counterarguments.

06

ANIME, GAMES, CHARACTERS / Violence and Sex in Anime

⁰⁶ アニメ映画の名作──AKIRA、ポスト宮崎駿…

日本のアニメ映画の歴史は、20世紀前半から始まります。1958年、日本
初のカラー長編アニメ映画『白蛇伝』^{※15} は、国内外の映画祭で受賞を重ね
ました。

1988年の『AKIRA』^{※16} は、当時の技術の粋を極めて作られたSFアニメ
映画の金字塔です。舞台は未来の暗黒街──まるで大人向け実写映画のよ
うな、サイバーパンク^{※17} なドラマを、アニメーションならではの表現で打
ち出したのです。そのリアルな世界観やドライブ感、壮大で複雑なストーリ
ーは、海外でも衝撃的に受けとめられて、アニメ映画の芸術性が見直され
るきっかけとなりました。以来、1995年の『攻殻機動隊』^{※18}、2004年の
『APPLESEED』^{※19} と、このジャンルの傑作が続きます。

2000年代半ばには、日本アニメの世界的なブームが追い風となり、表現の
可能性を拡げる、意欲的な映画がいくつも登場しました。実写を交えたシ
ュールな映像の洪水のような『マインド・ゲーム』^{※20}、独特なタッチの漫
画を原作とする『鉄コン筋クリート』^{※21}……。

日本では、しばらく前から、「ポスト宮崎駿」は誰だ? というのも話題に
なっています。ジブリの後輩に限らず、万人に好まれる質の高い日本アニメ
を創る監督ということですが、細田守や新海誠の名がよく挙がっています。

Notes

※15 脚本・演出：藪下泰司　※16 原作・監督：大友克洋　※17 SFのサブジャンル。人間が機械化し、
意識が巨大なネットワークに取り込まれた状態と、反体制思想を描く。　※18 監督：押井守、原作：士郎
正宗　※19 監督：荒牧伸志、原作：士郎正宗　※20 2004年、監督：湯浅政明、原作：ろびん西
※21 2006年、監督：マイケル・アリアス、原作：松本大洋

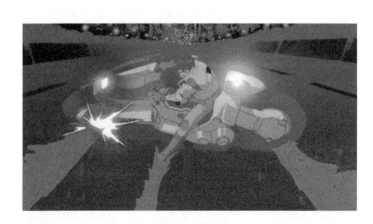

⁰⁶ *Akira* and the Post-Miyazaki Era

Japan's association with animated film dates back to the early decades of the 20th century. The country's first full-length feature animation in color, *Hakujaden* (*The Tale of the White Serpent*), came out in 1958 and won prizes at film festivals both in Japan and elsewhere.

Akira, a 1988 film that utilized the state-of-the-art animation technology of the day, is still regarded as the crowning achievement of Japanese sci-fi anime. Set in a dystopian underworld of the near future, the production gave full play to animation's expressive powers in the service of a cyberpunkish drama of the sort that had been seen only in adult-oriented live-action films.

The movie's realistic worldview, visual momentum, and sprawling, complex story line made it a sensation both domestically and abroad. *Akira* redefined anime as a legitimate artistic medium and inspired further masterworks of the genre, such as 1995's *Ghost in the Shell* and 2004's *Appleseed*.

By the mid-2000s Japanese animation was enjoying a worldwide boom that made conditions favorable for ambitious works that further extended anime's expressive palette. Standouts include *Mind Game*, which blends live-action footage with a flood of surreal imagery, and *Tekkonkinkreet*, based on a manga with a quirkily original touch.

For some time now anime fans have been asking themselves who the "next **Miyazaki**" will be. By this they mean a director—not necessarily from the **Ghibli** ranks—capable of making Japanese-flavored anime of high quality and broad appeal. Two frequently mentioned candidates are Hosoda Mamoru and Shinkai Makoto.

Vocabulary

state-of-the-art ｜最先端の、最新の
crowning achievement ｜最高の成果
dystopian underworld｜暗黒の（地下）世界、反ユートピア的裏社会

momentum ｜勢い
sprawling ｜広がりのある
redefine *A* as *B* ｜ A を B と再定義する
live-action footage ｜実写の場面

Left: アニメ映画『AKIRA』より
　　From the animated film *AKIRA*
Right: AKIRA［Blu-ray］
© 1988 マッシュルーム／アキラ製作委員会
発売元：NBC ユニバーサル・エンターテイメント

06

ANIME, GAMES, CHARACTERS / Akira and the Post-Miyazaki Era

コラム　クールジャパン

「クールジャパン」は、2002 年にアメリカのジャーナリスト、ダグラス・マグレイが『フォーリン・ポリシー』誌に寄せた記事で、「日本はクールな（かっこいい）文化を、ソフトパワー[22] として生かしきれていない」と論じてから、日本で広まった言葉です。90 年代イギリスで流行った、「クール・ブリタニア」の影響もあったでしょう。

キティに**ポケモン**、**ゴスロリ**、**すし**……と、現代日本の文化が世界で一躍脚光を浴びた時期でした。その頃から、海外市場を意識してか、**着物**や伝統芸能など、日本らしいテーマやアイコンを採り入れるコンテンツ[23] が、増えたように感じます。

一方、もとよりグローバル化のなかで、著作権保護問題などへの対応に迫られていた日本政府は、文化面での人気を、外交や輸出振興に結びつけようとする「クールジャパン」政策[24] に着手しました。2013 年からは予算を大幅にアップさせて、今後の動向が注目されています。

Notes

※ 22　国家が軍事や経済力等の圧力によらず、文化や価値観等の魅力で、国際社会の支持を得られる力のこと。提唱者のジョセフ・ナイは、国家が管理できないし、すべきでないとしている。　※ 23　メディアが伝達する内容、著作物。具体的には音楽、漫画、アニメ等。
※ 24　K- ポップ等を積極的に輸出している韓国の影響もあった。

Comment

僕の知る限り、現場のつくり手は、政策の行方をナナメに見てますね。アニメーターの労働条件の改善とか、創造的な環境づくりにつながればいいのですが……。
As far as I can tell, people actually producing the content associated with "Cool Japan" view the government's policy rather skeptically. If nothing else, they hope it will lead to improved working conditions for animators and an environment more conducive to creative endeavors in general.

07　海外とのアニメ共同制作

21 世紀に入る頃から、アニメ制作で、日本と海外のスタッフとのコラボレーションが展開されるようになりました。

たとえば、2003 年アメリカの実写映画『キル・ビル』には、日本のスタジ

→

^{COLUMN} **Cool Japan**

"Cool Japan" became a slogan in this country after an article by the American journalist Douglas McGray appeared in 2002. Writing in *Foreign Policy* magazine, McGray argued that Japan had not fully exploited its "soft power" potential as a "cool" culture. The term probably owes something to the catchphrase "Cool Brittania" that was heard in the U.K. in the 1990s.

This was a period when contemporary Japanese culture—from **Hello Kitty** and **Pokémon** to **GothLoli** and **sushi**—found itself in the global limelight. Since that time, perhaps with an eye to foreign markets, Japanese producers seem to have consciously added more Japanesque elements—**kimono**, traditional arts, and so on—to their content.

Meanwhile, the Japanese government, confronted with such globalization-related issues as copyright protection, has launched a "Cool Japan" initiative that it hopes will harness the popularity of Japanese culture in the services of diplomacy and increased exports. Having received a sizable budgetary boost in 2013, the program bears watching for future developments.

Vocabulary

exploit ... | …を生かす	confronted with ... | …に直面した、…を突
global limelight | 世界的な脚光	き付けられた
consciously | 意識的に	harness ... | …を利用する、役立てる

⁰⁷ Joint Anime Productions

The 21st century has ushered in an era of collaboration on anime work between production staffs inside and outside Japan. The 2003 American live-action film *Kill Bill*, for example, contained an animated sequence created by Production I.G, a studio in Japan.

Another U.S. live-action movie, 1999's *The Matrix*, drew its inspiration from the Japanese anime (see p. 147) feature *Ghost in the Shell*. It was followed in 2003 by the omnibus animation film *The Animatrix*, to which several Japanese creators, including Studio 4°C and Madhouse, contributed their animated takes on the *Matrix* world.

Hollywood has produced a number of live remakes of Japanese anime and **games**, such as *Speed Racer* and *Biohazard*. Plans for a live-action

→

←

オ「Production I. G」によるアニメのパートが挿入されています。

99 年アメリカの実写映画『マトリックス』は、日本の**アニメ映画**『攻殻機動隊』にインスパイアされた作品ですが、2003 年にはオムニバス・アニメーション映画『アニマトリックス』[※25] が登場。「Studio 4℃」や「マッドハウス」など、日本のクリエーターが多数参加して、マトリックスの世界観をアニメ化しました。

また、『スピード・レーサー』[※26] や『バイオハザード』のように、日本のアニメや**ゲーム**がハリウッドで実写版にリメイクされるケースもあり、今後も、『**AKIRA**』などの実写化が企画されています。

その他、しばらく前から日本のアニメ制作のかなりの部分が外注されているアジア各地や、EU、アフリカでも、日本のスタッフとのテレビアニメ共同制作の企画が起こっています。2012 年には、日本人なら誰でも知っている野球アニメ『巨人の星』（P. 74 参照）が、設定をクリケットに替えてインドでリメイクされました。タイトルは『スーラジ　ザ・ライジングスター』です。

Notes

※ 25　監督：アンディ・ジョーンズ、前田真宏、渡辺信一郎、川尻善昭、小池健、森本晃司、ピーター・チョン　※ 26　日本の原題は『マッハ GoGoGo』。

[08] アート・アニメーション（短編アニメーション）

日本には、大量に流通しているセルアニメ（P. 138 参照）だけでなく、パステルや絵の具、粘土、切り絵、人形など、さまざまな技法を使ったアニメーションがあります。個人作家などが自主的に制作した短編アニメーションは、「アート・アニメーション」と呼ばれることがあります。

この分野で有名な作品は、古典**落語**を現代の設定に置き換えた『頭山』[※27] や、海面上昇の影響で変わりゆく老人の生活を描いた『つみきのいえ』[※28] など。両方、アニメーション映画の賞を数々受賞しているので、どこかでご覧になったことがあるかもしれません。

Notes

※ 27　演出、アニメーション、美術、編集／山村浩二　※ 28　監督、アニメーション／加藤久仁生

06

アート・アニメーション
アニメ、ゲーム、キャラクター／海外とのアニメ共同制作／

←

version of **Akira** have also been announced.

For some years now, much of Japan's anime production has been outsourced to other parts of Asia, as well as the EU and Africa, giving rise to joint TV anime projects by Japanese and local studios.

In 2012, a remake of *Star of the Giants* (see p. 75), a TV anime series about baseball that every Japanese is familiar with, was released in India under the title *Suraj: The Rising Star*, with the game changed to cricket.

Vocabulary

usher｜先導役となる	be outsourced to ...｜…に外注される
omnibus｜オムニバスの	give rise to ...｜…を生じさせる

08 Art Animation

The Japanese animation world includes not only mass-distributed cel anime (see p. 139), but also works made by a diversity of techniques—pastels, paints, clay, cut paper, dolls. Short films of this kind, often created by individual animators, tend to be grouped under the rubric "art animation."

Among the better-known titles in this category are *Mt. Head*, which places a classic **Rakugo** tale in a contemporary setting, and *The House of Small Cubes*, which depicts how rising sea levels affect the life of an elderly man. Both of these films have won numerous awards, so you may have actually seen a clip or two somewhere.

Vocabulary

mass-distributed｜大量に流通している	rubric｜表題、項目、見出し
be grouped under ...｜…に分類される	rising sea levels｜海面の上昇

『頭山』より From *Mt. Head*, directed by Yamamura Koji
© Yamamura Animation

06

ANIME, GAMES, CHARACTERS / Joint Anime / Art Animation

⁰⁹ コンピューターゲーム

コンピューターゲーム^{※29} の開発は、日本が 20 世紀最後の数十年間で、一躍存在感を示した分野でした。

最初の大ヒットは、1978 年のアーケードゲーム「スペースインベーダー」。続いて「パックマン」も流行りました。

80 年代には、**任天堂**の携帯型「ゲーム＆ウォッチ」や、家でテレビとつなぐ「ファミリーコンピュータ（ファミコン）」が大ヒット。90 年代からは、任天堂とソニーが家庭用ゲーム機の開発競争を繰り広げるようになりました^{※30}。ゲームソフトでは、「スーパーマリオブラザーズ」が画期的でしたね。ゲームがアニメのような世界観をもつようになりました。

日本では RPG（ロールプレイングゲーム）の人気が高く、なかでも「**ポケットモンスター**」シリーズは世界を席巻しました。その他、鳥山明（漫画『ドラゴンボール』の作者）がキャラクターをデザインした「ドラゴンクエスト」や、CG 映画のような「ファイナルファンタジー」も有名です。

また、**オタク**趣味として知られる一大ジャンルに、**美少女**が出てくる「ギャルゲー（ギャル・ゲーム）」や、そのなかでキャラクターと仮想恋愛を体験する「恋愛ゲーム」があります。

2000 年代には、「Wii Sports」（P. 154 参照）や「脳トレ」（脳をトレーニングするクイズやパズル）など、大人のライトユーザー^{※31} 向けゲームがヒットしました。

近年は世界的に、オンラインゲームやソーシャルゲーム^{※32} がさかんですね。課金制でギャンブル性の高いものは、社会問題になりました。

海外では映像のリアルな銃撃戦のゲームが流行りで、あいかわらずアニメのような絵の日本製 RPG は、今では昔懐かしいイメージになってしまったと聞きますが、それでも一定の人気は保っているようです。また、スマートフォンでゲームをする人が急速に増えたので、空き時間に断続的に遊べる「パズル＆ドラゴンズ」（パズルと RPG を組み合わせた「パズル RPG」という新ジャンルのゲーム）が、ひさびさの世界的ヒットとなりました。

Notes

※29 和製英語。米で computer game はパソコンのゲーム。 ※30 2000 年代にはマイクロソフトが参入。 ※31 ゲームに不慣れで利用時間の短い人（light user）。heavy user の対義語。英語では、ゲームの場合、casual user の方がよく使われる。 ※32 人とネットを通して競争や協力等ができるゲーム。日本では主に、携帯電話を通して SNS 上で行うゲームを指す。

⁰⁹ Video Games

Japan burst onto the scene as a developer of video games during the final decades of the 20th century. The first big hit was *Space Invaders*, an arcade game that made its debut in 1978, shortly followed by the equally popular *Pac-Man*.

With the 1980s came **Nintendo**'s handheld Game & Watch and the *Famicon* (short for Family Computer, the domestic version of the Nintendo Entertainment System), which is hooked up to a TV set at home. By the 1990s Nintendo and Sony were engaged in an escalating race to develop home video game consoles. In the 2000s Microsoft also entered the fray.

In the game software realm, *Super Mario Bros.* was a landmark success, signaling the emergence of video games that rival anime in their ability to conjure up entire realities.

Role-playing games (RPGs) are big in Japan, with the **Pokémon** franchise branching out to take the entire world by storm. Other best-selling series are *Dragon Quest* (with characters designed by Toriyama Akira, creator of the hit manga *Dragon Ball*) and *Final Fantasy*, which resembles a movie made with computer graphics.

A major category that caters to **otaku** tastes is the "gal game," featuring **bishojo** characters; a "romance game" subgenre allows players to engage in virtual love affairs with the characters. The 2000s saw the advent of *Wii Sports* (see p. 155) as well as brain-training games aimed at the adult casual-user market. Today online and social games are played all over the world. In Japan, controversy has erupted about "pay-to-play" games that encourage a mindset similar to gambling.

Overseas, where shooting games with realistic footage are in vogue, one hears that Japan-made RPGs with their anime-style illustrations have acquired an old-fashioned retro image, yet still retain a degree of popularity. Meanwhile, now that so many people play games on their smart phones, *Puzzle & Dragons*, a puzzle RPG that can be played off and on during one's spare moments, has become the first global hit in some time for Japan's game industry.

Vocabulary

video game ｜電子ゲーム全般［テレビゲーム（console game）、ゲームセンターのゲーム（arcade game）等が含まれる］
burst onto the scene ｜一躍その場に現れる
handheld ｜携帯型の、手で持って操作できる

escalating race ｜過熱する競争
fray ｜争い
conjure up ... ｜...を描く、出現させる
erupt ｜噴出する

10 任天堂と宮本茂

任天堂はテレビゲーム[33]のハードとソフトを開発・販売している会社。80年代半ばから90年代半ばまで、国内で圧倒的シェアを誇り、アメリカでも当時、ニンテンドーといえば、そのままテレビゲームを指していました。

同社のマリオや「ゼルダの伝説」シリーズなどをプロデュースしたゲームクリエーター・宮本茂（1952～）は、『TIME』誌ほかの海外メディアで「現代ビデオゲームの父」と呼ばれ、フランスの芸術文化勲章シュヴァリエ章など、数々の賞を受賞しています。

2000年代にも任天堂は、老若男女が直感的に操作できる家庭用ゲーム機「Wii」や、携帯型ゲーム機「DS」を発表して大ヒットさせました。Wiiの専用ソフト「Wii Sports」は、テレビ画面に合わせて体全体を動かし、テニスや野球などのポーズを取るゲームです。

Notes

※33 テレビゲームは和製英語で、おもに家庭用据え置き型ゲーム機。

11 ポケットモンスター（ポケモン）[34]

日本のゲームソフト[35]の名前で、そのなかに出てくる架空の生き物のこと。日本での正式名称はポケットモンスター。「ポケモン」はその略称です。96年の発売以来、アニメや「ポケモンカード」と呼ばれるカードゲーム、関連イベントなどを次々と派生させて、世界的なキャラクター・フランチャイズになりました。

その圧倒的な知名度から、98年の劇場版アニメ第一作『ミュウツーの逆襲』は大ヒットして、アメリカでも「日本映画初の週間興行ランキング初登場第1位」を記録しました。

アニメ版『ポケットモンスター』で、主人公のサトシと旅するポケモンは、ピカチュウといいます。

Notes

※34 ポケモンが正式名の国が多い。　※35 当初は任天堂から発売され、現在は株式会社ポケモンが発売。ソフト開発は株式会社ゲームフリーク。

¹⁰ Nintendo and Miyamoto Shigeru

The Nintendo company develops and sells video-game hardware and software. From the mid-1980s to the mid-1990s it dominated the Japanese market, and even in the U.S. the name Nintendo became synonymous with game consoles.

Game creator Miyamoto Shigeru (1952-), who produced such hit Nintendo series as *The Legend of Zelda* and the *Mario* franchise, has been hailed by *Time* magazine as the "father of modern video gaming." The recipient of numerous prizes, he was made a *Chevalier* of France's Ordre des Arts et des Lettres.

Nintendo continued to turn out hits in the 2000s, notably the DS handheld console and the Wii, a game console designed to be user-intuitive to players of all ages. *Wii Sports*, played on a Wii console connected to a TV screen, lets the user simulate the movements of tennis, baseball, and several other sports with the entire body.

Vocabulary

become synonymous with ... ｜…と同義語になる   user-intuitive ｜ユーザーが直感で使える
be hailed as ... ｜…と呼ばれる、評価される

¹¹ Pokémon

The name of a Japanese video game franchise as well as of the imaginary creatures that populate it, *Pokémon* is short for "Pocket Monsters," as the game was originally titled in Japan. Since the first games appeared in 1996, the franchise has become an ever-expanding universe that encompasses events, merchandise, anime series, and a Pokémon Trading Card Game.

In 1998 this overwhelming brand recognition propelled the inaugural *Pokémon* theatrical feature, *Pokémon: The First Movie—Mewtwo Strikes Back*, to the top of U.S. box office charts on its opening weekend, making it the first Japanese film to accomplish that.

The mascot of the franchise is Pikachu, a Pokémon who appears as the hero Satoshi's sidekick in the anime series.

Vocabulary

ever-expanding ｜拡大し続ける   propel ... ｜…を促す
encompass ... ｜…を網羅する   inaugural ｜シリーズ最初の
overwhelming ｜圧倒的な   sidekick ｜親友、相棒

¹² **オタク**

オタクは、日本でアニメや漫画、テレビゲーム、鉄道などのマニアを指すスラング。英語（米）にもナードやギークなど、似た意味のスラングがありますが、海外では日本のアニメや漫画などのファンだけを、otaku と呼ぶようになりました。

日本語の「おたく」は、もともと相手の家を指す一般的な言葉で、「あなた」の丁寧語でもあります。それがマニアを表すようになった起源は、一説によると 80 年代頃、SF 大会で、若者に似合わず、ほかの人を「おたく」と丁寧に呼ぶリーダー格のグループがいて、彼らがアニメ・ファンたちの人気者だったので、周囲も真似したといいます。

しかしその後、オタクと呼び合う人たちのイメージは悪くなり（P. 144 参照）、「現実世界と折り合えずにヴァーチャルな世界※36 に引きこもる人」という意味で、この言葉が使われるようになります。

最近では、悪いイメージは薄れてきて、「美少女キャラクターに萌える人」※37 という意味合いが強まっています。一方で、言葉が一般化して、各分野における玄人としてのこだわりを「オタク的」と言ったりします。

2000 年前後には、オタク文化が現代日本のひとつの象徴として、海外で紹介されるようになりました※38。

Notes

※36　コンピューターの中の、仮想の「現実世界」（virtual reality）。　※37　インターネットの電子掲示板への書き込みを元にした恋愛物語『電車男』（2004）の影響が強い。同作は映画／ドラマ化もされた。英語タイトルは『Train Man』。　※38　早い例としては 1994 年、フランスの TV でドキュメンタリー番組『おたく（Otaku: fils de l'empire virtuel）』（ジャン＝ジャック・ベネックス監督）が放送された。　※39　鉄道ファンを表す英語には train buff や、イギリスでは trainspotter（ホームで列車の車両番号を記録する趣味の人）等がある。

Comment

アメリカで otaku といえば、「海外文化に精通したクールな人」っていう、いい意味に使われていると聞いたけど、実際はどうなのかな？

I've heard that in America, *otaku* is a word with a positive image, something like "a cool, cosmopolitan person"... Really?!

Comment

オタクのなかでも、ガンダムのオタクは「ガンオタ」、鉄道オタク※39 は「鉄オタ」っていいます。私は「エヴァオタ」かな。高校の頃、エヴァンゲリオンに、はまりました。

Japan is populated by a variety of otaku: Gundam fans are called *Gun-ota*, and train buffs are *tetsu-ota* (from *tetsudo*, meaning railroad). I guess I'm an *Eva-ota* because when I was in high school I was totally hooked on *Evangelion*.

¹² Otaku

In Japan, *otaku* is a slang term for someone obsessed with such things as anime, manga, **video games**, and trains. Its connotation is similar to that of English words like nerd and geek, but outside Japan, "otaku" has come to mean a fan of anime, manga, or other Japanese pop-culture phenomena.

Otaku in Japanese is originally just a word for "your home," as well as a polite way of saying "you." As for how it came to refer to a certain kind of hobby fanatic, one anecdote has it that sometime in the 1980s, some preppy fans at a science-fiction convention were addressing other people with the overly polite "otaku," which sounded especially odd coming from young people. But since the group in question played a leading role in the anime fan world, listeners quickly began imitating them, according to this explanation.

Subsequently, however, the image of nerds who call each other otaku began to suffer (see p. 145), as the word acquired the nuance of an individual who finds it hard to cope with the real world and seeks refuge in virtual reality.

That negative image has improved since then, but nowadays the word tends to get applied to people fixated on **bishojo** characters from manga or anime. On the other hand, its usage has also broadened, so that having a specialized knowledge in a given field can be labeled "otaku-ish."

Since around the year 2000, otaku culture has acquired an image overseas as an iconic element of contemporary Japan.

06

ANIME, GAMES, CHARACTERS / Otaku

Vocabulary

obsessed with ... | …で頭がいっぱいな	subsequently | その後
connotation | 言外の意味、含意	nuance | ニュアンス
anecdote | 逸話	broaden | 広がる
overly | あまりにも	

仏・パリのジャパン・エキスポ
Japan Expo in Paris, France, 2013
© Circle.ms

13 コスプレ

コスプレとは、扮装をしてポーズを決め、アニメや漫画、**ゲーム**などのキャラクターになりきる遊び。コスチューム・プレイという和製英語をもとにした言葉です。コミックマーケット（漫画**同人誌**即売会）など関連イベントの参加者の間で広まりました。

2000 年代になると、東京の秋葉原という**オタク**・スポットに「メイドカフェ」が次々と出来て、話題を呼びました。店を訪れると、19 世紀英国のメイドをイメージしたコスプレのウェイトレスたちが、「おかえりなさい、ご主人様」と呼びかける、テーマパークのようなカフェです。

今では海外のコスプレ愛好者も増えて、2003 年から年 1 回、名古屋で「世界コスプレサミット」[40] が開催されるようになりました。イタリア、フランス、中国、ブラジルなど、世界各国の代表コスプレーヤーがパフォーマンスを行い、グランドチャンピオンが選ばれます。

Notes

[40] 外務省、テレビ愛知等で構成される「世界コスプレサミット実行委員会」の主催。

東京ゲームショウでのコスプレーヤーたち
Cosplayers at Tokyo Game Show, 2013
Photo: Miura Yoshiaki (The Japan Times)

14 フィギュア

日本でフィギュア[41] といえば、アニメや**ゲーム**のキャラクターを立体化した、樹脂製（PVC やレジン）の像のこと。それぞれのキャラクターらしいポーズを、おもに型取りで作っています。なかでも**美少女**フィギュアの製作や収集は、典型的な**オタク**趣味ととらえられています。髪の毛やスカートが揺れているなど、瞬間的なシーンを閉じ込めたような表現が、美少女フィギュアのポイントです。**現代アート**作家の**村上隆**は、こうしたフィギュアのスタイルを踏襲した彫刻を発表しています。

また、関節が可動式になっている、**ロボット**などのアクション・フィギュア

→

¹³ Cosplay

A Japanese truncation of "costume play," *cosplay* is the practice of dressing up, posing, or performing as a character from the anime/manga/**game** world. It first caught on with participants at events like Comiket, the manga **doujinshi** market.

During the 2000s, "maid cafés" began to spring up around the Tokyo **otaku** mecca of Akihabara and became a much talked about phenomenon. These are theme-park-like establishments where young women, dressed in maid costumes inspired by those of 19th-century England, wait upon customers whom they greet with "Welcome home, Master."

Cosplay enthusiasts have also proliferated outside Japan. Since 2003 a World Cosplay Summit has taken place once a year in Nagoya. Cosplayers representing such countries as Italy, France, China, and Brazil gather to perform and compete for grand-champion status.

Vocabulary

truncation｜略語［truncate で「(長い文章を) 切り詰める」の意］	greet with ...｜...という言葉で出迎える
establishment｜店舗	enthusiast｜ファン
	proliferate｜急増する

¹⁴ Figures

In Japan, a "figure" is a three-dimensional PVC or resin model, usually cast from a mold, of an anime or **game** character in a pose identified with the character. Making or collecting **bishojo** figures is regarded as an archetypal **otaku** pastime; these figures often capture the character in a dramatic moment—with her hair or skirt swaying, for example. Contemporary artist **Murakami Takashi** has produced sculptures in the likeness of character-type figures of this sort.

Another popular genre is the action figure, typified by **robots** with movable joints.

Vocabulary

PVC｜ポリ塩化ビニル［polyvinyl chloride の略］	pastime｜趣味、娯楽
cast from a mold｜型から作られた	capture ...｜...をとらえる、形のあるものにする
archetypal｜典型的な	movable joint｜動かせる関節

←
も人気です。

Notes

※ 41　食玩フィギュアのブーム以来、人以外のミニチュアも指す。髪や服等の素材をボディと変えたものは「ドール」と呼ばれる。

15　マスコット・キャラクター

現代日本には、アニメ風のマスコット・キャラクターがあふれています。おもちゃやコンテンツの企業だけでなく、信頼性の重視される銀行や、警視庁などの省庁まで、**カワイイキャラクター**をシンボルにして、親しみを PR しているのです。

各地方自治体が設定している「ご当地キャラクター」には、かつて役場の職員や住民などの素人がデザインしたものがよくあり、そのあか抜けない魅力が注目されて、「ゆるキャラ」※ 42（ゆるいキャラクター）と呼ばれるブームになっていました。

ところが最近では、プロデューサーやデザイナーが入って大きくビジネス展開する、ゆるキャラ風でも、全然ゆるくないキャラクターが増えています。たとえば熊本県の「くまモン」など。

また、船橋市の一市民が、勝手にゆるキャラ風の着ぐるみを着て、パフォーマンスを始めた「ふなっしー」は、市の公認を得ないまま、人気者になりました。

しかし、どうして日本人は、こんなにキャラクター好きなのでしょうか？それは社会学者や精神科医を交えて、諸説飛び交うテーマとなっています。こうした現象には、無害で愛らしいキャラクターのイメージで物事が判断されて、肝心の内容が軽視されるという懸念もあります。

Notes

※ 42　みうらじゅんの命名。

アニメ、ゲーム、キャラクター／フィギュア／マスコット・キャラクター

¹⁵ Mascot Characters

Japan today is overrun with anime-style mascot characters. No longer just the purview of toy companies and content makers, these *kawaii* characters are the stars of PR campaigns to foster friendly feelings toward banks, police departments, and other institutions that seek the public's trust.

At one time, the characters devised by regional governments to represent their locality tended to be amateurish designs by office employees or local citizens. Their artless appeal sparked a boom in what came to be called *yuru-kyara*, short for "*yurui* (loose, relaxed) character."

Lately, however, producers, designers, and other professionals have moved into what is now a thriving business, creating mascot characters that look like the old yuru-kyara but are too slick to be yurui. A popular example is Kumamon, the official mascot of Kumamoto Prefecture.

On the other hand we have Funassyi, a character designed by a private citizen of the city of Funabashi (who dresses in a Funassyi costume and gives performances in character). Funassyi has become a nationwide hit despite lacking official recognition by the city itself.

So why do Japanese like mascot characters so much? The question has become fodder for sociologists and psychologists, who offer a host of explanations. Not a few people believe that tying these cute, harmless images to institutions or events lulls the public into overlooking the actual behavior of such entities.

Vocabulary

be overrun with ...	…であふれている	fodder	素材、ネタ
purview	範囲	harmless	害のない
foster ...	…を心に抱かせる	lull *someone* into ...	（人を）安心させて…の状態
thriving	さかんな、盛況な	にする
slick	巧妙な	entity	組織、存在物

06

16 初音ミク

「初音ミク」は、**美少女**アニメのような絵の仮想アイドル歌手です。2007年、パソコン用「歌声合成ソフトウェア（ボーカロイド※43）」の製品名、かつそのパッケージに描かれたキャラクター名として登場しました。これは、パソコンに曲の歌詞とメロディ（音符）を入力すると、合成した女性の声※44で歌ってくれるソフトです。

以来、ユーザーが作ったミクの曲が、「ニコニコ動画」※45という日本の動画投稿サイトに投稿されるようになり、やがて人気曲に合わせたイラストやアニメも投稿され、ミクを踊らせる3Dソフトが無償でリリースされ……と無数の人が介入して、多彩なミク像が育まれていきました。

初音ミクの絵は、青緑色をしたツインテールの髪が特徴。発売元の「クリプトン・フューチャー・メディア」は、16歳という年齢など、彼女の基本データをいくつか設定していますが、絵の非営利利用や改変を、積極的に認めています※46。それで、**二次創作**や見知らぬ同士のコラボレーションが、連鎖的に起こっているのです。

ゲーム、小説、漫画、**フィギュア**……といった商業展開もされていて、今や初音ミクの映像が、ステージで歌い踊る「コンサート」には、15,000人の観客が集まるようになりました。また、芸術家たちもミクに注目し、ミクとオーケストラの共演や※47、ミクがヒロインの新作オペラ※48も出来ています。そして2014年には、レディ・ガガの全米コンサートツアーに、ミクが出演して話題を呼びました。

Notes

※43　音声作成の技術（技術開発は「ヤマハ」）や製品、キャラクターもボーカロイドと呼ぶことがある。
※44　声優・藤田咲の声を録音して合成している。　※45　YouTubeと違う点は、流れる画面上に直接、声援等のコメントが書き込める。　※46　独自のピアプロ・キャラクター・ライセンスを設定。「公序良俗に反する」利用は認めていない。2012年からクリエイティブ・コモンズ・ライセンスも採用。　※47　『イーハトーヴ交響曲』（2012年、冨田勲・作曲）。　※48　ボーカロイド・オペラ『The End』（2013年、渋谷慶一郎・作曲）。

Comment

ミクの公式イラストは、「**萌え**」キャラとちょっと違って、わざと人形みたいに無機的なイメージにしてあるらしい。そのせいでオタクだけでなく、わりと誰にでも好かれてる。あまりメジャーになって、ミクのイメージが崩れないかは、心配だな。
Official illustrations of Miku differ from the typical **moé** character in that they seem intended to portray her as doll-like and a bit mechanical. But for just that reason she has a relatively broad appeal not limited to the otaku market. Let's hope her image doesn't take a beating if she gets too big!

¹⁶ Hatsune Miku

Hatsune Miku is a virtual idol, an imaginary pop singer who looks like a **bishojo** anime character. She made her debut, both as a Vocaloid singing-voice synthesizing software product and as a character on the software package, in 2007. The software generates a tune sung in a female voice when the user inputs the melody and lyrics into a personal computer.

Users began submitting songs they had written for Miku to Nico Nico Douga, a Japanese video-sharing site, which inspired others to send in pictures and anime to accompany their favorite tunes. The spread of free software that lets users create 3D Miku animation led to a further surge in fan participation. Thus a myriad Mikus were born.

The Miku character is readily identified by her long turquoise-colored pigtails. Her creator, the Crypton Future Media company, describes her as a 16-year-old girl, along with a very few other details, but actively encourages modifications of her image and its use for nonprofit purposes. The result is a rapidly growing chain of **derivative works** and serial collaborations between mutual strangers.

The Hatsune Miku franchise now extends to games, manga, novels, and **figures**. "Concerts" in which the image of Miku appears onstage have taken place before audiences of 15,000. The virtual diva has attracted the notice of artists who have come up with such productions as an orchestral performance accompanying Miku, and a Vocaloid opera. In 2014 Miku caused a sensation when she made an appearance on Lady Gaga's U.S. tour.

06

ANIME, GAMES, CHARACTERS / Hatsune Miku

Vocabulary

singing-voice synthesizing ｜歌声の合成	readily ｜すぐに、容易に
generate ... ｜…を作り出す	nonprofit purpose ｜非営利目的
myriad ｜無数の	virtual diva ｜仮想の歌姫［ミクのこと］

海外におけるアニメ

日本のアニメは、世界の広範囲な地域に輸出されています。近年では anime や manga といえば、日本の（スタイルの）アニメやコミックを指す世界語として、通用するようになりました。

アメリカでは早くも 60 年代に、『鉄腕アトム』や『エイトマン』などがヒットしましたが、ほとんどの視聴者は、それらが日本製とは知りませんでした。70〜80 年代には、日本の情報に詳しい熱心なファンが上映会の開催を始めます。やがて『科学忍者隊ガッチャマン』などが、はっきり日本製として放送されるようになりました。もっとも、この作品は大幅に再編集されたそうです。

ヨーロッパでは 70 年代、まずはイタリアとフランスで、版権料の安かった日本のアニメのテレビ放送が始まりました。80 年代にはこれらの国で民営テレビ局が出来て、チャンネルが増えたことから、大量に放送されるようになります。

当時、日本のアニメが子ども向け番組の 9 割ほどに及んだフランスでは、拒絶反応も噴出しました。83 年、ラング文化相は、日本アニメを「文化侵略」と公言。『キン肉マン』※49 や『北斗の拳』は、暴力シーンなどが問題となって、放送中止に至りました。90 年代の一時期、日本アニメはフランスの地上波からほとんど姿を消し、衛星放送や OVA（P. 144 参照）に移って、日本からのグッズやマンガを直輸入する業者が登場しました。

やがて、『AKIRA』やジブリ・アニメなどの芸術性が世界的に認められたことは、日本アニメをひとつにくくらず、作品ごとの評価が重視されるきっかけになりました※50。また、原型を損なうほど、テレビアニメを再編集することも減ったといいます。

海外における日本アニメのブームは、2000 年代半ばをピークに一時、落ち着いていました。しかし、インターネット配信がさかんになって、業界に活況が戻ってきているようです。

Notes

※ 49 『キン肉マン』にでてくるキャラクターの衣装が、ナチの軍服に酷似していたのが直接の原因。　※ 50 90 年代頃まで、米を中心に「ジャパニメーション」という言葉が使われた。

劇場版アニメ『時をかける少女』（2006 年、監督：細田守）。原作は 1967 年、筒井康隆の小説。これ
まで何度も実写映像化されてきたが、アニメーション化はこの作品がはじめて。
The Girl Who Leapt Through Time (2006), an animated film directed by Hosoda Mamoru. Based
on the 1967 novel by Tsutsui Yasutaka, this was the first animated release following several live-
action versions.
© 「時をかける少女」製作委員会 2006

07

RELIGION AND SPIRITUALITY

宗教・精神論

01 日本の宗教観や精神論

日本人の宗教にまつわる感覚はあいまいで、理解しづらいかもしれません。たとえば無宗教を自認する人が、正月には神社で手を合わせて、結婚式は**キリスト教会**で挙げ、葬式は**仏教式**……といったことが、当たり前のように行われています。こうした行事は、文化や風俗ととらえられていて、あまり宗教活動と認識されていないのです。

日本の「宗教」という言葉[1] は、じつは近代になって西洋から輸入された翻訳語で、言葉の意味は、聖書などの正典を固く信じたり、新しい宗教団体（P. 176 参照）で熱心に活動したりすることだと、とらえられる傾向があります。一方、自然崇拝を中心とした、教義のない民間信仰については、宗教と思っていない人がいるわけです。また、日本に古くから根付いている仏教の行事も、信仰心は漠然としたままでも、習慣的に繰り返されています。東アジアでさかんな儒教は、宗教というより道徳的規範としての影響が残っています。そして、クリスマスパーティーなどキリスト教行事のいくつかは、商業展開によって、現代の娯楽となりました。

理由としては、日本ではもともとの民間信仰が多神教だから、新しい宗教が入ってきても、寛容に受け入れて融合していくのだという人もいます。日本の神々は多彩で、god、deity、spirit といった訳語が当てられています。**宮崎駿**の『千と千尋の神隠し』に出てきた、湯屋の客たちのようなイメージもありますね。

このような日本人が無意識にもつ価値観を、「日本教」と表現した評論家[2] がいました。日本では近代以降、さまざまな**日本文化論**が流行ってきたのです。海外では、日本の精神論として、**禅**や**武士道**が知られていますね。

昨今は世界的に、スピリチュアル[3] なものを求める潮流がありますが、日本においては、それが土着的な信仰の再発見と結びつきやすい傾向があります。

Notes

※1 古くは仏教において、宗旨の教えといった意味で使われていたが、翻訳語としては、明治時代に登場。
※2 『日本人とユダヤ人』のイザヤ・ベンダソン（著者のベンダソンは、評論家の山本七平とされる）。
※3 60年代の米西海岸に起こった、近代文明の行きづまりからの解放をめざすニューエイジ運動 等。

Comment

私は海外に行くようになって、「何教の信者ですか？」とよく聞かれて初めて、宗教について考えるようになりました。私に言えるのは、どんな宗教もいいところは尊重したいということでしょうか。
When I started traveling abroad, I was often asked what religion I belonged to. That was really the first time I had ever stopped to think about religious matters. I guess all I can say is that I try to respect the good things about every religion.

01 Japanese Views of Religion

The prevailing Japanese attitude toward religion is rather ambiguous, and probably difficult for many non-Japanese to understand. Even people who consider themselves non-religious may think it perfectly natural to pray at a shrine on the New Year, hold a wedding in a **Christian** chapel, and have a funeral at a **Buddhist** temple. They tend to treat such rituals as cultural practices or customs, not religious activities.

Even the Japanese word for religion, *shukyo*, was imported into the country in modern times as a translation of the Western concept. Many Japanese, when they hear this word, are inclined to think of people who devoutly believe in the Bible or some other holy scripture, or the fervent members of new religious groups (see p. 177).

Those same people may not view nature worship or other folk beliefs lacking in dogma as a kind of religion. The Japanese also make a habit of participating in Buddhist ceremonies that have been a part of community or family life since ancient times, but never with more than a vague sense of their religious significance. Even Confucianism, which is so much a part of East Asian society, retains its influence in Japan more as a set of moral standards than as a religion. Meanwhile, commercialization has turned Christmas parties and other Christianity-derived activities into contemporary forms of entertainment.

Some people argue that it is because Japan's indigenous folk beliefs are polytheistic that the culture tolerantly absorbs any new religion that arrives here and mixes it in with all the others. Japan is home to a vast diversity of *kami*—a word that embraces gods, deities, spirits, even the creatures of **Miyazaki Hayao**'s imagination in his animated film *Spirited Away*.

At least one pundit has given this unconscious Japanese value system a name of its own: *Nihon-kyo*, literally "Japan-ism." This is just one of a host of theories of Japanese culture that have gained cachet since Japan entered the modern era. Overseas, Japanese spiritual values are best known through such philosophies as **Zen** and **bushido**.

Recent years have seen a global trend of growing interest in spirituality. In Japan this frequently takes the form of rediscovery of the culture's native folk beliefs.

Vocabulary

prevailing ｜支配的な、一般的な	indigenous ｜土着の、固有の
ritual ｜儀式	polytheistic ｜多神教の
be inclined to *do* ｜…しがちである	tolerantly ｜寛大に
devoutly ｜敬虔に、熱心に	pundit ｜評論家
vague ｜あいまいな、はっきりしない	gain cachet ｜流行する

02 神道

神道とは、この列島の各地に残された、自然や先祖の霊、あるいは万物を神格化する民間信仰と、それをもとにした宗教活動の総称です。

神を祀る神社は日本中いたるところにあり、鳥居という門で見分けられます。多くの日本人は、何かを祈願するときや観光の一環として、気軽に神社にお参りします。

神社はもともと山や木立など、神域とする自然のなかに建てられたものが多く、そういう場所は空気がよくて、訪れるとすがすがしい気持ちになります（P. 288 参照）。境内ではよく、おみくじやお守りを「受ける」※4 ことができ、各種の祭りも行われています。また、結婚式など個人的な儀式を、神社で執り行うこともできます。

もうひとつの側面として、神道は皇室との結びつきが深く、かつて天皇は「現人神（あらひとがみ）」とされてきました（P. 96 参照）。特に、日本が帝国主義を推し進めた、19 世紀後半から第二次世界大戦終結までは、政府が国民の意識をまとめるために、天皇信仰を強化した歴史があります。

Notes

※4 神社では、お守りなどを「買う」ではなく「受ける」という。

神社の鳥居
Torii gate of a shrine
Photo: Hara Shoko

03 仏教

仏教は 6 世紀以前に大陸から伝来し、**神道**と並ぶ二大宗教として日本に浸透しています。仏教用語から日本語になった言葉※5 がたくさんあり、ヒーローとしての僧侶たちが何人も歴史に名を残しています。

仏教はアジア各地で、民間信仰と融合しているそうですが、日本でも土着の神々と仏を同一視する信仰が生まれました。1868 年に成立した明治政府が神道を国教のようにあつかい、仏教と分ける政策をとりましたが、今でも両者の混合した感覚は残っています。

→

⁰² Shinto

Shinto (literally the "way of kami") is a general term for religious practices linked to ancient folkways in different regions of Japan that treat all sorts of entities, including the spirits of ancestors and natural phenomena, as kami.

Shinto shrines or *jinja*, easily identified by their distinctive *torii* gates, can be found throughout Japan. Jinja retain their popularity with Japanese today as places to pray for good fortune, or simply to sightsee.

Traditionally, most jinja have been built in mountains, forests, and other natural spots that were considered sacred. Such places are blessed with clean air, and visitors find them peaceful and rejuvenating (see p. 289). Within the shrine precincts you can often obtain good-luck charms or written fortunes. Jinja hold a variety of festivals as well as providing facilities for weddings and other private ceremonies.

Another aspect of Shinto is its close association with the Imperial Family. In the past the emperor was even treated as a "living god" (see p. 97). This was especially true in the years of Japan's imperial expansion, from the late 19th century until the end of World War II. During this time the government promoted emperor worship as a way of unifying the country behind its policies.

Vocabulary

entity｜存在、実在	rejuvenating｜リフレッシュするような
retain *one's* popularity｜人気がある	precincts｜（神社やお寺の）境内 [通例複数形]

⁰³ Buddhism

Buddhism arrived in Japan from the Asian continent in the sixth century or earlier and is, along with **Shinto**, one of Japan's "two great religions." Many Buddhist terms have found their way into the language, and Buddhist monks have figured as heroes in Japanese history.

Throughout Asia, Buddhism has had a tendency to blend with indigenous folk beliefs, and Japan is no exception. Here a composite faith arose that viewed Buddhas and the native kami as one and the same. The Meiji government that took over in 1868 established a policy of treating Shinto as if it were a state religion and separating it from Buddhism. Yet even today, the practices of the two often seem to merge together in people's minds.

The focus of Buddhism is not on the Buddha as a "one and only" divinity, but on the Dharma—the cosmic order or law. The term Buddha, in fact, means "the awakened one," someone who comprehends the Dharma. Over time, various Buddhas became objects of worship, but the word can also refer

➔

←

「仏」について補足すると、仏教では「唯一神」の代わりにまず「法（ダルマ）」があって、仏とはもともと、法を悟った者のことです。やがて時代が下ると、仏が信仰の対象[6]になりました。仏教の開祖・釈迦[7]のみを、仏というときもあります。

仏教には決まった啓典がなく（膨大な数の経典が書かれています）、地域や宗派によって教義がかなり異なります。日本には、おもに大乗仏教[8]が伝わりました。そして、宗派が続々と生まれ、19世紀まで政治と密接に結びつくなど、独特の展開をしてきました。

たとえば、アジアの他国の仏教徒には驚かれますが、日本の僧侶は結婚が認められていて、寺の住職といえば世襲が多くなっています。

また、釈迦は葬送を重視しなかったのに対して、日本の葬式や先祖供養の儀式は、おもに仏教式です。むしろ生前の行いとは関係なく、そうした儀式に安楽な死や生まれ変わりを期待する傾向が強くて、形骸化した「葬式仏教」だと揶揄されています。これには、古来の死生観が影響しているという研究者もいます。

統計をみると、伝統的宗派で信者数が多いのは、念仏を唱える浄土系宗派。これはおもに、その家の先祖代々の宗派と考えられます（江戸時代に、全世帯が地域の寺に登録される義務[9]があったなごりとして）。また、仏教をもとにした**新宗教**で、20世紀に大きく勢力を伸ばした団体が、いくつかあります。

ここ数年は、歴史上初めて、初期仏教や上座部仏教[10]への関心が高まり、関連書籍が増えています。

Notes

※5 縁、空、苦、因果、三昧、果報、有頂天、玄関 等。　※6 釈迦牟尼仏（釈迦如来）、阿弥陀仏、薬師仏 等。　※7 紀元前7〜紀元前4世紀頃、古代インド（現在のネパール）で誕生。　※8 自己の修行や解脱より、万人の救済を重視する流派。釈迦の死から数百年後に起こり、中国を経て日本に伝わる。　※9 檀家制度。先祖代々、特定の寺に葬祭供養を委託。　※10 スリランカ、ミャンマー、タイなどの仏教。小乗仏教という言葉もあるが、否定的表現として最近はあまり使われない。

Comment

お経はたいていサンスクリット語や漢語で書かれているので、法事などのときには、みんな意味がわからないで唱えています。だけど、仏教をわかりやすく解き明かそうという試みは、わりと多いですね。ちょっと前には、**初音ミク**の般若心経ロックに、スラング調の現代語訳が付いて話題になりました。

Most Buddhist sutras are written in Sanskrit or Classical Chinese, so few Japanese understand the meaning of the words they chant at memorial services and the like. There have been attempts to make Buddhist teachings easier to understand; not too long ago an uploaded clip of the Vocaloid **Hatsune Miku** singing the Heart Sutra as a rock tune, with subtitles in slangy contemporary Japanese, made quite a splash.

specifically to Sakyamuni, the "historical Buddha" who founded Buddhism.

Buddhism does not have a definitive sacred text (there are a vast quantity of sutras or scriptures), and its practices vary among sects and regions. Most sects in Japan belong to the Mahayana tradition. Buddhism has diversified into numerous schools, and until the Meiji Restoration of the mid-19th century it enjoyed strong political connections, giving Japanese Buddhism a flavor all its own. For example, Japanese monks are allowed to marry, a tenet that would surprise Buddhists in other Asian countries. Indeed, the position of chief priest is usually hereditary nowadays.

Notwithstanding the fact that the historical Buddha attached little importance to funerals, in Japan memorial services and other rituals for the dead are generally conducted Buddhist-style. Many Japanese sects view such ceremonies as a way to ensure a happy afterlife and rebirth for the deceased, regardless of their behavior while in the world of the living. This tendency has earned Buddhism in Japan a negative reputation as "funeral Buddhism," more concerned with formalities than substance. At least one scholar has attributed this point of view to a Japanese perspective on life and death that has persisted since ancient times.

Statistics show that of the traditional Buddhist sects in Japan, the one with the most adherents is Pure Land Buddhism, which advocates chanting the name of the Buddha Amida. But membership in a particular sect is typically something passed down in a family from generation to generation—a holdover from the Edo period (1603-1868), when every household in the country was required to register with a local temple.

A number of "**new religions**" based on Buddhism have also emerged, with several such organizations growing rapidly during the 20th century.

In recent years, for the first time in their history, people in Japan have begun to display an interest in Early Buddhism and Theravada Buddhism, and books on these subjects have proliferated.

07

RELIGION AND SPIRITUALITY / Buddhism

Vocabulary

one and the same ｜まったく同一の
merge together ｜融合する
comprehend ... ｜…を理解する、悟る
historical Buddha ｜釈迦
sect ｜宗派
tenet ｜教義、主義
priest ｜位の高い僧 [monk は僧侶（キリスト教や他の宗教の聖職者にも使われる）]

notwithstanding ｜それにもかかわらず
perspective on life and death ｜生死観
adherent ｜信奉者 [follower も同義語]
advocate ... ｜…を唱道する、推奨する
chant ... ｜（お経等）を唱える
holdover ｜なごり、遺物
proliferate ｜急増する

04 禅

禅はインドのヨーガをもとにした修行法、またはその修行をおもに行う**仏教**の諸宗派を指します。

禅の各宗派は、5〜6世紀頃中国で活動したインドの僧侶・達磨を始祖とあおいでいます。日本には13世紀以降に広まりました。

20世紀には、日本の仏教学者や禅僧たちの活動を通して、禅が欧米に伝わります。そうして、Zenは日本語から国際語（P. 182参照）になりました。同時に、禅の影響を受けた文化芸術（**書道**、**茶道**、**庭園**など）も広まっています。

禅の修行法としては、坐禅がおもに行われています。ある宗派では、ただ静かに坐って、身体、呼吸、心をととのえることで、無駄な迷いや執着心が取りはらわれて、「今、ここ」を生きる感覚が沸いてくるといいます。また「公案」といって、師匠から与えられたなぞかけのような問いについて、じっくりと考える修行法もあります。

こうした仏教の修行でたどりつく世界を、「悟り」とか「無我の境地」ということがあります。無我とは何か？——禅の世界では、言葉が誤解や固定概念を生むことをきらうので、それを説明するのは無理かもしれません。修行においては、師の心が弟子の心へ直接伝わること、また自ら体験することが重んじられています。

05 キリスト教とイスラム教

日本におけるキリスト教は、人口比では1%ほどなものの、**神道**、**仏教**につづいて3番目に信者が多い宗教です[※11]。16世紀、イエズス教会の宣教師フランシスコ・ザビエルが、初めて日本に伝えたといわれています。

キリスト教は日本の医療、教育、文化などに、大きな影響を及ぼしてきました。しかし、西洋列強の支配力拡大などを恐れた権力者たちが、禁止令を出して、信者が厳しい弾圧を受けた時代も長くありました。

憲法で信教の自由が認められている現代では、カトリック、プロテスタントなどの各宗派が日本で活動しています。また、クリスマスや教会で挙げるロマンチックな結婚式などが、信仰とは関係なく普及しています。

関連業界の宣伝効果もあるのでしょう。たとえば日本のクリスマスは、家族で静かに祝うというより、子どもの楽しいイベントか、恋人たちのデートの

→

04 Zen

"Zen" is the name of a spiritual discipline that has its origins in Indian yoga, as well as a general term for **Buddhist** sects that emphasize this type of training. All Zen sects consider their founding father to be Bodhidharma, an Indian monk who introduced the teachings in China sometime during the fifth and/or sixth century. Zen began to flourish in Japan from the 13th century on.

The 20th century saw the spread of Zen to the West through the activities of Japanese Buddhist scholars and Zen priests. Today "Zen" is part of the global vocabulary, as are such Zen-influenced arts as **calligraphy**, **tea ceremony**, and **gardens**.

The primary training method of Zen is the seated meditation known as *zazen*. In one form of zazen, practitioners simply sit quietly and compose the body, mind, and breath so that superfluous anxieties and attachments will fall away, producing a sense of being in the "here and now." Another technique is to ponder a *koan*—a riddle-like question posed by one's teacher.

The state of mind one aims to achieve through this practice is described by such terms as *satori* (awakening) or "no-self." Just what is no-self? In the world of Zen, which treats words with suspicion as a source of misunderstandings and rigid preconceptions, you should not expect an explanation. Zen training stresses personal experience and the direct transmission of wisdom from the mind of the teacher to that of the student.

Vocabulary

meditation｜瞑想	ponder ...｜…を熟考する
compose ...｜…を落ち着かせる、ととのえる	riddle-like｜なぞなぞのように難解な
superfluous｜余計な	aim to *do*｜…しようとする
attachment｜執着、愛着	preconception｜先入観、偏見

05 Christianity and Islam

Although Christians make up only one percent of the population, Christianity claims the third highest number of adherents among religions in Japan, surpassed only by **Shinto** and **Buddhism**. Francis Xavier, a Jesuit missionary, is credited with introducing the religion to Japan in the 16th century.

Christianity has had a significant influence on Japanese medicine, education, and culture. But there was also a long period of the nation's history when the authorities, fearing that Christianity would open Japan to domination by the Western powers, banned the religion and harshly suppressed its followers.

➔

←

機会になっています。こうした状況は、商業主義ともみられますが、キリスト教のいいイメージが広まるひとつのきっかけにもなっているようです。

一方、同じく世界宗教といわれるイスラム教は、大々的に日本に伝来した歴史がなく、多くの日本人にとってなじみの薄い宗教です。それでも国内にはモスク（礼拝堂）が最低でも数十カ所あって、いくつかはイスラム文化センターを併設しています。

Notes

※11 2014年公表の政府統計より（ただし、各宗教の信者合計が日本の人口を上回る）。

06 新宗教

日本では、ここ100年余りのうちに成立した、新しい宗教団体も数多く活動しています。

現代人の心の問題に対応する役割が高まっているのでしょうか、団体によっては膨大な数の信者を抱えるようになり、特色のある学校や美術館の運営に関わっていたり、目を引く宗教建築を建てていたりします。

「創価学会」や「幸福の科学」は特に巨大で、政党の支持母体※12 となっています。

しかし、1994〜95年に「オウム真理教」が引き起こした、恐ろしいサリン殺人事件は、世界を震撼させました。

そんなこともあって、熱心に布教活動する宗教団体がある一方で、新宗教をすごく警戒する人もいます。また、これは明治時代の政策の影響だといいますが、「信仰は個人の心のなかに留めておくもの」として、宗教について話題にしない人も多いのです。

Notes

※12 現行の憲法に「政教分離」の言葉はないが、それにあたる内容として、宗教団体への特権付与、宗教団体の政治権力行使、国の宗教的活動がそれぞれ禁止されている。宗教団体のバックアップが大きく、政治的影響力の強い政党は、「宗教団体の政治権力行使」にあたるのではないかとの議論が度々起こっている。

←

Today, with the Constitution guaranteeing freedom of religion, Catholic, Protestant, and other denominations of Christianity are all active in Japan. Many Japanese indulge in customs associated with Christianity, such as Christmas and church weddings, without attributing any religious significance to them. Much of this appears to be inspired by corporate advertising. Christmas, for instance, is packaged not as a time for quiet family gatherings, but as an exciting event for children or an occasion for couples to go out on a date.

Though this treatment of Christian celebrations gets criticized for its commercialism, it apparently has had some effect in popularizing the image of Christianity.

By contrast, another of the world's great religions, Islam, has not made any major inroads into Japan, and remains relatively unfamiliar to most Japanese. Yet there are several dozen mosques in the country, some of which also serve as Islamic cultural centers.

Vocabulary

surpassed by ... | …に越される［「…につづく」ということ］
suppress ... | …を抑圧する

denomination | 宗派［しばしば sect より大きい］
indulge in ... | …を楽しむ
make inroads into ... | …に食い込む

⁰⁶ New Religions

Japan is home to numerous "new" religious groups that were established within the past century or so.

Perhaps because they offer solutions to the spiritual woes of people in contemporary society, some of these groups have attracted huge numbers of devotees. Many build conspicuously designed religious facilities and operate schools and museums with their own unique characteristics.

Particularly large organizations like Soka Gakkai and Happy Science maintain close ties with political parties, to which they provide substantial support.

However, the deadly sarin gas attacks perpetrated by Aum Shinrikyo in 1994 and 1995 shocked the world and contributed to a deep mistrust felt by some Japanese toward new religions in general. These religions may also stand out because they challenge the still-prevailing notion—fostered, one scholar says, by Meiji-era government policies—that religious faith is a personal matter and should be kept private.

Vocabulary

devotee | (熱心な) 信者
conspicuously | 著しく、目立って
perpetrated by ... | (犯罪など) …が犯した

still-prevailing notion | 今なお通説となっている考え
fostered | 育成された

⁰⁷ わび・さび・幽玄

わび・さび・幽玄は、日本の伝統的な美意識。禅ブームの頃から、海外でもよく知られるようになりました。

「わび」や「さび」は、もともといい意味ではありませんでした。わびは貧しくわびしいこと、さびは古びてさびしいこと。禅などの影響でそれが転じて、閑寂ななかに奥深さ、心の充足を見いだす価値観になりました。訳語としては、わびには「ひなびた」、「静寂」、さびには「風化した」、「古色をおびた」などが当てられます。「簡素」はどちらにも使いますね。「わびさび」と合わせて、「不足の美」として語られることもよくあります。現代では、わびは茶の湯、さびは俳句の代名詞のようになっています。

「幽玄」はもともと中国の思想的な用語で、深淵でたやすく理解できないことを意味していました。日本ではおもに芸術的な用語となり、優美さや超越性など、さまざまな意味合いが表現されてきました。現代では、能の神秘的な美を表す言葉として、よく使われています。

Comment

わびとさびの違いは、僕にもはっきりわからないよ。同じような意味で使われている気がするな。
You know, I can't even figure out the difference between wabi and sabi myself.
I think people often use them to mean the same thing.

⁰⁸ 武士道

武士道は、直訳すると「サムライの道」。1900年、教育者でキリスト教徒だった新渡戸稲造の著書『武士道』が英語で出版されて、この言葉が世界に広まりました。

新渡戸は武士道を、西洋における騎士道の「ノーブレス・オブリージュ（高い地位に伴う義務）」にあたるものと説明しました。また、武士道の徳目として「義、勇、仁、礼、誠、名誉、忠義」を挙げ、禅や神道、儒教の影響を指摘しています。

しかしこの本は、実際の武士がいなくなった近代に書かれたものです。武士が戦いを繰り広げていた戦国時代、武士道はもっと生々しい兵法などを指していました。

武家政権が安定した18世紀頃になると、為政者としての武士に、ストイックな倫理性が求められるようになります。そして、19世紀末の武士階級廃止からほどなく、近代日本の国民道徳として、アレンジされた武士道が謳

→

07 Wabi, Sabi, Yugen

As concepts that embody traditional Japanese aesthetics, *wabi*, *sabi*, and *yugen* have become familiar terms to non-Japanese thanks to the "**Zen** boom."

Wabi and sabi initially had less than positive connotations. Wabi referred to something poor and meager, sabi to something old and lonely. The influence of Zen turned these notions on their head so that the words came to epitomize the value of spiritual profundity and fulfillment found in tranquil solitude. Wabi is now defined by such terms as "rustic" and "quiet"; sabi by "weathered" and "elegantly aged." The word "simple" is often used as a translation for both. They are also spoken of as one concept, *wabi-sabi*, associated with the beauty in imperfection. These days wabi is nearly synonymous with the **tea ceremony** and sabi with **haiku**.

Originally a Chinese philosophical term, yugen once referred to something deep, subtle, and not readily understood. In Japan it became an artistic concept with multiple meanings, ranging from elegance to transcendence. Today it is frequently used to express the mystical aesthetic of **Noh** drama.

Vocabulary

embody … │ …を体現する	profundity │ 奥深さ
connotation │ 含意、含み	fulfillment │ 充足感、達成感
epitomize … │ …を要約する、…の典型となる	subtle │ 微妙な、とらえがたい

08 Bushido

A literal translation of *bushido* is "the way of the samurai." The word became known around the world when Nitobe Inazo, an educator and a **Christian**, published his book *Bushido: The Soul of Japan* in English in 1900.

Nitobe described bushido as equivalent to the noblesse oblige of Western chivalry and ascribed to it the virtues of "rectitude, courage, benevolence, respect, honesty, honor, and loyalty." He saw in bushido influences from **Zen**, **Shinto**, and Confucianism.

However, Nitobe wrote his book in the modern era, when actual samurai were no longer around. During the Sengoku period (1493-1590), when the samurai were at their most warlike, bushido stood for a far bloodier, cruder "art of war."

By the 18th century the samurai-run government of the Shogunate had firmly established itself and military men, now serving as statesmen, were expected to exhibit a stoic integrity. Not long after the samurai class had been abolished in the late 19th century, bushido came to be extolled as a model of "national morality" for the modern era, thus functioning as both a spiritual cornerstone for national consensus and a keyword for Japanese values as perceived by the outside world.

➔

われるようになったのです――一方で国民をまとめる精神的支柱として。もう一方で国外に日本の価値観を理解させるキーワードとして。

こうした武士道の復興は、18世紀の一武士が心得を説いた、書物『葉隠（はがくれ）』の発掘評価につながります。「武士道と云ふは死ぬことと見つけたり」という、強烈なフレーズが一人歩きしやすい本書は、同時代には異端視され、第二次世界大戦時に熱狂的に広められました。

現代の日本でも、武士道という言葉は、「潔い決断と行動」、「フェアプレイ」といった、人によっていくぶん振り幅のあるイメージをもって息づいています。

Comment

滝沢馬琴の『南総里見八犬伝』には、ご興味を持たれるかもしれません。江戸時代に書かれた、勧善懲悪で武士道の香りがする長編ファンタジーです。現代でも映画や漫画、アニメなどに翻案されていますよ。

You might enjoy reading *Nanso Satomi Hakkenden* (The Eight Dog Chronicles) by Takizawa Bakin, an Edo-era fantasy novel with a strong bushido flavor to its moralistic narrative. It remains popular today through adaptations to manga, anime, and film.

コラム　**切腹**

武士が腹を切って自死する「切腹」は、日本の現代人にとって――少なくとも私には、理解しづらいものです。

戦国時代の初めには、敵に追い詰められたときなどに散見されましたが、次第に役目が果たせなかった償いや殉死など、名誉ある武士の死に方として定着し、江戸時代には処刑方法となりました。そして礼法が整えられ、首を切る介錯人が付きました。

ではなぜ、武士たちは自分の腹を切ったのでしょう？　武士としての勇ましさを示したい面もあったでしょうが、新渡戸稲造は、人間の腹に「霊魂と愛情が宿る」という古来の信仰からだと説明しています（著書『武士道』より）。魂をあらわにして、主君への忠義や身の潔白などを証明するのです。

また、場合によっては、切腹することで部下や子孫が優遇されたためともいいます。

近代以降も、軍人などは切腹することがありました。

←

This revitalization of the bushido concept was closely associated with the discovery and reappraisal of *Hagakure* ("Hidden by Leaves"), a book of teachings by an 18th-century samurai. One of the provocative aphorisms in that volume, "The way of the samurai is in death," took on a life of its own. Though viewed as heresy in its own time, the book acquired a fanatic following during World War II.

In present-day Japan, the word bushido has slightly different connotations to different people, such as fair play or courage in thought and action.

Vocabulary

chivalry｜騎士道（精神）
benevolence｜善意、博愛
be extolled as ...｜…としてほめそやされる

cornerstone｜基礎、土台
reappraisal｜再評価
aphorism｜格言、金言、警句

RELIGION AND SPIRITUALITY / Bushido / Hara-kiri

COLUMN **Hara-kiri**

Hara-kiri or, as it is generally known in Japan, *seppuku*—the samurai ritual of suicide by disembowelment—is something that contemporary Japanese find difficult to comprehend. At least, I do.

Early in the Sengoku period, there were scattered instances of warriors committing seppuku in desperate situations, as when surrounded by the enemy. Gradually, the practice took hold among samurai as a means of dying honorably, in atonement for failing to carry out one's duties or to follow one's master in death, for example. During the Edo period it became a method of execution. A specific protocol was established, with an attendant standing by to behead the samurai after he had cut his own belly.

Why did samurai disembowel themselves? As a way to demonstrate their courage, certainly—but Nitobe Inazo further asserts that seppuku derives from an ancient belief that the belly is the "seat of the soul and of the affections." By thus exposing his soul, the warrior proves his loyalty to his master and the purity of his motives.

Another objective of seppuku on occasion was to secure favorable treatment for one's subordinates or offspring.

Even in the modern era, Japanese soldiers have sometimes committed seppuku.

Vocabulary

disembowelment｜切腹 [disembowel *oneself* で「切腹する」]
scattered instances｜散見される例

atonement｜償い
subordinate｜部下
offspring｜子孫

181

国際語になった Zen

アメリカでは禅の紹介者として、特に「二人の鈴木」が知られています。一人目は、1897 年に初渡米した仏教学者の鈴木大拙。禅や仏教をテーマに、多数の本を英語で発表しました。

もう一人は、1960 年代サンフランシスコに禅センターを開設した曹洞宗の僧侶・鈴木俊隆。彼の『Zen Mind, Beginner's Mind（禅マインド ビギナーズ・マインド）』(1970) は、禅入門書の決定版とされています。

その他、ドイツ人哲学者オイゲン・ヘリゲルが、日本の弓道（the way of the bow）に禅の精神をみてとった『Zen in the Art of Archery（弓と禅）』(1948) も、欧米における禅への関心を高めました。

1950 年代、ジャック・ケルアックをはじめとするビートニクの作家たちが、禅をスローガンのように掲げた頃から、欧米では、潜在能力の解放に興味をもつ若い世代が、坐禅などの修行に取り組み始めます。近年では、アップル創業者のスティーヴ・ジョブズが、禅の影響を受けていたと話題になりました。

今や Zen という言葉はすっかり国際語として定着し、なんとなくシンプルで癒されるもの、あるいは先進的で洗練されたものといった意味合いで使われています。

英語で「a Zen moment」といえば、一瞬の気づきという意味だそうです。そして、Zen や Zazen という名前が、リゾートホテルからコンピューターソフト、睡眠薬にまで付けられているのです。

07

宗教・精神論／国際語になったＺｅｎ／日本文化（日本人）論

京都・龍安寺の石庭（枯山水）
Kare-sansui (dry-landscape) garden at Ryoan-ji, a Zen temple in Kyoto
Photo: oben901 – Fotolia.com

日本文化（日本人）論とNihonjinron

Googleのデータベースで、1500～2008年に発行された英語書籍のデータ[※13]に含まれる、Japanese cultureという語の割合を検索してみました。すると明治維新後から増え始め、大戦前の1940年頃にひとつの山があり、1990年代にピークを迎えています。

日本文化[※14]について書いた作家といえば、明治時代に来日したラフカディオ・ハーン（小泉八雲）が有名です。英語から日本語への翻訳は大正末期に始まり、近年はその思想性や内容の信ぴょう性を再検討する試みがさかんになりました。またルース・ベネディクトの『菊と刀』は、戦争直後の1946年に発表されています。

一方日本では、戦後1978年までに日本文化論に類する本が698冊発行されたという数字[※15]があります。中根千枝の『タテ社会の人間関係』（1967）などは、日本語から各国語に訳されました。こうした書物には、全般的な傾向に対する批判も出ています。まずは「日本文化」を単一的にとらえ過ぎなこと。それに対・世界ではなく、対・欧米という図式に偏りがちなこと（日本語で書かれたものか、外国語かを問わず）。多くは強国との関係を意識して、生まれたものだからでしょう。李御寧（イ・オリョン）の『「縮み」志向の日本人』（1982）は、韓国との比較を展開して、話題を呼びました。

1986年にピーター・N・デールは、英語の著書で「nihonjinron」を民族主義的だと分析しています。そのせいか、この言葉に悪いイメージを持つ英語話者に時々出会います。またハルミ・ベフは、日本人による日本文化論を、体制に役立つ「イデオロギー」のためのもの、あるいは「大衆消費財」だと論じています。なお、自国に批判的な日本文化論の本もかなりあります。

日本文化論は、思考の材料としては有意義ですが、日本人が沿うべき枠ととらえるような、行動のかせにはしたくないものです。

07

Notes

※13 Google Books Ngram Viewer。mangaの頻度は増え続けている。　※14「文化」は明治時代に、culture等、欧米語を訳した語。社会の風習・精神活動のすべてを指す場合と、高尚なものという意味で使う人がいる。　※15 野村総合研究所による。翻訳書も含む。

08

GEIDO,
THE WAY OF THE ARTS
芸道

⁰¹ 芸道とは？

日本には、数百年から千年以上も起源がたどれる、伝統的な芸能・技芸の数々が、社会の近代化とともに形を変えながら残っています。

それらの多くは、「柔術」は**「柔道」**、「茶の湯」は**「茶道」**……と、徐々に「道」の付いた名で呼ばれるようになりました。100 年ほど前、新渡戸稲造が**『武士道』**をアメリカで著して、人気を得た影響かもしれません。芸道^{※1}はそれらの総称です。

「道」は直訳すると way（道）。中国^{※2}では、万物の法則などを表す言葉（英語でいう Tao）です。一方、日本で「〇〇道」といえば、修行を重ねて、技術と精神が高まる過程や境地を指します。そして芸の向上は、人格の向上によると考えられているのです。

多くの芸道では、決まった「型」を体で覚えることから、修行が始まります。型が身についてはじめて、型を破って、自分の個性が発揮できる^{※3}というわけです。

師弟関係に重きを置くのも、芸道の特徴です。こうした世界の教授法は、もともと秘伝や言葉で伝えにくい感覚を、師匠から子どもや弟子に、直接伝授するものでした。今でも玄人の養成では、変わらないようです。芸道の伝わる家、またはその家の当主は、「家元」や「宗家」^{※4}と呼ばれています。しかし江戸時代から現代にかけて、芸道は大衆に開かれていき、流儀がテキストなどで、公開されるようになりました。

いくつかの芸道では、家元を中心に、素人の修行者を統括し、能力認定する全国組織が発達しました。これは家元制度といわれています。**茶道**や**華道**はその典型で、20 世紀には女性のたしなみとして繁栄しました。

また、こうした技芸のいくつかは、近代的ジャンルの「芸術」としても解釈され、1950 年代には前衛運動と結び付くなど、新しい創造活動が展開されています（P. 50、188、190、192 参照）。

Notes

※1 「道」は付かないが、邦楽（第1章）、能、歌舞伎、日本舞踊（第5章）も芸道の一種とされることが多い（本書ではページを分けた）。　※2 現代北京語での「道」の発音は「dao」。　※3 「守・破・離」という（型を守る、破る、型から離れる）。　※4 家元と宗家が両方置かれる流派もあり、役割分担は多様。

01 **What Is Geido?**

Japan is blessed with a great number of traditional art forms that date back hundreds of years or more and have survived to the present.

In the course of weathering the changes that accompanied the modernization and westernization of the country, many of these arts gradually came to be labeled with the suffix *do*, meaning "way" or "path," a trend highlighted by Nitobe Inazo's 1900 book ***Bushido*** ("the way of the warrior"), which was published in the United States. Examples include ***judo*** ("the gentle way") and ***sado*** ("the way of tea"). *Geido* is a general term for all of these arts.

In China the same word, pronounced *dao* (and frequently spelled "Tao" in the West), can refer to the "way" of the universe, the principle underlying all creation. In Japan *do* signifies a path of seeking and achieving, through rigorous practice, a high degree of artistic and spiritual attainment. It is understood that improving the self is key to improvement in artistic endeavors.

In most traditional Japanese arts, training begins with the commitment to physical memory of certain *kata* or forms. Only after you have fully internalized the kata can you break away from them and develop your own mode of expression, the thinking goes.

Another hallmark of geido is an emphasis on the relationship between teacher and pupil. Traditionally, the techniques of geido arts have been transmitted directly from master to disciple (often the teacher's own child) through secret teachings or non-verbal actions. Master practitioners are still trained in this manner today. The families and family heads who are the hereditary leaders of particular schools of geido are known by such honorific terms as *iemoto* and *souke*.

08

Since the Edo period (1603-1868), these schools have been opened to the public at large and their teachings disseminated through texts and other media. In what is called the iemoto system, some genres of geido have set up nationwide organizations that unify the teaching and certification of students under one iemoto.

Typical examples of the iemoto system are found in the worlds of ***sado*** and ***kado*** ("the way of flowers," i.e., ikebana), both of which enjoyed a heyday in the 20th century as essential accomplishments for women.

From another perspective, the various geido can be viewed as modern forms of fine art that interacted with the avant-garde movement of the 1950s and continue to evolve to this day (see pp. 51, 189, 191, and 193).

Vocabulary

weather the changes｜変化を乗り切る	**internalize** ...｜…を自分のものにする
suffix｜接尾辞、末尾に追加したもの	**hereditary**｜世襲の
artistic endeavor｜芸に関する試み	**disseminate**｜（情報が）広まる

02 茶道（茶の湯）

茶道は、英語でよく「茶の儀式」と翻訳されていますが、ひととき日常を離れて茶を点て、自然や道具の美を愛で、客をもてなすことに、思想的な意味合いを求める芸道です。

今日、茶道は日本文化の神髄とされ、茶事（少人数での正式な会）における建築、**庭園**、**花**、**掛物**、道具、**香**、料理（P. 276、44、230 参照）などの要素とあいまって、総合芸術ととらえられています。

茶道では、抹茶というパウダー状の緑茶を使います。主人は客の前で抹茶を茶碗に入れ、湯をそそぎ、竹製の茶筅をふるって、なめらかな泡を立てます。この茶を点てる一連の動作を「点前」といい、手先の細かい動かし方まで定められています。これはパフォーマンスとして美しいとされるだけでなく、身体の動きを規制することによって、精神をコントロールすることが求められているのです。

世界的にもめずらしい、こうした茶の文化がなぜ生まれたのかについては、神秘的な伝承が多く、実質的な研究は始まったばかりです。茶自体は一説によると 8 世紀に中国から伝わって[5]、僧侶が薬効を説き、やがて庶民にも普及しました。将軍や豪商などの有力者は、舶来の美術品を飾った、豪華な茶会を催しました。

現在の茶道[6] は、16 世紀に千利休が大成した、後にいう「わび茶」の流れをくむとされています。わび茶（草庵の茶）は生活雑器などを用いて、簡素の美を追求する茶で、禅の影響が強いといわれます。現在は流儀が固定化していますが、当時は各茶人の創意工夫が求められたようです。

意外なことに、わび茶にカトリックのミサの影響[7]を指摘する説もあります。利休の出身地・堺は貿易港で、ヨーロッパから多数の宣教師が来ていました。

Notes

※5 抹茶について日本最古の記録を残した僧侶の栄西（1141〜1215）が、茶の実や抹茶を伝えたという俗説があるが、最近の研究によると、抹茶は 11 世紀までに中国から伝わったと考えられる。現代の中国で抹茶は廃れているが、「茶芸」というおいしく茶を入れる作法があり、日本の茶道の影響といわれる。　※6 煎茶を用いた煎茶道もある。※7 武者小路千家の 14 代家元・千宗守も支持。

Comment

茶道に「一期一会」という、いい言葉があるんですよ。「一生に一度の会合」──つまり「こうしてお会いしている時間は、二度とない機会だと思って、誠意をもってふるまいなさい」という意味です。

There is a really nice expression used in sado: *ichigo-ichie*, a "once-in-a-lifetime meeting." It means that you should treat a gathering like the tea ceremony with reverence, because the same circumstances will never be repeated.

⁰² Sado, the Way of Tea

Sado (also pronounced *chado*) is usually translated as "tea ceremony," but it literally means "the way of tea," a philosophical activity in which the serving and drinking of tea affords participants an opportunity to retreat from the everyday world and savor the beauty of nature and art in an atmosphere of cordial hospitality. These days, sado is considered the quintessence of Japanese culture. Formal tea gatherings (*chaji*) of a few selected guests combine such elements as architecture, **gardens, flower arrangements, hanging scrolls**, utensils, **incense**, and cuisine (see pp. 277, 45, and 231) in what could be described as a composite art form.

The beverage used in sado is *matcha*, a powdered green tea. The host places the matcha in a tea bowl, pours in hot water, whips the mixture into a froth with a bamboo whisk, and presents the bowl to the guest to drink.

This tea-preparation procedure or *temae* is determined down to such minute details as the motion of the fingers. The temae is admired not only for its beauty as a performance, but for the self-discipline practitioners cultivate through mastery of the strict rules it imposes on one's physical movement.

How did this unique culture of tea arise? Veiled as it is in numerous mystical teachings, sado has only recently become a subject of substantive research. Tea itself came to Japan from China in the eighth century, according to one estimate. Buddhist priests praised the medicinal virtues of the beverage, and eventually its use spread among the general population. Shoguns, wealthy merchants, and other persons of influence held elaborate tea gatherings at which they displayed imported works of art.

Sado in its present form began with the style, later known as *wabi-cha* ("rustic tea"), perfected by Sen no Rikyu during the 16th century. The wabi-cha ceremony uses everyday utensils, seeks beauty in simplicity, and is said to be heavily influenced by **Zen** Buddhism. Though its practices are rigidly defined today, in the beginning individual tea masters were expected to devise their own original approaches.

Interestingly, there is a theory that wabi-cha was influenced by the Catholic mass. We do know that Rikyu's hometown of Sakai was a trading port with a sizable population of European missionaries.

Vocabulary

afford *AB* ｜ A に B を提供する	veiled ｜ベールをかぶった、不明瞭な
cordial ｜心のこもった	substantive ｜実質的な
quintessence ｜エッセンス、真髄	elaborate ｜手の込んだ
composite ｜複合的な、合成された	devise ... ｜…を工夫する、考案する
impose on ... ｜…に負担をかける	sizable ｜かなり多くの

03 いけばな（華道、花道）

花をいける日本の伝統的な芸術を、いけばな、または華道（花道）といいます。**仏教**の供花をもとに、住空間や多様な場を飾る花へと発展したものです。最古の流派は 15 世紀に源をもとめる池坊で、現在は 300 以上の流派が活動しています。

花のいけ方には、流派によっていくつかの型があります。

代表的な型は、江戸時代に発展した生花（せいか、しょうか）。3 本の枝のポイントが不等辺三角形をかたちづくる、アシンメトリーな構成です。

欧米のフラワーデザインでは、おもに花の部分を組み合わせるのに対して、いけばなでは木の枝のしなったラインや、葉の持ち味も生かして、構成のポイントに使います。

しかし近代以降は、両者が影響しあい、今では欧米のデザインにもライン・アレンジメントがありますし、日本のいけばなにも型のないジャンルができました。

また、かつていけばなは**床の間**などに置かれ、正面からだけ鑑賞するものでしたが、生活環境の変化にともなって、洋室（P. 284 参照）やホテルのロビーなどを飾る、見る方向を選ばない作品が増えました。

一方、1950 年代頃、草月流の創始者・勅使河原蒼風などを中心に「前衛いけばな」が盛り上がった時代があります。しばしば植物以外の素材と合わせた、彫刻とも呼べる作品が発表されて、「これはいけばなか否か」といった議論が巻き起こりました。

たとえば、流派に属さない作家・中川幸夫の『花坊主』(1973) は、カーネーション 900 本分の花びらをガラス器に詰め、真っ赤な花液がにじみ出るというショッキングな作品でした。

04 香道

香道とは、東南アジアから渡った香木のかけらを温めて、たちのぼる香を楽しむ芸道です。

日本には**仏教**とともに、香木などの粉をブレンドして焚く文化が伝わりました[8]。粉を練り合わせた練香が、貴族の間で流行した時代もあります（P. 90 参照）。やがて武士たちは、香木のなかでも「沈香」[9]のみの香りを賛美するようになり、それが香道へと発展しました（流派によっては白檀も使う）。

03 Kado, the Way of Flowers

The traditional Japanese art of flower arrangement is called *kado* or ikebana. It began with the **Buddhist** practice of flower offerings, and spread to the use of flowers to decorate homes and other locations. Ikenobo, the oldest ikebana school, was founded in the 15th century; currently over 300 schools are active. There are a number of kata or styles, varying from school to school, in which the flowers are arranged.

The most representative style is *seika* or *shoka* (literally, "living flowers"), which first flourished during the Edo period. The flowers and stems are arranged asymmetrically in a three-pointed, triangular format.

Whereas Western floral design tends to focus on the flowers themselves, ikebana is concerned with compositions that highlight such elements as the curving lines of branches and stalks, or the distinctive patterns of leaves. In modern times, both Japanese and Western traditions have influenced each other, so that Western floral designs now include line arrangements, and kata-less styles of ikebana have caught on in Japan.

In the past, ikebana arrangements were usually placed in the special **tokonoma** alcoves of Japanese homes, where one could only see them from the front. As lifestyles have changed, ikebana designed for viewing from any angle can now be found decorating Western-style rooms (see p. 285), hotel lobbies, and the like.

During the 1950s, "avant-garde ikebana" became popular, notably through the activities of Teshigahara Sofu, founder of the Sogetsu School. These works, which frequently incorporated non-plant materials and resembled sculptures more than flower arrangements, sparked debate over whether they really qualified as ikebana or not.

One work that many viewers found shocking was *Flowery Priestess* (1973) by Nakagawa Yukio, an artist who was not affiliated with any ikebana school. It consisted of petals from 900 carnations squeezed into a glass container, with a bright-red liquid oozing from them.

Vocabulary

stem｜茎、枝 [stalk も同義]	be affiliated with …｜…に所属している
triangular｜三角形の	petal｜花弁、花びら
composition｜構図	squeezed into …｜…に詰め込まれた
highlight …｜…を強調する	oozing from …｜…からにじみ出ている

04 Kodo, the Way of Incense

Kodo is a type of geido in which participants savor the scent wafting from heated pieces of aromatic wood from Southeast Asia.

←

最初は大量に焚いていた沈香ですが、日本では江戸時代に貿易が厳しく制限されたので、燃やさずに温めて、再利用するようになりました。そうして何百年も、受け継がれている名香もあるのです。沈香のなかでも高品質のものは、「伽羅」と呼ばれます。

具体的には、カップ（聞香炉）に灰を入れたなかに、小さな炭団をおこして仕込んでおいて、灰の上に雲母を敷き、3ミリほどの乾燥した沈香のかけらを載せます（写真・下）。そして、カップを顔に寄せ、香を聞き[10]ます。季節や古典文学『源氏物語』などをテーマに、沈香の銘柄を何種類か組み合わせて、客が香を聞き分けるゲームもあります。すべて作法に基づいて、礼儀正しく行われます。

Notes

※8 それ以前の神聖な香りは、日本にある檜等の自然な香りだった。線香は伝来の歴史が比較的浅いと考えられ、江戸時代から日本に普及。　※9 沈香の最古の記録として、『日本書紀』に淡路島への漂着が記されている（6世紀）。また正倉院に保存されている沈香の原木「蘭奢待（らんじゃたい）」は、織田信長等の権力者達に削り分けた跡がある。　※10 日本や中国では、香を嗅ぐことを「聞く」と表現する。

Photo courtesy of Yamada-Matsu Co., Ltd.

05 書道（書）

中国をはじめとする漢字圏には（P. 94参照）、墨と筆を使って文字を書く芸術があり、日本では「書道」として発展しました。通常は和紙の上に、縦書きで右から左に書きます。

漢字のほか、日本で作られた文字のひらがなも書かれ、一字一字をはっきり書く楷書、文字をくずしてつなげる草書、その中間の行書といったスタイルがあります。

筆運びは一瞬で決まり、ごまかしがきかないので、書は心を表すといわれます。**茶道**の茶事では、禅の高僧による書がよく鑑賞されてきました。また、日本の小学校では、毛筆でお手本通りに字を書く授業があります。

今では普段の生活で、わざわざ毛筆を使う機会はあまりありませんが、慶事など儀式的な場面では、毛筆が正式とされています。また、正月には新

→

The practice of burning blended powders of incense wood and other materials arrived in Japan along with **Buddhism**. Kneaded mixtures of aromatic powders known as *neriko* gained favor among the medieval aristocracy (see p. 91). Later, the samurai class came to prize agarwood (*jinko*) above all other scents, and this appreciation evolved into the pastime of kodo. (Some schools also use sandalwood.)

At first Japanese incense connoisseurs burned agarwood in great quantities, but when the Edo Shogunate imposed tight restrictions on overseas trade, people began to heat the wood rather than burn it, so that it could be reused. As a result, some famous incenses have been preserved for hundreds of years. High-grade jinko is called *kyara*.

For the incense-appreciation ceremony, a smoldering charcoal briquette is embedded in ashes in a cup (*kikigoro*), a chip of mica is laid over the ashes, and a bit of dried agarwood about three millimeters long is placed atop the mica (image on left). The participant brings the cup close to the face and "listens" (as it is said in Japanese) to the scent.

Kodo enthusiasts also play games—based on such themes as the seasons or the classical novel *The Tale of Genji*—in which various types of agarwood are combined together and participants try to identify them. Kodo games and ceremonies alike are conducted according to established rules of etiquette.

Vocabulary

wafting from ...	…から漂っている	smoldering charcoal	くすぶっている木炭
kneaded mixtures of ...	…を練ったもの	be embedded	埋め込む
evolve into ...	…に発展する	mica	雲母

08

⁰⁵ Shodo, the Way of Calligraphy

In China and other countries that use Chinese characters (*kanji* in Japanese, see p. 95), the writing of text with brush and ink is an art form. In Japan it is called *shodo*, literally "the way of writing," or simply *sho*. The calligraphy is written vertically from the right side of the sheet, usually on traditional-style *washi* paper.

Besides kanji, the Japanese also create calligraphy with the indigenous syllabic characters known as *hiragana*. There are three principal shodo styles: *kaisho* (block or print style), *sosho* (cursive), and *gyosho* (semi-cursive).

Because the movement of the brush occurs in an instant, with no room for second-guessing or fixing, shodo is said to reveal the inner spirit of the practitioner. In the **sado** tradition, tea gatherings have often included the viewing of calligraphy created by high-ranking **Zen** priests.

→

年の抱負などを書で表す「書き初め」という習慣があります。

革新的な動きとして、1950 年代頃に「前衛書道」（墨象_{ぼくしょう}）がさかんになりました。これは字を書くというより、抽象的な美術作品のように、筆の軌跡や、垂れる墨滴、余白の美などの造形性を追求するもので、今日ではジャンルとして定着しています※11（図版 P. 203）。巨大な紙の上に、モップのような大筆を振り回して文字を書く、ライブ・パフォーマンスもみられるようになりました。

近年は女子高校生を中心に、10 人ほどのチームで音楽やダンスに合わせて行う書道パフォーマンスが流行し、選手権大会が開催されています。

Notes

※11 欧米の即興的な抽象絵画運動、アンフォルメル（仏）、アクション・ペインティング（米）等と影響を与え合ったと考えられる。

Photo courtesy of Kandakashojuen

06 **盆栽**

盆栽とは、小さな鉢などに木を植え込んで、ミニチュアの大木のような姿に育てていく、いわば「生きた芸術」です。中国の「盆景_{ぼんけい}」が起源といわれ、日本の bonsai を通して世界に普及しました。

樹形にはいくつかの型があります。木が風に耐えて曲がった姿や、崖の上から垂れ下がっている姿など、自然の情景を模した、ストーリー性を感じさせるかたちです。

ふつうの園芸とは木の育て方が違い、枝を切ったり、針金で幹や枝の方向づけをしたりして、とても手間がかかります。鉢も大事な要素で、土にはたいてい苔を敷きつめ、緑の大地を表します。

木の種類は、縁起物の松が代表格。国内では、古くから日本にあった種類の木が、おもに使われます。海外では、その土地の植物も使われています。高さは数センチから、1 メートル以上のものも。時を経るほどに風格が増し、

→

At Japanese elementary schools, training in the use of brush and ink to copy characters is part of the standard curriculum.

Although there are few opportunities to write with a brush in the course of life in the present day, brush-written characters are still considered appropriate for formal occasions. It is also customary to write New Year resolutions with a brush.

In the 1950s, "avant-garde shodo" came into vogue. This bears less resemblance to calligraphy than it does to abstract art, with such elements as brush traces, ink droplets, and white space brought to the fore. Today it is an established genre of shodo (image on p. 203).

Also a part of the contemporary art scene are live performances in which a shodo artist draws characters on large sheets of paper with a huge, mop-like brush.

Recently, a new style of calligraphy event has become popular, particularly among female high school students. Teams with as many as ten members put on shodo performances to music or dance, sometimes in national competitions.

Vocabulary

vertically｜縦に	New Year resolution｜書き初め
reveal ...｜…を明らかにする	bear a resemblance to ...｜…と似ている
in the course of life｜日常生活の中で	brought to the fore｜前面に出された、目立った

08

⁰⁶ Bonsai

Bonsai is a kind of "living art" in which a tree is planted in a small pot or tray and grown into what looks like a miniature version of a full-sized tree (image at left). Although it is said to originate with the *penjing* ("tray scenery") of China, the practice has become known throughout the world by the Japanese name *bonsai*, which means "tray planting."

There are a number of standard kata or forms for the trees. The shapes—a tree bent by the wind, or leaning over the top of a cliff, and so forth—are meant to evoke natural landscapes and tell a story to the viewer.

Bonsai tree cultivation requires techniques quite different from those of ordinary gardening. A bonsai grower must invest a lot of time and effort in pruning the branches and attaching wires to shape the direction of growth of the branches and trunk. The container is also an important element of the total work, as is moss, often used to cover the soil to suggest a grassy green expanse.

The primary tree of choice for bonsai is the pine, an auspicious plant in Japan. Most trees used in Japanese bonsai are indigenous or long-

→

百年以上受け継がれる名木には、何百万～何千万円の値が付くものもあります。それで盆栽は、お金持ちで暇があるご隠居の趣味といったイメージが持たれています。

そうした先入観がなかった欧米などでは、老若男女が芽から育てて、日々の変化を味わう、盆栽の楽しみ方が広がっているようです。

盆栽は従来、**床の間**や専用の棚に飾られていました。最近はモダンな鉢を使って、観葉植物のように室内を飾るスタイルが流行り出しています。

Comment

盆栽は、木をむりやり型にはめるものではありません。木の持ち味をくみ取って、それを生かすように、手をかけていくのです。
Bonsai isn't concerned about forcing a tree into a specific form, but about cherishing the essence of the tree and turning it into art!

ホノルル合気道道場（米・ハワイイ）
Aikido of Honolulu dojo in Hawaii, USA, 2003
Photo: Miura Fumiko

07 **武道**

武道とは、かつての武士の戦闘技法が、近代以降、スポーツ兼精神修養法として、再構成されたものです。

格闘技ととらえられることもありますが、礼に厳しく自制的なところが、武道の武道たるゆえんです。日本では、武道が中学校の体育授業に取り入れられています。

武道のなかでも**柔道**は、唯一のオリンピック正式種目で、世界中に愛好者がいます。

剣道は剣術の稽古を競技にしたもので、防具（面、胴、小手、垂れ）を付けて、竹刀を用い、一対一で打ち合います。

合気道は平和貢献を理念とし、勝敗を競わず、素手で型の修行に徹します。暴徒などから攻撃されたら、相手にひどい傷を負わせずにかわして、「被害者も加害者も作らない」のが心得。健康法としても、広く人気を集めてい

established species (overseas, local species are also used). The trees can range from a few centimeters to over a meter high. Their beauty is said to ripen over time, and some famous trees that have survived for over a century sell for tens of millions of yen. For these various reasons bonsai has a bit of a reputation in Japan as a hobby for wealthy retirees with plenty of time on their hands.

In Western countries, where this stereotype doesn't exist, bonsai attracts enthusiasts of all ages who enjoy growing the trees from seedlings and watching the changes they undergo as the days and years pass by.

In the past, bonsai typically adorned **tokonoma** alcoves or special shelves, but nowadays we see them placed in modern-looking pots, decorating interior spaces in the style of houseplants.

Vocabulary

bent by ... ｜…のために曲がった	soil ｜土
cultivation ｜栽培	auspicious ｜縁起の良い
pruning the branches ｜（余計な）枝を切ること	adorn ... ｜…を飾る

⁰⁷ Budo

A general term for the martial arts, *budo*—literally "the way of war"—began as the practice of fighting techniques by the samurai. In modern times, however, it has been reinvented as a sport as well as a means of cultivating mental discipline.

Budo tends to be thought of as a type of combat sport, but what makes it unique is its emphasis on strictly observed etiquette and self-restraint. Budo is a part of the physical education curriculum in Japanese middle schools.

Judo, the only type of budo that is formally recognized as an Olympic sport, has fans and practitioners all over the world.

Kendo ("the way of the sword") is a competitive sport derived from swordsmanship techniques. Opponents wearing a variety of protective gear—helmet and mask, breastplate, gauntlets, groin and leg protectors—engage in one-to-one matches with bamboo swords.

Aikido ("the way of harmonious spirit") is based on a philosophy of contributing to universal peace. Rather than compete to win, students focus on mastering kata for unarmed combat. The creed of aikido is to "create neither victim nor offender"—i.e., to respond to attackers in a way that does not injure them. It has grown popular as a regimen for maintaining personal health as well.

Karate (also known as *karate-do*, "the way of the empty hand") originated

➔

08

197

←

るようです。

空手道[12] は沖縄（琉球王国）発祥で、突きや蹴りなどの打撃技を特徴とする武道です。分派を繰り返していて、相手の体の直前で打撃を止める（もしくは、ダメージを与えない程度にあてる）流派と、防具を付けて打撃する流派、直接打撃する流派があります。武道としてより、むしろ格闘技のカラテとして世界中に広まっています。

Notes

※ 12 中国拳法とは別物だが、影響は受けている。また、少林寺拳法は日本で成立（少林拳は中国武術）。

08 柔道と柔術

柔道は素手で組み合い、投げ技や固め技などで勝敗を決める**武道**です。国内では、明治時代に創設された、講道館[13] の柔道が主流になっています。柔道の「柔」は、「柔らかい、柔軟性がある」という意味で、「柔よく剛を制す」[14] という理念からきています。相手の体制をくずすことによって、強い相手を最小限の力で倒せるということです。

道着の上に締める帯の色が、段位によって変わるシステムは、柔道で始められ、ほかの武道に波及しました。よく黒帯が一番強いように誤解されていますが、黒帯は上級者と認められる初段からで、最高位は赤帯[15] です（初段以上は黒を締めてもかまいません）。

「柔術」は柔道のもとになった武術で、かつてはさまざまな流派がありましたが、国内ではほとんど廃れてしまいました。しかし 100 年余り前から海外に渡って教える人たちがいたので、ほかの格闘技と融合したりしながら、各地で異なったスタイルの柔術が発展しました。特に、ブラジリアン柔術やヨーロッパの IJJF 柔術が普及しているようです。

Notes

※ 13 創設者は嘉納治五郎。　※ 14 古代中国の兵法の書『三略』より。　※ 15 原則として 13 歳以上の四〜五級および初心者が白帯、一〜三級が茶帯、初段〜五段が黒帯、六〜八段が紅白帯、九（女子は八）〜十段が紅（赤）帯。

Comment

柔道が 60 年代に世界的なスポーツとして普及していく上で、重量制が導入されたのは、柔道のよさを損ないましたね。とはいえ、日本柔道に本家意識が強くて、客観性を欠くのは問題で、そろそろ他国の柔道に学ぶ時期かもしれません。

When judo became a world-class sport and introduced weight divisions in the 1960s, it lost part of what made it so appealing. On the other hand, the Japanese judo community tends to think too much of itself as the originator of the sport. Maybe it's time we thought about learning something from judo in other countries!

in the Ryukyu Kingdom (now Okinawa) and is known for its punching and kicking techniques. Today there are many different schools, with varying approaches: some permit direct blows to the body, others require that the attacker stop just short of striking the body (or strike lightly so as to avoid injury), and still others practice with protective gear. The style of karate that has spread around the world is more of a combat sport than a form of budo.

Vocabulary

self-restraint｜自制	creed｜モットー、主義
swordsmanship｜剣術	regimen｜養生法

08 Judo and Jujutsu

Judo is a category of **budo** in which two people wrestle barehanded using a variety of throwing and grappling techniques to determine the winner. The mainstream form, Kodokan Judo, was established during the Meiji period (1868-1912).

The *ju* of *judo* means soft or flexible, reflecting judo's origins in the idea that "softness overcomes hardness"—in other words, that you can defeat a strong opponent with minimal strength on your part, by destroying the opponent's balance.

The system of identifying ranks of mastery by the color of the belt worn around the uniform began with judo and spread to other kinds of budo. Though people sometimes mistakenly believe that the black belt represents the highest rank, it is actually used from the first-dan level (the lowest rank among the top class of practitioners) on up. Those at the very top are allowed to wear a red belt.

The martial art from which judo developed is *jujutsu* (or *jijitsu*)—"the gentle art." Although a variety of schools of jujutsu once existed, most of them are no longer active in Japan. However, thanks to practitioners who emigrated and taught jujutsu overseas during the past century or so, diverse styles (sometimes merged with other combat sports) have developed in different parts of the world. Two prominent examples are Brazilian jiu-jitsu and Europe's International Jujitsu Federation (IJJF).

08

Vocabulary

barehanded｜素手で	emigrate｜移住する
grappling technique｜（一般的な）組み合う技、	merge with ...｜…と融合する
（柔道の）固め技	

⁰⁹ 相撲

相撲はよくレスリングの一種と説明されていますが、古代に発祥した神事でもあります。また、戦国時代には武術で、現在に続く興行は、江戸時代から始まりました。相撲には、こうした歴史の軌跡が色濃く残っていて、日本の国技^{※16} と認識されています。

今でも力士は男性のみで、江戸時代のように髷を結い（P. 254 参照）、裸の巨体にまわしだけを付けて取り組みます。土俵は丸く（直径 4 メートル 55 センチ）土を固めたもので、取り組み前に力士が塩をまくのは、清めの儀式です。そして相手と組み合い、押したり投げたり……。どちらかが土俵の外に出るか、倒れて足裏以外に土が付いたら、即負け^{※17} です。プロレスのように血を流しながら攻撃し続けたりしないので、老若男女が安心して観戦できます。

重量は無差別なので、力士はたくさん食べて体重を重くします。それでも日頃のトレーニングによって、体脂肪率を標準以下に保つ力士もいるそうです。また、小さい力士が、技で巨漢を倒すのも、相撲の醍醐味のひとつです。

相撲には力士の格付けがあって（場所前に番付で発表される）、最高位の横綱には、強いだけでなく人格者であることが期待されています。

相撲の社会は封建的で厳しく、近年は日本人の新弟子が減るなか、番付の上位にハワイ、モンゴル、東欧などを出身とする外国人力士が増えました。2011 年、相撲界では八百長や賭博が発覚して大騒ぎになり、力士や関係者が何人も解雇処分になりました。相撲界では信頼回復に努めるとともに、これからの相撲文化のありようが模索されているところです。

Notes

※16　日本に法で定められた国技はない。1909 年に専用の競技場「国技館」が開設され、国技と認識されるようになった。日本相撲協会は公益財団法人。　※17　反則をしたり、まわしが取れても負け。

Comment

江戸時代の**落語**や**歌舞伎**には、病気の母親を持つ力士にわざと負けるといった「人情相撲」の話があります。つまり、昨今の問題は、金儲け主義が暴走してしまったことなどで、取り組みで加減すること自体は必ずしも悪くないと、考える人がいるのです。

Edo-era **Rakugo** storytellers and **Kabuki** plays told tales of "compassionate sumo," in which a wrestler voluntarily loses to a colleague caring for a sick mother. Some fans still view this attitude as part of sumo culture, blaming the recent scandals on excessive greed and arguing that "flexibility" in the ring is not necessarily a bad thing in itself.

⁰⁹ Sumo

Frequently described merely as a type of wrestling, sumo is also a religious ritual that dates back to ancient times. During Japan's turbulent Sengoku ("Warring States") period it was regarded as a martial art. Not until the subsequent Edo period did sumo come into its own as the spectator sport we know today. Thanks to the colorful traces it retains of its historical roots, sumo is commonly recognized as the national sport of Japan.

As in the past, only men can compete. They wear their hair in *mage* topknots (see p. 255), Edo-style, and wrestle with their bulky bodies clad only in thick *mawashi* loincloths. The wrestling ring or *dohyo* is a raised circle of packed earth, 4.55 meters in diameter. Before each bout, the wrestlers toss salt in a purification ritual.

The bout begins with two wrestlers charging at each other in the middle of the dohyo. Each attempts to push his opponent out or toss him down. The match is over the instant one wrestler steps or falls outside the ring, or when any part of his body other than the soles of his feet touches the ground. Unlike pro wrestling, sumo does not involve prolonged, bloody attacks, and the matches are quickly resolved, making it a remarkably genteel sport enjoyed by men and women, young and old alike.

Because there are no weight divisions or restrictions, sumo wrestlers eat a lot and try to bulk up as much as they can. Even so, many wrestlers are said to have lower-than-average body fat ratios, thanks to their intensive daily training. One of the great pleasures of sumo is seeing a small wrestler use his technical skills to defeat a much bigger opponent.

Sumo has rankings, published in a list called the *banzuke* before each tournament. Those holding the highest rank of *yokozuna*, or grand champion, are expected not only to win consistently, but to behave with dignity.

The sumo world is feudalistic and tough. In recent years, as fewer young Japanese have shown interest in joining, the *banzuke* has featured growing numbers of non-Japanese wrestlers from such places as Hawaii, Mongolia, and Eastern Europe.

In 2011 sumo was rocked by scandals involving fixed matches and gambling, and a number of wrestlers were forced to resign. These days the sumo community appears to be grappling with efforts to regain the public's trust and with questions about the future of sumo culture.

Vocabulary

merely｜ただ、単に	**clad in** ...｜…を身にまとって
turbulent｜荒れた、激動の	**... meters in diameter**｜直径…メートル
spectator sport｜観戦のためのスポーツ	**bout**｜試合、取り組み
bulky｜〔体が〕大きい	**toss ... down**｜…を投げる

世界における武道

国際柔道連盟の加盟国は、199 カ国／地域。特に柔道人気が高いフランスでは、登録競技人口が 60 万人を超え、日本の登録競技人口の約 16 万人[18] に比べて、人口比で約 7 倍となっています（ただし、日本の学校の授業で柔道を習う人口などは未知数）。日本では、学校で一度柔道を経験しながら、大人になると観戦するだけの層が厚いのに対して、フランスでは生涯続けるスポーツとして、普及しているようです。また、指導者に国家資格制度があることも注目されます。

日本では廃れてしまった講道館以外の柔術／柔道が、海外で流れを保っているケースもみられます。明治時代に欧米で日本ブーム[19] が起こったときにも、柔術や柔道が紹介されましたし、戦後、GHQ が武道禁止令を出したときに、海を渡った柔術／柔道家も少なくありませんでした。たとえば生涯無敗で、ヘーシング選手（東京オリンピック無差別級優勝）を育てた柔道家・道上伯（1912〜2002）は、日本ではあまり知られていませんが、フランスなどで著名です。その他の武道人口をみると、剣道は日本で約 47 万人[20] が「活動」中。海外では韓国で数万〜数 10 万人、その他の国で数万人以上が活動中と考えられています。合気道は比較的新しく成立した武道ながら、世界全体の活動人口が約 58 万人（日本で約 8 万人）[21]。また空手の愛好者は、世界で 1 億人ともいわれます[22]。弓道（the way of the bow）は国内の登録競技人口約 14 万人[23] 中、半数以上が高校生（学校の部活動が主）です。海外の活動人口は約 3,000 人と多くないものの、ドイツのヘリゲルが著した『弓と禅』（P. 182 参照）などの影響で知られています。

Notes

※18 日本柔道連盟の大会に出場できる登録者数（2013 年度）。フランスとは登録の内容が異なるので、単純比較はできない。 ※19 その頃書かれたアルセーヌ・ルパン（フランスの探偵小説の主人公）も、柔術や柔道の心得がある設定。 ※20 全日本剣道連盟の 2007 年の調査が元。60〜70 万人という推定もある。 ※21 合気道による。国内の数字は 2012 年の概算。世界の数字は、各連盟の申告を元に類推。 ※22 世界空手道連盟エスピノス会長の発言（報道）。 ※23 全日本弓道連盟による。

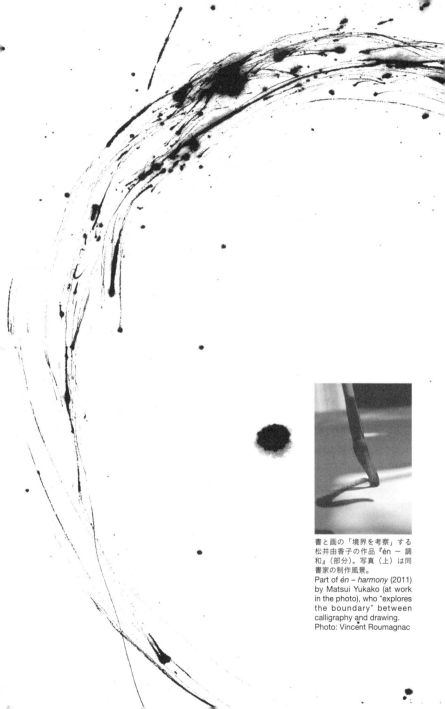

書と画の「境界を考察」する
松井由香子の作品『én — 調
和』（部分）。写真（上）は同
書家の制作風景。
Part of *én – harmony* (2011)
by Matsui Yukako (at work
in the photo), who "explores
the boundary" between
calligraphy and drawing.
Photo: Vincent Roumagnac

09

CINEMA
映画

日本映画をめぐる状況

かつて**黒澤明**、**小津安二郎**などの巨匠を輩出し、1990年代以降ふたたび国際映画祭で受賞を重ねている日本映画は、世界でも評価の高いブランドとなっています。

日本は20世紀前半^{※1}にはすでに、アメリカに次いで世界第二の年間生産数を誇る映画大国でした。といっても、そのほとんどは、海外のアート系映画館で上映されるようなタイプの日本映画ではなく、娯楽映画や子ども向け映画が大人気だったのです。**時代劇**、**ヤクザ映画**、アクション、怪獣映画（P. 214参照）、人情喜劇やメロドラマ……。戦中^{※2}のブランクを経て、50〜60年代の黄金期には、大手映画会社6社がこうした人気路線の映画を量産し、気を吐く独立プロの作品とともに、日本映画の土壌を作ってきました。

その後、テレビやビデオの普及によって映画産業は低迷し、大手映画会社の撮影所や専属映画館は閉鎖していきます。代わって80〜90年代は、個性的な作品を上映するミニシアターがたくさん出来て、インディペンデント映画（P. 222参照）が台頭しました。以前はめずらしかった他業種出身者や女性監督も、映画制作に参入しやすくなり、やがて**北野武**、河瀬直美などが国際的な脚光を浴びます。また、日本の**アニメ映画**が、各国で社会現象を巻き起こすほどの人気となりました。

近年は、シネマコンプレックスが郊外に普及し、テレビ会社が製作に参加するテレビドラマのような映画が多くなっています。また、アジア各国やハリウッド、フランスなどとの間で、監督や役者などが行き来する国際共同製作が活発になり、「日本映画」でくくれない世界の映画文化の動向が注目されます。

Notes

※1 日本で初めて映画が撮られたのは1898年。フランスでリュミエール兄弟がシネマトグラフを発明した3年後。　※2 第二次世界大戦まで、日本の占領地では国策映画が制作されていた。現在の中国にあった「満州映画」等。

Comment

3D映画は、『アバター』が流行った頃から、日本でもよく作られているよ。だけど、3D対応の映画館では、割増料金が取られるんだ。
Ever since *Avatar* became a big hit, Japan has been making lots of 3D films too, you know! But movie theaters equipped for 3D add an extra charge to their ticket prices.

01 **The State of Film in Japan**

Japanese cinema, which once produced such masters as **Kurosawa Akira** and **Ozu Yasujiro**, experienced a revival in the 1990s that saw Japanese movies win numerous prizes at international film festivals. Today it is an internationally recognized brand.

By the first half of the 20th century, Japan had already become a cinema superpower, ranking second behind the United States in the number of movies produced annually. However, most of these were not like the Japanese films often shown overseas in art-house theaters, but were primarily for entertainment or aimed at children. They ranged from *jidaigeki*, **yakuza** and action movies to *kaiju* films (see p. 217), human interest and comedy movies, and melodramas. After a hiatus during the war years, Japanese film enjoyed a golden age in the 1950s and '60s during which·the six top studios mass-produced movies in these and other popular genres. Together with progressive independent producers they formed a fertile breeding ground for Japanese cinema.

Later, with the spread of television and video, the movie industry went into decline, leading to the closure of several major studios and their theater chains. In the 1980s and '90s, mini-theaters specializing in auteur films sprang up in their place as indie cinema (see p. 223) came to the fore. It became easier for artists from other professions and women, until then a rarity in the industry, to enter the movie world, and soon people like **Kitano Takeshi** and Kawase Naomi were basking in the international limelight. Meanwhile, Japanese **animated movies** were also growing so popular that they became a cultural phenomenon in some countries.

Recently, cinema complexes have become a common sight in the suburbs, and the number of movies that resemble television dramas made in collaboration with broadcasting companies has increased. There has also been an upsurge in international—especially Asian, French and Hollywood—co-productions, a development that highlights the trend toward a global cinema culture beyond the confines of "Japanese cinema."

09

Vocabulary

cinema｜映画（全般）、映画制作、映画界、（英では特に）映画館
recognized｜評価された
art-house theater｜アート系の映画館
be aimed at ...｜…向けである
hiatus｜中断、空白
breeding ground for ...｜…の土壌、環境
go into decline｜衰退する

lead to ...｜結果として…になる
auteur film｜作家性の高い映画［auteur はフランス語］
come to the fore｜目立つ、台頭する
upsurge｜急増
highlight ...｜…を強調する、浮き彫りにする
confines｜境界、範囲［通例複数形］

02 時代劇

時代劇は、江戸時代以前の日本を舞台にした、演劇や映画のジャンルです。大半はサムライ（P. 296 参照）が主人公で、クライマックスは日本刀を交える戦いのシーン。演武のような所作で華々しく演出します。昔の映画では、役者は斬られても血が出ませんでした。

かつては勧善懲悪型の娯楽映画が大量に作られていましたが、60 年代以降、その路線は『水戸黄門』※3、『遠山の金さん』などのテレビドラマに引き継がれました。また、『座頭市』（P. 224 参照）※4 や『子連れ狼』（P. 72 参照）※5 などのシリーズはハードボイルド・タッチで、海外でも人気を博しました。

まだ着物を着る人の多かった 20 世紀前半と違い、サムライたちの時代が実感できないほど遠くなった今、時代劇は日本人にとってもエキゾチックなドラマとなりました。近年は、コンピューターグラフィックス（CG）を駆使したり、古くからの演目を大胆な解釈や演出で描いたりと、新しいスタイルの時代劇がみられるようになっています。

Notes

※3『水戸黄門』の物語は講談が最初と考えられ、テレビシリーズは 1954 〜2011 年、断続的に放送された。
※4　第一作／1962 年公開（以下、映画の年は公開年）、監督：三隅研次、出演：勝新太郎 他。同シリーズはキューバで国民的人気。香港のカンフー映画への影響も大きい。　※5　第一作／1972 年、監督：三隅研次、出演：若山富三郎 他

Comment

昔の子どもたちはよく、空き地で棒をもって、チャンバラごっこをしたものです。チャンバラというのは日本刀で戦うシーンが出てくる時代劇のこと。「ちゃんちゃんばらばら」という刀の音からきたといわれています。
In the old days, children used to meet in vacant lots to play *chanbara*—sword fighting with wooden sticks. *Chanbara*, a word for jidaigeki with sword-fighting scenes, derives from the "chan-chan bara-bara" sound the swords make.

03 サイレント映画と活動弁士

サイレント映画の時代、日本では「活動弁士」と呼ばれる映画館専属のナレーターが大活躍しました。彼らはたくみな話術で、映画の上映前に解説をしたり、上映中にさまざまな声色で台詞を語ったりしました。観客は映画の俳優や内容でなく、生出演する弁士の名調子を目当てに、映画を選ぶことがあったのです。日本にはもともと、落語や講談などの話芸や、能や文楽など、演者とは別の人が舞台脇でストーリーを説明する芸能があったので、自然と弁士が人気を集めたと考えられています。日本以外では、影絵芝居のあるタイでも、サイレント映画における説明者の役割が重要だったそ

→

02 Jidaigeki

The *jidaigeki* is a genre of film and theater set in the Japan of the Edo period (1603-1868) or earlier. In most cases the main characters are samurai (see p. 296), and the climax is usually a sword-fighting scene. These fight sequences are spectacularly staged with actors using the exaggerated movements of a martial arts display. In the older movies there is no bloodshed—even when the characters are slashed with swords.

In the past, jidaigeki with moralistic plots and an emphasis on entertainment were produced in large numbers, but since the 1960s this genre has been taken over by television dramas like *Mito Komon and Toyama no Kin-san*, while hard-boiled series such as *Zatoichi* (see p. 225) and *Lone Wolf and Cub* (see p. 73) have earned followings overseas.

Today, unlike the early 20th century, when many people still wore **kimono**, the age of the samurai is so much a part of the distant past that people have no real sense of what it was like. Thus for many Japanese, too, jidaigeki have become exotic fare. Recent years have seen the emergence of new styles of jidaigeki that use a lot of computer graphics or offer bold new interpretations of well-established storylines.

Vocabulary

spectacularly｜華々しく、劇的に	moralistic plot｜道徳的な筋書き
exaggerated｜誇張された	bold｜大胆な、冒険的な
be slashed with ...｜…で斬られる	interpretation｜解釈

03 Silent Movies and Benshi

During the silent-movie era, Japan's cinemas employed live narrators called *benshi*. Using their storytelling skills, they explained the film before it screened and spoke the lines in different voices as it played. Sometimes audiences chose which movie to go to based not on the actors or the story, but on the eloquence of the benshi. It's possible the popularity of these benshi was due to the existence in Japan of such storytelling traditions as **Rakugo** and Kodan, and of performing arts like **Noh** or **Bunraku** in which non-acting narrators tell the story from the side of the stage. Outside of Japan, too—in Thailand, for example, where shadow plays are popular—narrators apparently played an important role in silent movies.

Today, there are only a few benshi left, but vestiges of the tradition remain in Japanese film. There may be a narration at the start of a movie in a voice different from any of the actors, or a spoken explanation of what the main character is thinking in the middle of the action. The prevalence

うです。

現在、弁士はほとんどいなくなりましたが、その面影は今でも日本映画に残っています。たとえば映画の冒頭などに、登場人物とは別の声でナレーションが入ったり、映画の途中で、主人公の心中が、長々と説明されたりすることがあります。また日本映画が長回しを得意とするのも、絵巻物の影響とともに、弁士が口上を述べる間を取っていたなごりだとも考えられます。

小津安二郎『東京物語』（製作：松竹）
Ozu's *Tokyo Story* (Shochiku Co., Ltd.), 1953

04 巨匠の時代──黒澤、溝口、小津

黒澤明（1910〜98）は、20世紀を代表する映画監督として、世界の映画人の尊敬を集める存在です。1951年、モノクロの**時代劇**『羅生門』[※6] が、ヴェネツィア国際映画祭で金獅子賞を受賞。この作品は、3人の登場人物それぞれの証言によって、ひとつの事件が異なる話で再現されるというもので、以後の映画手法に大きな影響を与えました。

また、彼の最高傑作とうたわれる『七人の侍』[※7] は、アメリカの『荒野の七人』、イタリアの『黄金の七人』、香港の『忠烈圖』……とたくさんの翻案があります。若い頃、画家志望だった黒澤は映像美にも厳しく、撮影の邪魔になる民家の一部を壊して、撮影後に直したなど、演出のための逸話が多く残っています。

溝口健二（1898〜1956）は1950年代に、黒澤とともに国際映画祭で受賞を重ねました。『雨月物語』[※8] は彼の伝統的な日本絵画への傾倒がよく表れた作品です。溝口はとりわけヨーロッパの**ヌーヴェルヴァーグ**の作家たちに愛されました。

黒澤より若干上の世代の小津安二郎（1903〜63）は、生前から日本の映画界の重鎮でしたが、海外では没後に評価が高まりました。『東京物語』[※9] を

→

←

of long takes in Japanese films may be due to the influence of picture scrolls, but it may also be a holdover from when extra time would be provided for the benshi to speak.

Vocabulary

narrator	語り手、ナレーター	vestige	痕跡、なごり
storytelling skill	物語を話す技術	prevalence	普及、はやり
eloquence	流暢な話しぶり、能弁	holdover	なごり

04 The Age of the Masters: Kurosawa, Mizoguchi, Ozu

Kurosawa Akira (1910-98) is revered by movie buffs around the world as one of the leading filmmakers of the 20th century. In 1951, his black-and-white **period drama** *Rashomon* won the Golden Lion at the Venice Film Festival. In this work, a single episode is re-enacted in different ways based on the testimony of three different characters, a technique that was adopted by other directors and had a major impact on cinema.

Seven Samurai, which many regard as Kurosawa's best work, spawned numerous adaptations, including *The Magnificent Seven* in the U.S., *Seven Golden Men* in Italy, and *The Valiant Ones* in Hong Kong. Kurosawa, who originally aspired to become a painter, was extremely strict when it came to visual aesthetics, and there are many anecdotes describing the lengths he went to in this regard, such as demolishing part of a house that stood in the way of a shot and rebuilding it afterwards.

Like Kurosawa, Mizoguchi Kenji (1898-1956) won numerous awards at international film festivals in the 1950s. His admiration for the traditional Japanese pictorial arts is expressed in such movies as *Ugetsu*. Mizoguchi was a particular favorite of the European **New Wave** filmmakers.

Ozu Yasujiro (1903-63), who was slightly older than Kurosawa, was a leading figure in Japanese cinema, although it was not until after his death that his reputation grew overseas. He is known as the quintessential Japanese director

黒澤明『羅生門』のポスター
（製作：大映）
Movie poster for Kurosawa's *Rashomon* (Daiei), 1950

→

09

←

はじめとする、正面からのローアングルで、家族のありようを淡々と描いた
作品によって、「もっとも日本的な映画監督」として知られています。

Notes

※6 1950 年、出演：三船敏郎、京マチ子 他　※7 1954 年、出演：三船敏郎、志村喬、木村功 他。ヴェ
ネツィア国際映画祭銀獅子賞受賞。　※8 1953 年、出演：京マチ子、森雅之 他　※9 1953 年、出演：笠
智衆、原節子 他

Comment

三船敏郎は、黒沢映画に欠かせない俳優として、世界的に有名ですね。また原節子は、小津映画で
の演技がとても印象的でした。当時のシステムとして、二人とも役者を始めたときには、映画会社
の社員だったんですよ。

Thanks to his indispensable role in so many Kurosawa films, Mifune Toshiro
attained worldwide fame. Hara Setsuko, too, left a strong impression as an actress
in Ozu's works. Under the system in place at the time, both of them began their
acting careers as film studio employees.

05 ヤクザ映画

日本には、「ヤクザ」と呼ばれるアウトローの世界を描いた映画のジャンル
があります。

60 年代に大ブームとなった「任侠もの」路線は、勧善懲悪型のストーリー
です。「任侠」とは、義理と人情を重んじ、弱者のために体を張る精神のこ
と。筋立ては大体パターンが決まっていて、主人公は「任侠道」に生きる、
伝統的なヤクザです。卑劣な新興ヤクザなどの悪者と対立し、最後には着
流し姿に日本刀で殴り込み。名ゼリフが決まると、観客はスクリーンに向か
って声をかけたといいます。代表的な作品は、『昭和残侠伝』※10 など。そ
れらの多くで、高倉健が主演しました（寡黙に筋を通す男性像を演じ続け
た日本のスター／1931 〜2014）。

任侠ものが飽きられてきた 70 年代、実話を元に戦後の暴力団抗争を描いた
『仁義なき戦い』※11 が登場します。この映画は義理などを無視した裏切り
の連続で、リアルな迫力が大反響を呼びました。以来、ヤクザ映画に「実
録もの」と呼ばれる路線が形成されました。

ヤクザ映画は、暴力を肯定し、ヤクザを美化していると批判されつつも、
その後の日本映画や、香港のジョン・ウー監督、アメリカのクエンティン・
タランティーノ監督などにも、大きな影響を与えています。

Notes

※10 1965 年の第一作（監督：佐伯清）から、シリーズで 9 作品が制作された。
※11 第一作／1973 年、監督：深作欣二、出演：菅原文太 他

映画／巨匠の時代──黒澤、溝口、小津／ヤクザ映画

09

←

for works, most famously *Tokyo Story*, that portray family life in a quietly flowing style with an emphasis on low-angle, front-on shots.

Vocabulary

be re-enacted｜再現される	anecdote｜逸話
spawn ...｜…を生む、発生させる	demolish ...｜…を取り壊す
aspire to ...｜…を切望する	admiration｜称賛、憧れ
aesthetic｜美意識	quintessential｜典型的な、真髄の

05 Yakuza Movies

In Japan, there is a special genre of film that depicts the outlaw world of the so-called yakuza.

The popular yakuza movies of the 1960s, known as *ninkyo-mono*, had moralistic storylines. *Ninkyo* refers to the chivalrous spirit of honoring duty and humanity and putting one's body on the line to protect the weak. The plots tended to stick to the same pattern; the protagonist was a traditional yakuza who embodied the ninkyo spirit, confronting the newly emerging class of unprincipled yakuza and mounting a sword attack at the end while clad in kimono. Upon delivery of the climactic lines, ardent fans would shout words of encouragement at the screen. Classic yakuza films like *Showa Zankyoden* featured Takakura Ken (1931-2014), a Japanese star who appeared in countless works of the genre and went on to play taciturnly righteous male characters for much of the rest of his career.

In the 1970s, when people were tiring of ninkyo-mono, *Battles Without Honor and Humanity*, a movie portraying the real-life postwar struggle between organized crime groups, appeared. The powerful realism of this tale of a series of betrayals that show no regard for such virtues as loyalty caused a sensation. Its release sparked the rise of a sub-genre of yakuza movies — mixing fact and fiction, known as *jitsuroku-mono* — "true stories."

While criticized for glorifying violence and the yakuza, the genre has exerted a huge influence on later Japanese movies as well as overseas filmmakers like Hong Kong's John Woo and America's Quentin Tarantino.

Vocabulary

chivalrous｜騎士道的な、義侠的な	would｜（よく）…したものだった［過去の習慣を
put *one's* body on the line｜自身を危険にさら	表す］
す、体を張る	words of encouragement｜励ましの言葉
embody ...｜…を体現する	taciturnly｜無口に
unprincipled｜無節操な	righteous｜高潔な、正義の
mount｜（攻撃を）仕掛ける	betrayal｜裏切り
ardent fan｜熱狂的なファン	

09

コラム **ヤクザと刺青**

ヤクザには独特の風習があって、なかでも背中全面に一枚の絵のように彫られた、龍や桜など伝統的な絵柄の刺青は、ヤクザの象徴となっています。また、親分子分や兄弟分の関係になるときに、儀式として「盃」をかわし、なにか不始末を起こしたときは、詫びのしるしに「指詰め」といって指を切ることも、ヤクザ映画を通して広く知られています。

日本の映画を観ていると、特にヤクザ映画でなくても、服の下に刺青を隠した人が登場することがあります。すると、その人物が、裏の世界に生きていることや、人に言えない過去を背負っていることなどがわかるのです。

とはいえ、ヤクザ社会の実態は、私をふくめ接点のない人々にとって、謎につつまれています。ヤクザに詳しいあるジャーナリストは、「実録もの」でも事実は2割程度だといいます。

06 ゴジラと **Godzilla**

『ゴジラ』は60年続いている、世界最長の映画シリーズです。口から火を噴く恐竜のようなその姿は、海外でも長らく日本のB級ポップカルチャーとしておなじみでしたが、2014年にアメリカ映画のシリアスな『Godzilla』[※12]が大ヒットして、大分イメージが変わったようですね。

日本のもっとも古いファンにとって、ゴジラは悲劇のヒーローでした。1954年の第一作[※13]で描かれたゴジラは、古代から海底に棲んでいた生き物で、水爆実験で環境を壊され、陸へ上がって大暴れするという設定です。人間の被害者として現れて、人間を脅かす「自然」の象徴でしょうか。その年は、戦後GHQの統治が終わった直後で、第五福竜丸が水爆実験で被爆した年です。人々は娯楽映画のなかにも、トラウマの癒しと政治的表明を求めていました。

シリーズが進むにつれ『ゴジラ』は娯楽性を強め、子ども向けになります。そしてゴジラを原型に、日本映画に「怪獣映画」というジャンルが形成されました。モスラ、ガメラなど映画ごとに生み出されるユニークな「怪獣」

Yakuza and Tattoos

The yakuza have their own unique manners and customs. One in particular—painting-like tattoos that cover the entire back and feature such traditional motifs as dragons and cherry blossoms— has come to symbolize the yakuza. Other practices seen in yakuza movies include the ceremonial sharing of sake from a single cup to formalize an *oyabun-kobun* (boss-henchman) or sworn-brotherhood relationship, and *yubitsume*, the cutting off of one's finger to atone for a wrongdoing.

Even Japanese films that are not yakuza movies sometimes show characters with tattoos hidden under their clothing. The audience knows from this that the character is involved in the underworld or is burdened with a past he cannot reveal.

In point of fact, the yakuza world remains a mystery to those not directly connected to it, including this writer. According to one journalist, even scenarios of the jitsuroku-mono genre are only about 20 percent "true."

Vocabulary

henchman｜子分、取り巻き	atone for a wrongdoing｜不始末を償う
sworn brotherhood｜兄弟分の誓い	be burdened with ...｜…を背負う

06 Gojira and Godzilla

At 60 years of age, *Godzilla* (pronounced *Gojira* in Japanese) is the longest running movie series in the world. For much of that time the fire-breathing, dinosaur-like monster has enjoyed notoriety abroad as an icon of grade-B Japanese pop culture. In 2014 a more "serious" made-in-USA *Godzilla* became a megahit, giving the big lizard a bit of an image makeover.

To his oldest fans in Japan, in fact, Godzilla was a tragic hero.

In the first film of the series, *Godzilla* (1954), the creature has lived at the bottom of the sea since ancient times, but his habitat is destroyed by the testing of a hydrogen bomb, causing him to come ashore and go on the rampage. For many he symbolizes nature as a victim of humanity that in turn threatens humanity. In 1954 the postwar occupation of Japan had just ended, and it was also the year that the Japanese fishing boat *Daigo Fukuryu Maru* was exposed to nuclear fallout during the testing of an

→

← たちは、どれも普通の兵器では倒すことができず、科学で解明できない不思議な能力を持っているのが特徴です。

Notes

※12 監督：ギャレス・エドワーズ、出演：アーロン・テイラー＝ジョンソン、渡辺謙、エリザベス・オルセン他。1998 年にも、アメリカ版『Godzilla』が製作されている。　※13 監督：本多猪四郎、出演：志村喬、河内桃子、宝田明 他。同作はアメリカ公開時に再編集されて、元のメッセージが伝わっていなかったが、現在はオリジナル版の DVD が発売されている。なお、この作品には、前年のアメリカ映画『原始怪獣あらわる』の影響が指摘されている。

Comment

今度のアメリカ版『ゴジラ』には、現実の核にまつわるエピソードや原発事故を連想させるイメージが出てきますね。世界の人々が共有する、現代の危機感を表しているのかもしれません。実際の被害は、あんなものではないでしょうが……。
The latest U.S. version of *Godzilla* has episodes evoking hydrogen bomb tests and nuclear power plant disasters. Maybe it reflects a sense of crisis shared by people all over the world these days. Then again, the destruction they show in the film is nothing like what we face in reality...

07 「特撮の神様」 円谷英二とウルトラ・シリーズ

『ゴジラ』の特殊撮影は、「特撮の神様」といわれた円谷英二（1901〜70）が担当しています。黎明期から日本映画の世界に入った円谷は、現在のような CG がないなか、独自の撮影技術を開発していきました。60 年代には、特撮映像スタジオ「円谷プロダクション」を設立。テレビドラマ『ウルトラマン』を生み出しました。

ウルトラマンは、鉄仮面のような姿で身長 40 メートルの巨大な宇宙人。人類の味方をして、次々と現れる怪獣たちと戦います。ウルトラマンから派生した、「ウルトラ・シリーズ」は、子ども向け特撮テレビ番組の定番※14 として、現在まで続いています。

Notes

※14 70 年代に放送が始まった「仮面ライダー・シリーズ」、「スーパー戦隊シリーズ」も、特撮テレビシリーズとして長寿となった。

Comment

怪獣やウルトラマンは、着ぐるみのなかに人が入っているとわかるんだけど、それはお約束。演技や全体の迫力で、映像の世界に引き込まれるんだ。あれが CG になっちゃつまらない。仮面劇みたいなものかな。
You can tell that Ultraman and the various kaiju are just people in suits, but that's one of the accepted conventions of the genre. It's the dynamic acting and action that draw you in. It wouldn't be interesting with computer graphics, anyway. I guess you could say it's a bit like the masked Noh drama.

← H-bomb on Bikini Atoll. Even in films for entertainment, people sought healing from such traumas and an expression of political concerns.

As the series continued, *Godzilla* grew increasingly entertainment-oriented and aimed at younger audiences. Eventually, it became the model for a new genre of *kaiju* (monster) films. Typically, the kaiju in these movies, including such notables as Mothra and Gamera, cannot be defeated with normal weapons and possess mysterious powers that defy scientific explanation.

『ゴジラ』第一作のポスター
（製作：東宝）
Movie poster for *Godzilla* (Toho Company Ltd.), 1954

Vocabulary

the longest running｜もっとも長く続いている	come ashore｜上陸する
fire-breathing｜火を噴く	go on the rampage｜暴れ回る
habitat｜生息地	be exposed to ...｜…に巻き込まれる
hydrogen bomb｜水素爆弾	nuclear fallout｜核の降下物

07 The "God of SFX": Tsuburaya Eiji and the Ultra Series

The special effects in **Godzilla** were handled by Tsuburaya Eiji (1901-70), hailed as Japan's "god of special effects." Because there were none of the computer graphics we see today, Tsuburaya, who entered the film world at the dawning of cinema in Japan, had to develop his own SFX techniques. In the 1960s he established a studio, Tsuburaya Productions, that produced the television drama *Ultraman*, about a 40-meter-tall space alien, wearing what appears to be an iron mask, who fights alongside humans against various kaiju that appear one after another. The Ultra Series, a successor to *Ultraman*, continues to thrive as a staple of special-effects TV programming geared for kids.

09

Vocabulary

special effects｜特殊効果［略語は SFX］	what appears to be ...｜…のようなもの
hailed as ...｜…として称えられた	thrive as ...｜…として成功する
dawning｜始まり、幕開け	staple｜定番、必需品

08 ヌーヴェルヴァーグと大島渚

50年代後半から、フランスの「ヌーヴェルヴァーグ」など、世界的な映画運動と呼応するように、日本でも若い監督たちによる、新しい傾向の映画がみられるようになります。

なかでも大島渚（1932〜2013）は、社会に問題提起する意欲作を次々と発表して、「松竹ヌーヴェルヴァーグ」の旗手と呼ばれました。松竹は彼が所属していた大手映画会社ですが、後に独立。そして70年代、『愛のコリーダ』※15 で世界に衝撃を与えます。

1930年代の猟奇的な殺人事件を題材にしたこの映画は、一組の男女の極限的な関係を描いています。軍靴の響く時代背景にそぐわず、全編を満たすその挑発的な性描写は、国内外でわいせつ性をめぐる裁判や、上映禁止などの騒動を巻き起こしました。日本では大幅にカットされ、2000年に公開されたノーカット版も、ボカシが入っています。

80年代以降も大島は、政治討論のテレビ番組などで過激な言動を繰り返し、スキャンダルの象徴であり続けました。83年の国際合作映画『戦場のメリークリスマス』では、イギリスのミュージシャン、デヴィッド・ボウイのほか、ミュージシャンの**坂本龍一**、当時**お笑いタレント**だったビートたけし（**北野武**）など、俳優が本業でないユニークな出演者を起用。この映画は洗練された筆致で、坂本のテーマ曲とともに多くのファンを得ました。

Notes

※15　1976年、出演：藤竜也、松田英子 他

09

09 『男はつらいよ』 ※16

1969年から全48作が撮られたこの作品は、「一人の俳優が演じた世界最長の映画シリーズ」としてギネスブックに認定されています。同時代を舞台に、ノスタルジックな泣き笑いの人情を描いて、国民的人気を博し、95年に主演の渥美清が亡くなるまで続きました。

主人公の寅次郎、通称・寅さんは日本各地を渡り歩く的屋（てきや）──大道芸のような口上で客寄せをする露天商──です。東京の下町にある、実家の団子屋に時々ふらりと戻っては、騒動を起こして、母親違いの清楚な妹に心配をかけます。また毎回、人気女優によるマドンナが登場。寅さんは純情な恋心を抱くのですが、最後にはマドンナの恋人が発覚する……というのが

→

⁰⁸ The New Wave and Oshima Nagisa

In the late 1950s, as if in concert with the global movement in cinema that included the Nouvelle Vague, or French New Wave, there emerged in Japan, too, a new cinematic movement led by young filmmakers.

One of these directors was Oshima Nagisa (1932-2013), sometimes called the standard-bearer for the "Shochiku Nouvelle Vague," who released one provocative work after another that addressed social issues. Shochiku was the name of the major movie studio he worked for, although he later went independent. In the 1970s Oshima shocked the world with his film *In the Realm of the Senses*. Based on a bizarre murder that occurred in the 1930s, the movie explores the no-holds-barred relationship that develops between a man and a woman out of step with the militarization of the society around them. Its sexual explicitness sparked legal action over its alleged obscenity and bans both at home and abroad. In Japan the film was cut extensively, and the uncut version released in 2000 was digitally masked in places.

From the 1980s onwards, Oshima perpetuated his scandalous reputation with outbursts of radical speech and behavior on TV shows and elsewhere. In the 1983 international co-production *Merry Christmas, Mr. Lawrence*, he cast a number of unique entertainers not previously known for their acting, including English musician David Bowie, Japanese musician **Sakamoto Ryuichi**, and comedian Beat (**Kitano**) **Takeshi**. The film won many fans on account of its sophisticated style as well as the theme song by Sakamoto.

Vocabulary

no-holds-barred ｜制限のない	alleged obscenity ｜わいせつ疑惑
explicitness ｜きわどさ、露骨さ	ban ｜（上映）禁止

09

⁰⁹ *Otoko wa Tsurai yo*

With 48 installments released since 1969, *Otoko wa Tsurai yo* ("It's Tough Being a Man") is recognized by the Guinness Book of World Records as the world's longest running movie series starring the same actor. Always set in the same time period, it earned nationwide popularity with its evocation of human nostalgia—both tears and laughter—and continued up until the death of the leading actor, Atsumi Kiyoshi, in 1995.

The protagonist, Kuruma Torajiro (a.k.a. Tora-san), is a silver-tongued street vendor who wanders all over Japan hawking his wares. From time to time he returns to his home, a *dango* (rice dumpling) shop in the old *shitamachi* area of Tokyo, but he always causes a ruckus and upsets his prim half-sister. Every installment also features a leading lady, known to fans as the "Madonna" character, played by a different popular actress each time. The standard storyline sees Tora-san naively falling in love with this Madonna, only to learn

→

定番のストーリーです。

当初は破天荒なはみ出し者だった寅さんも、シリーズが家族向け映画として定着するにつれ、性格が丸くなっていきます。やがて、寅さんの甥っ子の成長物語にもなりました。

Notes

※16 原作・脚本・監督は山田洋二（第3作監督は森崎東、第4作は小林俊一）。出演：倍賞千恵子 他

Comment

この映画は子どもの頃、毎年、正月に公開されるごとに家族で観ていました。寅さん一家がスクリーンに出てくると、まるでほんとうにいる友人たちに再会したように感じていましたよ。
When I was a little kid I watched these movies with my family during every New Year holiday. When Tora-san and his family appeared on screen it was as if I'd been reunited with real-life friends.

10 伊丹十三

伊丹十三（1933〜97）は、俳優、ドキュメンタリー映像作家、グラフィックデザイナーなど、さまざまな職を経て、1984年に『お葬式』（主演：山崎努）を初監督。一躍、日本を代表する映画監督になりました。それからというもの、人間の欲望と死に目を向け、日本の社会問題に鋭く斬り込みながら、同時にウィットに富んだ娯楽映画を次々と世に出しました。ラーメンを題材にした西部劇のパロディ『タンポポ』（1985／主演：同上）は、特に海外にファンの多い作品です。作品中のヒロインは、ほとんどが妻の宮本信子です。

11 『Shall we ダンス？』

1996年の大ヒット映画。監督は周防正行。役所広司演じる平凡なサラリーマンが、ある日、美しいダンス講師に目を奪われ、妻子に内緒で社交ダンスを習い始めます。竹中直人など個性豊かな脇役たちが笑いを誘うなか、次第にダンスにのめり込み、輝き出す主人公。そんな彼に刺激されて、心に傷を抱えたヒロインのダンス講師（草刈民代）や、一時は彼の浮気を疑った妻も変わっていきます……。この映画をきっかけに、古くさいイメージだった社交ダンスが脚光を浴びました。

中年の危機と心の解放を描いたこの作品は、世界各国で共感を呼びました。アメリカではアジアの実写映画の興行収入記録を更新。2004年にリメイク版が作られました。

映画／『男はつらいよ』／伊丹十三／『Shall we ダンス？』

09

←

at the end that she already has a sweetheart.

As the series grew more family-oriented, the spirited maverick character of Tora-san mellowed. Towards the end, the films even included episodes focusing on the romances of Tora-san's nephew.

Vocabulary

silver-tongued｜弁の立つ、雄弁な	**hawk** *one's* **wares**｜商品を売り歩く
street vendor｜露天商	**half-sister**｜父親か母親が異なる姉／妹

¹⁰ Itami Juzo

Itami Juzo (1933-97) worked in various occupations—among them actor, documentary filmmaker, and graphic designer—before making his directorial debut with *The Funeral* (1984), starring Yamazaki Tsutomu. The movie catapulted him to the ranks of Japan's foremost film directors. Itami produced witty and entertaining movies that still managed to get to the heart of such issues as desire, death, and social problems. *Tampopo* (1985), also with Yamazaki, a parody of the Spaghetti Western genre that looked at the world of ramen, has a particularly strong overseas following. The heroine in most of Itami's films was played by his wife, Miyamoto Nobuko.

Vocabulary

catapult *someone* **to** ...｜（人）を…に押し上げる	**Spaghetti Western**｜マカロニ・ウエスタン［イタ
foremost｜主要な	リア製の西部劇］

¹¹ *Shall We Dance?*

This huge hit from 1996 was directed by Suo Masayuki. An ordinary salaryman, played by Yakusho Koji, becomes enamored of a beautiful dance instructor, and without telling his wife or daughter starts taking ballroom-dancing lessons. While Takenaka Naoto and the rest of the idiosyncratic supporting cast elicit laughs from the audience, the protagonist becomes absorbed in and transformed by his dancing. Inspired by him, both the emotionally scarred dance instructor (Kusakari Tamiyo) and the protagonist's wife, who at one point suspects he is having an affair, begin to change. As a result of this movie's success, ballroom dancing, which many people had regarded as old-fashioned, was thrust once more into the limelight.

Touching as it does on the themes of mid-life crisis and emotional liberation, *Shall We Dance* evoked a favorable response around the world. In the U.S. it set a new box-office record for a live-action movie from Asia, and was remade as a Hollywood film in 2004.

Vocabulary

become enamored of ...｜…に夢中になる	**emotionally scarred**｜心に傷のある

CINEMA / Otoko wa Tsurai yo / Itami Juzo / Shall We Dance?

221

89 年、塚本晋也監督が自宅アパートで少数のスタッフと制作し、初めて一般公開した作品『鉄男』[17] は、いきなり世界各地でカルト的な評判を呼びます。この頃から、かつては必要とされていた映画会社の助監督修業を経ていない監督たち——園子温、岩井俊二、是枝裕和、青山真治などが、新鮮な視点を携えて次々とデビュー。90 年代後半には、ベテラン、若手の作品ともに、日本映画が 50 年代以来ひさしぶりに海外の映画祭の常連になりました。

また、低迷からの脱出を模索する古くからの会社などは、低予算のポルノ映画やビデオ映画に乗り出していましたが、そこでも周防正行や黒沢清など、作家性を追求しようとする才能が育ちました。

それまではめずらしかった女性の監督も、活躍が目立ち始めます。河瀬直美は、2007 年、劇映画『殯の森』[18] でカンヌ国際映画祭グランプリを受賞。下の世代では西川美和が、『ゆれる』(2006) [19] で大型の才能を印象付けました。

ドキュメンタリーも、多様な視点の作品が現れています。89 年に始まって、以来 2 年ごとに開催されている「山形国際ドキュメンタリー映画祭」[20] は、アジアにおけるドキュメンタリー映画の活性化に、大きく貢献しています。

Notes

※ 17　出演：田口トモロヲ、藤原京、石橋蓮司 他　※ 18　2007 年、出演：うだしげき、尾野真千子、渡辺真起子 他　※ 19　出演：オダギリジョー、香川照之 他　※ 20　その他の主な映画祭：「東京国際映画祭」、アジア作品を中心とする「東京フィルメックス」等。

Comment

さびしいことに、ミニシアターは、ここ数年でずいぶん閉鎖してしまいました。私の地元にもマイナーな作品を上映する名物映画館があって、ファンたちがボランティアで手伝ったりして、支えています。
Sadly, an awful lot of mini-theaters have closed their doors in recent years. In my hometown we have a popular cinema that screens lesser-known films with support from volunteers.

¹² Filmmakers Since the 1990s

The 1989 film *Tetsuo: The Iron Man*, the first feature released by director Tsukamoto Shinya, who shot it with a small crew in his own apartment, earned an unexpected cult following overseas. From around the same time, film directors like Sono Shion, Iwai Shunji, Koreeda Hirokazu and Aoyama Shinji who had not trained as in-house assistant directors— once regarded as essential—debuted in quick succession, bringing fresh perspectives to Japanese cinema. In the late 1990s, Japanese works by veteran and new-generation directors alike began to screen regularly at international film festivals for the first time since the 1950s.

Meanwhile, established studios sought to recover from their slump by churning out low-budget porn films and videos, in the process inadvertently fostering such creative and ambitious talents as Suo Masayuki and Kurosawa Kiyoshi.

More and more female directors, previously extremely rare, also began to make their mark with spectacular results. In 2007 Kawase Naomi won the Grand Prix at the Cannes Film Festival with *The Mourning Forest*. Among the younger generation of female filmmakers is Nishikawa Miwa, who impressed audiences with *Sway* (2006).

Documentaries, too, seek to explore subjects from more varied points of view these days. The Yamagata International Documentary Film Festival, which has taken place every two years since 1989, has made a significant contribution to documentary filmmaking in Asia.

09

Vocabulary

cult following｜カルト的な人気	inadvertently｜偶然にも
perspective｜視点、観点	extremely rare｜非常にまれな
churn out ...｜…を量産する	impress *A* with *B*｜A を B で印象づける

広島市のミニシアター「横川シネマ」。インディペンデント映画の上映をはじめ、各種イベントが開催され、地域の文化拠点に。
The Yokogawa Cinema, a mini-theater in Hiroshima, is a local cultural enclave that screens independent films and holds a variety of events.
Photo: Miura Fumiko

[13] 北野武

お笑いタレントとして人気絶頂だったビートたけしが、映画監督・北野武[21]として話題作を次々と発表し始めたのは、90年代の大事件でした。彼の映像は斬新で、唐突に不条理な暴力シーンが出てくるのですが、クールなニヒリズムとして国内よりも海外で評価が高まりました。また、正面から撮ったショットが多く、台詞や表情が最小限に抑えられているのも特徴です。『ソナチネ』（1993）[22]など初期には青を基調とする作品が多く、キタノブルーといわれました。

北野はテレビ番組の司会者などを務めながら、出資者に恵まれて、自分の撮りたい映画をコンスタントに発表できる立場にあります。それで、彼の心理状況や遊びの要素などが、作品に現れやすいのでしょう。98年には『HANA-BI』（1998）[23]が、ヴェネツィア国際映画祭で金獅子賞を受賞しました。『座頭市』（2003）[24]はめずらしく依頼によって撮られた**時代劇**（かつて映画やテレビで人気を博したシリーズ）ですが、日本の大衆芸能が各種盛り込まれたエンターテイメント映画で、大きなヒットとなりました。

Notes

※21 1947年生まれ。89年公開『その男、凶暴につき』（出演：ビートたけし、白竜、川上麻衣子）で映画監督デビュー　※22 出演：ビートたけし、国舞亜矢、渡辺哲 他　※23 出演：ビートたけし、岸本加代子、大杉漣 他　※24 出演：ビートたけし、浅野忠信、夏川結衣 他　※25 1999年、出演：ビートたけし、岸本加代子 他

Comment

たけしの映画は、暴力的過ぎて私は苦手です。だけど『菊次郎の夏』[25]は、少し人情味を感じさせる作品ですね。この映画を日本人が観ると、昔のビートたけしを思い出させるコントの要素があちこちに出てきます。彼のブラックな笑いは、海外の人にはどう映るでしょうか。
Most of Takeshi's movies are too violent for my tastes. But I know he's also made films that tug at the heart—like *Kikujiro*, for example. It's peppered with skit-like elements that remind Japanese audiences of the Beat Takeshi of old. I wonder what people overseas make of his black humor.

右：北野武『HANA-BI』より
Right: From Kitano's *Hana-bi*
© 1997 バンダイビジュアル・テレビ東京・TOKYO FM／オフィス北野

Kitano Takeshi

Beat Takeshi was at the height of his popularity as a **comedy** star in the 1990s, so when he began directing a succession of high-profile movies under his real name, Kitano Takeshi, it caused a sensation. His visual style is unconventional and his works are often punctuated by abrupt outbursts of absurd violence, which combined with their cool nihilism have gained them more of a following overseas than in Japan. Other hallmarks of Kitano's films include numerous front-on shots and an almost deadpan acting style with minimal dialogue and expression. Many of his early works, such as *Sonatine* (1993), had a distinctive blue tone that came to be called "Kitano blue."

Blessed with investor backing, Kitano is in the position of being able to make the movies he wants while continuing to work as a TV host. This may explain why his movies often reveal aspects of his own psychological state or indulge in playfulness. In 1998, *Hana-bi* (1998) won the Golden Lion at the Venice Film Festival. *Zatoichi* (2003) is a **jidaigeki** that he made under commission, a rarity for Kitano. Based on an older film and TV series, it went on to become a hit with its engaging style and its incorporation of Japanese popular entertainment.

Vocabulary

high-profile｜注目を集める	absurd｜不条理な
cause a sensation｜大騒ぎを起こす	hallmark｜特徴
unconventional｜型にはまらない	deadpan｜無表情な
be punctuated by ...｜…を差しはさまれる	playfulness｜遊び心
abrupt｜不意の、突然の	tug at the heart｜心の琴線に触れる

10

CUISINE
料理

日本料理と食文化

すしをはじめとする日本料理は、カロリーや脂肪が少なく、穀物の**発酵食品**を多用したヘルシーフードとして、世界的に人気を集めています[1]。近代以前は、**仏教**の影響で、肉があまり食べられていなかったので、豊富な魚介や海藻、米、豆、そして山菜などを使った、淡泊な料理となりました。

また、**会席**に代表される美しい盛り付けや、季節の素材を生かしたミニマルな調理法は、日本料理の美学として知られています。

一方、近代以降に海外の料理をアレンジした洋食や中華料理も、日本にすっかり定着しています[2]。なかでも**ラーメン**（中国の料理をもとにした汁そば）や**カレーライス**は、すでに日本の大衆食を代表するメニューとなりました。各国の本格的なレストランがたくさん出来た昨今でも、和風スパゲッティなどの折衷料理が、日々生み出されています。

日本の家庭料理の献立は、一汁三菜[3]、一汁一菜などといって、主食のごはんのほか、汁物とおかずが一品か三品に、**漬物**を卓上に並べるのが基本といわれます。食堂で和風の定食を頼んでも、こうしたスタイルで出てきますね。とはいえ手軽な食事では、前述のカレーライスや丼——丼とは大きな鉢——など、ごはんにおかずが乗っているものもありますし、卓上コンロで鍋をぐつぐつ煮る鍋料理は、冬の定番メニューです。

50年代以降は、インスタント食品の開発が進みました。そのうち即席ラーメンは、世界中で年間 1,000 億食以上も食べられています。

飲食店の形式としては、居酒屋が海外でも有名になりつつありますね。仲間同士でさまざまな料理がシェアできる、気軽な酒場のことです。

また食といえば最近、安全性に対する意識が高まっています。おしゃれな雰囲気の店にも、あらためて健康志向を打ち出すところが増えました。

Notes

※1 2013 年、和食（日本の伝統的食文化）がユネスコの無形文化遺産に登録された。申請に際しては、自然の尊重や年中行事との関わりも強調された。 ※2 天ぷらは、大航海時代に伝わった料理が元といわれる。 ※3 「菜」は「おかず」の意味。四は縁起が悪いので四菜といわず、奇数がよいとされる。家庭料理の「三菜」は主菜と副菜 2 種（一汁三菜は本膳料理からきていて、本膳料理の「三菜」は、なます、煮物、焼物）。 ※4 外国人に「箸の使い方が上手ですね」とほめるのは、子ども扱いで失礼という意見もある。

Comment

日本では、おもに木の箸を使って食事します。箸の使い方[4]には、いろいろマナーがありますが、外国の人がマナーを間違うのは仕方ないと思う人が多いので、固くならなくても大丈夫ですよ。
Japanese food is generally eaten with wooden chopsticks. Although there are certain conventions for handling these utensils, few Japanese expect non-natives to have mastered them, so don't worry about your chopsticks technique while you're eating!

⁰¹ Japan's Food Culture

Japanese cuisine, including but not limited to **sushi**, has earned a global reputation as healthy, low-calorie, low-fat fare that makes ample use of **fermented** grains and vegetables. Until the modern era, Japanese ate little meat—a consequence of **Buddhism**'s influence—and instead developed a light, natural cuisine utilizing the country's abundance of seafood and seaweed, as well as rice, beans, and edible wild plants.

Japan's culinary culture is also famed for the aesthetics of its minimalist approach to food preparation, the use of in-season ingredients, and the exquisite arrangement of the dishes, exemplified by the traditional *kaiseki* style.

Additionally, Japan boasts its own distinctive versions of Chinese, Western, and other foreign cuisine, which caught on here after the advent of the Meiji era (1868-1912). Two such dishes—**ramen** (a noodle broth originally from China) and **curry rice**—have become standard bargain-menu items. Today, when restaurants here offer cuisine from all over the globe, the country continues to give birth to an ever-growing selection of fusion dishes like Japanese spaghetti.

A basic home-cooked Japanese meal is usually in a "one soup, three dishes" or "one soup, one dish" format (odd numbers are often considered auspicious in Japanese cuisine), with a bowl of **rice** as well as some *tsukemono* pickled vegetables on the side. That is also pretty much what you will get if you order a Japanese-style meal in a typical restaurant. But simpler fare is also popular—notably dishes that consist of rice with a topping, like the aforementioned curry, or the wide range of *donburi* rice-bowl dishes. A staple of winter menus is the *nabe*, a meal cooked in a large pot on a portable stove placed right on the table.

Precooked food has enjoyed dramatic growth in Japan since the 1950s. People around the world consume approximately 100 billion meals of instant ramen, a Japanese invention, every year.

Among Japan's diverse eating and drinking establishments, *izakaya* have acquired some cachet abroad of late. These are casual bars where people can gather and share a variety of a la carte dishes with friends over drinks.

With food safety a growing concern, even fashionable cafes and restaurants have recently been placing more emphasis on healthy food.

CUISINE / Japan's Food Culture

10

Vocabulary

fare｜料理	exemplified by ...｜…が良い例となった
fermented｜発酵した	broth｜だし汁、スープ
abundance｜豊富さ	odd numbers｜奇数
culinary｜料理の	staple｜主食、必需品

02 **会席と懐石**

現代において、もっとも洗練された形式の日本料理が、「会席」です。料亭という和風建築の高級料理店で出される酒宴のための料理で、形や大きさの違ういろいろな器に、少量ずつ美しく盛りつけられた料理がコースで出てきます。お腹をいっぱいにするものではなく、個室で花や調度品をながめつつ、時に**芸者**の歌舞音曲を楽しみながら、酒とともに、料理の趣向を味わうのです。

料亭のなかには紹介がないと入れない店もあり、以前は政治家や財界人などの限られた人しか利用できませんでしたが、最近は敷居が低くなってきているようです。

同じカイセキでも違う字を書く「懐石」（茶懐石）は、**茶道**にもとづいて、茶席で主人が客に出す軽い料理です（写真 P. 247）。わびた趣向で、簡素でありながら、旬の素材を使って手作りするのが、最高のもてなしとされています。

正統派の日本料理として、かつては数百年前に端を発する「本膳料理」がありました。畳（P. 282 参照）の部屋に座る客ひとり一人の前に、料理の乗った脚付きの角膳が運ばれてくるスタイルです。今では、**時代劇映画**のなか以外、ほとんど見られなくなりました。

Comment

実際の飲食店では、カイセキという言葉が両方、好き勝手に使われていますよ。少しずつ出てくるコース料理に「洋風懐石」と名づけているのも、よくみかけます。

In practice, you'll find that Japanese eateries and drinkeries use both forms of the word *kaiseki* rather loosely. For example, it's not uncommon to see "Western-style kaiseki" on the menu to indicate a multi-course meal where small dishes are brought out one at a time.

03 **板前とさしみ**

中国料理やフランス料理では、鍋やフライパンを持つシェフが厨房を仕切りますが、日本の**会席**料理では、「さしみ」を切る人がトップで、文字通り「板前」──「まな板の前」という意味──と呼ばれています。

さしみとは、生の魚介を切って盛り付けた料理です。日本料理ではこの「料理しない料理」が、素材そのものを味わう、最上の食べ方とされています。魚介を生でも食あたりなどおこさずに美味しく食べる[※5]には、素材の選別眼と、切り口が美しく、細胞をつぶさないように包丁を引く[※6]……など

→

料理／会席と懐石／板前とさしみ

10

⁰² Kaiseki and Kaiseki: Two Different Cuisines

The most sophisticated form of Japanese cuisine is *kaiseki*. This is the style of food served at banquets in *ryotei*, high-class restaurants of traditional Japanese design. Multiple courses in small, exquisitely arranged portions come in dishes of varying sizes and shapes. The point of the meal is not to fill yourself up, but to savor the delicious food and sake while enjoying the flowers and other attractive furnishings in the room, which may be augmented with songs and dances by **geisha**.

Some ryotei will not admit customers without an introduction. At one time such establishments catered exclusively to politicians and wealthy businessmen. Lately, however, there is a trend toward making ryotei more accessible to the average customer.

There is another kind of *kaiseki* as well—pronounced the same but spelled with different kanji characters (image on p. 247). Also called *cha-kaiseki*, this is the cuisine served to guests at formal tea gatherings as part of the *sado* tradition. Though these are light, simple meals, the host aspires to the highest form of hospitality by offering hand-prepared ingredients in season.

An even more classic form of Japanese cuisine is *honzen ryori*, which originated several hundred years ago. The food is served on a series of small, square, four-legged trays—one for each of the guests, who sit on a tatami-mat floor (see p. 283). Nowadays this style of presentation is no longer much in evidence, except in **jidaigeki** period dramas.

Vocabulary

be augmented with ...	…で補われる、強められる	aspire to ...	〔高いレベルにあるもの〕をめざす
accessible to ...	…に近づきやすい	in evidence	目立って、はっきりと見えて

⁰³ Itamae and Sashimi

In the Chinese and French culinary traditions, the cook who wields the pots and pans is the one who runs the kitchen. But with **kaiseki** cuisine, the man who cuts the sashimi is the boss. In fact, the word for chef, *itamae*, literally means "before the cutting board."

Sashimi—sliced raw fish—is considered the ultimate treat in Japan precisely because it is "uncooked cuisine" that lets you savor the ingredients just as they are. To ensure that the consumption of raw seafood is a delicious experience that does not result in food poisoning, the itamae must possess a number of well-honed skills, not least among them an eye for selecting ingredients, as well as a sure hand and artistic touch with the knife used to slice cleanly through the tissue.

→

の技術が要求されるのです。

さしみは、わさび（P. 244 参照）を少量のせて、小さな器に入ったしょう
ゆ（P. 236 参照）に少し付けて食べます。

Notes

※5 淡水魚は特に薬味と辛みを添えて、寄生虫などをふせぐ。　※6 素材によっては下処理も必要。

刺身　料理：柳原尚之（近茶流）
雑誌『婦人画報』2012 年 7 月号より
Sashimi prepared by chef Yanagihara
Naoyuki
From *Fujingaho* magazine (July 2012)
Photo: Kuma Masashi

04　だしと吸い物

「だし」と呼ばれるスープのもとは、多くの日本料理の決め手となっていま
す。現在もっともよく使われるのは、かつお節（かつおを燻製・発酵させ
て、固くなった塊を削ったもの）と、昆布のだし。材料を長く煮込んで濃厚
な味にするのではなくて、短時間で素材の風味を抽出するのが特徴です。
ほかにも、干しシイタケや煮干し、地方独特の素材からだしを取ることもあ
ります。現代の家庭では、液体やパウダー状のインスタントだしも普及して
います。

「吸い物」は、上質なだしそのものの風味を味わう透明なスープです。**会席**
などで出される吸い物には天然水が使われていて、シンプルですが玄人に
いわせると、**さしみ**と並ぶ日本料理の華です。漆（P. 42 参照）の椀[※7]で供
され、味、彩り、香りをもたらす三種の具──たとえば海老、三つ葉という
ハーブ、柚子という柑橘類の皮──が浮かび、塩やしょうゆ（P. 236 参照）
でほんのり味付けしてあります。

ほかにも、少なめのだしでさまざまな食材を煮る「煮物」、だしと溶き卵を
まぜて焼いた「だし巻き卵」……と、だしには無限の使い方があります。

→

←

One usually eats sashimi with a dab of wasabi (Japanese horseradish, see p. 245) and a quick dip in a small dish of soy sauce (see p. 237).

Vocabulary

wield ... │ …を巧みに使う	well-honed skill │ 研ぎ澄まされた技術
treat │ ごちそう、もてなし	tissue │ （細胞の）組織

くず豆腐と油目の煮物椀　料理：島谷宗宏
（京都「水簾」）『季節の椀もの入門』より
（誠文堂新光社・刊　制作：水谷和生）
An example of *nimono-wan* ("simmered-food bowl") cuisine featuring dashi soup with a generous helping of ingredients. Chef: Shimatani Munehiro. From the book *Kisetsu no Wanmono Nyumon* ("Introduction to Seasonal Soup Dishes"), produced by Mizutani Kazuo
Photo: Iwasaki Nanako

⁰⁴ Dashi and Suimono

Dashi—the stock used in Japanese soups—occupies an eminent position in the country's cuisine as the "clincher" that determines a meal's success. The most prevalent dashi is made of *katsuo-bushi* (flakes of smoke-dried and fermented bonito) and *konbu* (kelp). The secret of this type of dashi is not to boil the ingredients for a long time to produce a strong flavor, but rather to extract their essence through brief immersion in the broth. Other dashi include dried *shiitake* mushrooms and dried small sardines, as well as stock made with special local ingredients. These days, however, many households make do with instant dashi in liquid or powdered form.

Suimono is a clear soup that is designed to showcase the flavor of high-quality dashi. The suimono that accompanies **kaiseki** is prepared with natural water. It is a simple dish, but connoisseurs place it alongside **sashimi** at the pinnacle of Japanese cuisine. Served in a fine lacquer (see p. 43) bowl, suimono will typically contain small amounts of solid ingredients that provide the "three accents" of flavor, color, and aroma—examples might be shrimp, *mitsuba* leaf, and *yuzu* citron—with just a touch of salt or soy sauce.

The list of uses for dashi in Japanese cooking is practically endless. To name two, you can simmer foods in it to make *nimono*, stews that may contain a variety of ingredients, and you can mix it with eggs to make

→

←

料理にどんなだしが使われているかは見えにくくても、食べてみて、そのうま味※8 が感じられることを、「だしが効いている」といいます。

Notes

※7 漆器は耐熱性があり、口を付ける感触がいいことから。防虫効果もある（P. 44 参照）。　※8 科学用語としては、日本の学者・池田菊苗（きくなえ）が命名。苦味、酸味、甘味、塩味に加わる第五の味覚とされる。成分物質はグルタミン酸、イノシン酸、グアニル酸 等。一般用語としては、「おいしさ」という意味でも使う。

Comment

ほんとうの吸い物の味がわかる人が、めっきり少なくなりました。吸い物は、一口吸っただけでは、味が物足りなくて当たり前。全部が胃に入ってから、ゆっくりとおいしさを感じるものなのです。
Very few people are familiar with the taste of true suimono anymore. If you take only one sip, it is bound to strike you as a bit on the thin side. Only when you have imbibed an entire bowl, and the flavor slowly blooms in your mouth, will you appreciate just how delicious it is.

コラム　**米**

日本で、米はとても重視されている作物です。自給率はほぼ 100％で、米には高い輸入関税がかけられています※9。また**神道**では、米が神聖なものとされています。

日本で稲作が本格的に始まったのは 2000 年以上前で、稲作のカレンダーに沿って祭りなどの年中行事が行われてきました。また、米は税になり、江戸時代には武士の給与になり、領土の大きさが米の収穫高で示されていました。

歴史的にみると、米は長くぜいたく品で、現在のように米のごはんを毎日食べられた時代は短く、大半の人はおもに雑穀などを食べていたという説もあります。

米の消費量は 1960 年代前半にピークに達しましたが、その後の食生活の変化から、近年の消費量はほぼ半減しています。

Notes

※9 2014 年 12 月現在、TPP 交渉中。

05　ごはんと餅

日本の食事は、主食（日常的な食事の主体）と副食という概念※10 がはっきりしていて、米を炊いた※11 ものが一般的な主食になります。白米が主流で

→

dashi-maki tamago, a rolled omelette.

Though it is not always easy to tell what sort of dashi has been used in a particular dish, it makes its presence known when you taste that uniquely savory flavor of *umami*.

Vocabulary

eminent｜高い、傑出した	immersion｜浸すこと
clincher｜決定的要因、決め手	simmer ...｜…を弱火でゆっくり煮る［**boil** は「沸
prevalent｜広く行き渡った	かす、ぐつぐつ煮る、ゆでる」、**stew** は「煮込む」]
extract ...｜…を抽出する	

COLUMN **Rice**

Rice is an incredibly important crop in Japan. The country is nearly self-sufficient in the grain, and imposes a high tariff on imports. Indeed, **Shinto** beliefs have long treated rice as a sacred food.

Full-scale rice cultivation began in Japan over 2,000 years ago, and traditional festivals and other annual events largely follow the rice production cycle. In the past the grain has served as a tax, and, during the Edo period (1603-1868), as a salary for samurai and an index of the land value of their domains, assessed according to the amount of rice harvested.

Over most of Japan's history rice has been a luxury item, and it is relatively recently that the average Japanese has been able to eat it on a daily basis; people in earlier times generally ate other, coarser grains.

Japan's rice consumption peaked in the early 1960s; at present it has dropped to about half that level due to changes in eating habits.

Vocabulary

impose *A* on *B*｜A を B に課す	assessed according to ...｜…によって査
domain｜領土、領地	定された
	coarser grains｜雑穀、粗末な穀物

10

⁰⁵ Rice and Mochi

Japanese meals adhere to a concept that distinguishes between a staple food and other, secondary dishes. The standard staple in Japan is boiled **rice**—usually white rice, although brown rice and rice with the germ have

すが、玄米や胚芽米も健康食として見直されています。

日本の丸みをおびた米（ジャポニカ種※12）で炊くごはんは、ちょっとした
ねばりと弾力があります。

主食のごはんには味付けをせず、汁ものやおかず、**漬物**と交互に食べます。
ごはんの食べ方はほかにも、手づかみで食べる三角やたわら型の「**おにぎ
り**」（すしと違って酢飯ではなく、かるい塩味。中に**梅干し**や塩鮭などの具
を入れる）、茶碗の中のごはんに具をのせてお茶をかける「**お茶漬け**」、米
を炊くときに山菜や魚介類、調味料などをいっしょに入れる「**炊き込みごは
ん**」など、いろいろあります。

ねばりの強いもち米は、もともとおめでたいとき※13 に食べるものでした。
小豆と一緒に炊いて赤飯にしたり、炊いたもち米をついてねばらせ、食べ
やすい大きさの餅にしたりします。

現代は、パン※14 も日常的に食べられるようになりましたが、通常、和食を
食べるときにパンを合わせることはありません。

Notes

※10 東アジア、東南アジア他、太平洋諸島や東アフリカのいくつかの民族の間で、食事を主食と副食に分
ける習慣がある。対して、主菜（メインディッシュ）は、コースの目玉となる一品。　※11 欧米等では、ゆ
でた細い米をサラダにも使う。中国では米を「煮る」という。　※12 タイなどで食べられている細長い米
はインディカ種。　※13 アジアや東南アジアの各地に、もち米を重用したり、ハレの日に食べる地域が分
布している。　※14 パンはイギリス等では主食という認識はなく、主菜の付け合せのようなもの。

Comment

ごはんを炊いている鍋のふたは、開けないで。水分がなくなったら、最後は火を止めて蒸らして、
ふっくらさせるの。日本では、どこの家にも炊飯器があって、米と水を入れてボタンを押すだけで
炊けるんだけどね。
When you cook rice, don't remove the lid too soon! Even after the water boils away
and you shut off the flame, you need to let the rice sit and steam for a while to
plump it up. Of course, every Japanese household today has an automatic rice
cooker—all you have to do is add rice and water, push a button, and there you go.

⁰⁶ 発酵食品

日本料理で味や風味の決め手をになう食材には、発酵食品が多くあります。
もともと保存食だったものですが、近年は健康食としての価値が注目され
ています。

なかでも「**しょうゆ**」※15 は、和食になくてはならない液体調味料。大豆と
小麦を自然の菌で半年以上かけて発酵させるのが、本醸造と呼ばれる伝統
的な製法です。しょうゆは料理の味付けにも使いますし、しょうゆ差しを食

→

10

←

gradually gained acceptance as health foods.

Japanese rice (of the variety *Japonica*) is short-grained, oval in shape and, when boiled, somewhat sticky and chewy. When the Japanese serve rice with a meal, they seldom flavor it, but alternate between partaking of mouthfuls of rice and nibbling on the other dishes, soup, or pickles.

There are of course plenty of other ways to eat rice. *Onigiri* are clumps of boiled rice shaped into a triangle or oval and eaten by hand. The rice is lightly salted—not vinegared like **sushi** rice—and contains a savory filling such as **umeboshi** pickled plum or grilled salted salmon. *Ochazuke* consists of Japanese tea poured over a bowl of rice with some sort of topping. Vegetables, seafood, and various condiments may also be boiled together with the rice to make a pilaf-like *takikomi-gohan*.

Mochigome is a particularly glutinous rice that used to be consumed mainly on festive occasions. It is often boiled with red adzuki beans to produce *sekihan* ("red rice"), or pounded into a dough-like consistency and then shaped into *mochi* rice cakes for easy eating by hand.

Bread is also a daily staple in Japan now, but it is rarely if ever eaten with Japanese-style cuisine.

Vocabulary

adhere to …	…に忠実である	savory	味（香り、風味）が良い
chewy	かみ応えがある	vegetable	野菜、植物
partaking of …	…を食べる（飲む）こと	condiment	調味料、香辛料、薬味
(a) mouthful of …	一口の、口いっぱいの	glutinous rice	もち米
nibbling on …	…を少しずつ食べること	dough-like	パン生地のような
clump	かたまり	consistency	かたさ

06 Fermented Foods

Fermented foods make up a significant proportion of the ingredients considered key to the flavoring of Japanese cuisine. Fermentation originally functioned as a means of preservation, but lately these preparations have attracted notice for their healthful properties.

Soy sauce stands out amid fermented products as the liquid seasoning that Japanese food cannot do without. The traditional *hon-jozo* brewing method produces soy sauce by fermenting soybeans and wheat with naturally occurring molds for half a year or more. The condiment may be added while cooking, or during meals from the soy sauce pot that is a fixture on any Japanese dinner table.

Teriyaki, a style of cooking well known outside of Japan, consists of fish or meat broiled or grilled in a sweet-salty sauce prepared by mixing soy sauce with sugar and sake. The sugar adds a gloss to the surface that

→

10

←

卓に置いて、料理にかけたりもします。

海外で人気の「照り焼き」は、このしょうゆと砂糖や日本酒※16 を混ぜた甘辛いタレ※17 を、魚や肉に付けて焼く料理です。甘味のせいで、表面に「照り」が出るのが、照り焼きの名の由来です。アメリカなどで市販されている「テリヤキ・ソース」※18 は、ニンニクが入っていたりして、日本の照り焼きとは味が少し違いますね。

もうひとつ、重要な食材に「みそ」があります。大豆と穀物を発酵させたペーストで、古代から日本でつくられてきました。現在は調味料として使われることが多いですね。濃いめのだしにみそと具を入れたみそ汁は、家庭料理の定番です。

その他の発酵食品には、日本酒（米を発酵させて濾過した醸造酒）、かつお節（P. 232 参照）、**漬物**、納豆（蒸した大豆を発酵させた食品）、酢、塩こうじ（調味料）などがあります。

Notes

※15 大豆を使った液体調味料はアジア各地にあり、英語ではどれも soy sauce。　※16 日本語で「酒」はアルコール全般を指すが、海外では sake といえば日本酒のこと。　※17 タレには、日本酒の代わりにみりん（sweet cooking sake）を使うこともある。　※18 肉や豆腐などを付け込んで焼いたり、焼いた肉にかけたりするのに使い、照りを出すことは、あまり認識されていないよう。

Comment

納豆はねばねばと糸を引いて、においの強い、ユニークな食材。苦手な人は苦手です。日本に長く住む外国人の友達は、「納豆は食べられますか？」としょっちゅう聞かれていますよ。健康食品なので、じつは外国人のファンもわりといます。

With its gooey strings of slime and its powerful odor, natto guarantees a memorable dining experience! Some people simply can't stand it. My foreign friends who have lived in Japan a long time are frequently asked whether they can eat natto—but in fact, it seems to have quite a few non-Japanese fans.

WORLD CAFÉ **しょうゆ輸出の歴史**

日本のしょうゆは 17 世紀にオランダ東インド会社が輸出を開始し、18 世紀フランスの『百科全書』にも記載されています。1950 年代にはキッコーマンがアメリカに現地会社を設立し、今では世界 100 カ国以上でしょうゆを販売しています。

最近は、機械化されていない小規模な蔵で醸造される各地方のしょうゆの個性にも、注目が集まっています。

料理／発酵食品／しょうゆ輸出の歴史

10

gives teriyaki (literally "shiny-broiled") its name. The "teriyaki sauce" sold in such places as America contains ingredients like garlic that make it taste a little different from Japanese teriyaki.

Another essential foodstuff is *miso*, a paste of fermented soybeans and other grains that has been made in Japan for many centuries. These days it is used primarily as a flavoring. *Miso-shiru*, a soup prepared by adding miso and other ingredients to a robust **dashi** stock, is a staple of Japanese home cooking.

Other fermented items that figure prominently in Japanese cuisine are sake, which is brewed from fermented rice; katsuo-bushi bonito flakes (see p. 233); **tsukemono** pickles; *natto*, a food made by fermenting steamed soybeans; *shio-koji*, a mixture of malted rice and salt used as a seasoning; and vinegar.

Vocabulary

function as ...	…の機能を果たす	broiled or grilled	焼いた、 あぶった ［broil は
preservation	保存	「(肉等を) 直火や強火、 網で焼く」、 grill (おもに英)
property	特性、属性	は「(肉、 魚や野菜を) 網や鉄板で焼く」]
amid ...	…の中で	foodstuff	食材、食品
	prominently	目立って

10

丸中醤油（滋賀県）の 200 年続く蔵。そこに棲む微生物と自然の気温変化を利用した昔ながらの製法で、3 年前後もろみを熟成させるという。
A storehouse in use for 200 years at Marunaka Shouyu in Shiga Prefecture. The traditional production method makes use of the microorganisms that dwell here and natural air-temperature fluctuations to ferment soy sauce for around three years.
Photo courtesy of Marunaka Shouyu

07 ベジタリアン[19] に薦める日本料理

和食は一見、野菜や穀類だけにみえるメニューでも、魚でとっただしが使われていることが多いですね。だけど精進料理[20] という、伝統的な菜食料理がありますよ。もともとは寺で作られる僧侶の修行のための料理で、肉や魚はもとより、ねぎやニンニクなど、香りの強い野菜も使いません。

また最近は[21]、玄米食を中心とした「マクロビオティック」のカフェやレストランも出来ています。マクロビオティックは、1920年代に日本の桜沢如一[22] が提唱した食生活法です。彼と弟子たちの普及活動によって、日本よりもむしろ海外で知られていましたが、アメリカでマドンナなどのスターが実践していると報道されてから、逆輸入のようなかたちで静かなブームになっているのです。

マクロビオティックには陰陽論をもとにした思想があり、なるべく近隣で採れた自然農（P. 288参照）・有機農の作物や海藻を、皮や根も捨てずに丸ごと料理します。

Notes

※ 19　卵や乳製品をとらない厳密な菜食主義者は、英語圏でビーガン（vegan）という。また、ベジタリアン（vegetarian）にも程度差があり、例えば植物の他、魚をとる人をフィッシュ・ベジタリアン等という。
※ 20　中国や韓国等にもあるが、使う素材や味付けは異なる。　※ 21　食の安全を求める最新の動きとして、「放射能フリー」の店（厳しい自主基準で食品の放射能検査をしている店等）が登場している。
※ 22　George Ohsawa の名で、1960年代に『Zen Macrobiotics』を出版。

08 料理にかかわるメディアと人物

食に関するメディアの例として、古くは18世紀に、豆腐[23] の食べ方を百通り紹介した『豆腐百珍』という本が、ブームになったことがあります。

現代は、食にまつわる漫画がたくさん出ています。美食を追求する『美味しんぼ』は、30年以上雑誌の連載[24] が続いていますし、ワインをテーマにした『神の雫』は海外でも好評です。

また、90年代のテレビ番組『料理の鉄人』は、アメリカ版やイギリス版、タイ版などがつぎつぎと出来ました。スタジオにキッチンが設置され、料理人同士が試合形式で、料理の腕を競うショーです。

日本の美食家を象徴する人物としては、かつて北大路魯山人（1883～1959）という芸術家がいました。きたんのない言葉で芸術としての美食道を語り、料理に合う器も自ら作陶しました。

栗原はるみ[25]（1947～）は、「カリスマ主婦」として知られる料理家です。

→

⁰⁷ Japanese Cuisine for Vegetarians

Even Japanese meals that appear to consist of nothing but vegetables and grains often use fish-based **dashi** (soup stocks). There is, however, a purely vegetarian traditional cuisine as well. Originally developed in Buddhist temples to feed monks in training, *shojin ryori* not only contains no meat or fish, but also avoids vegetables with strong odors, such as leeks and garlic.

Recent years have seen the emergence of macrobiotic cafés and restaurants, featuring a cuisine centered around brown rice. The macrobiotic diet was introduced in the 1920s by Sakurazawa Yukikazu, a Japanese who also wrote under the name George Ohsawa and actively promoted the diet outside of Japan. In the wake of media reports of its popularity with Madonna and other American celebrities, macrobiotic cuisine has come full circle to enjoy a bit of a boom in its country of origin.

Macrobiotics is a philosophy based on the concept of yin-yang balance. It advocates the use of natural (see p. 289) or organic, locally grown grains, seaweed, and vegetables, which are cooked with skins and roots intact.

Vocabulary

in the wake of … │ …に引き続いて、…の結果として	yin-yang balance │ 陰陽のバランス
come full circle │ (一周して) 元の位置に戻る	intact │ 完全な、もとのままの

⁰⁸ Food Media and Food People

One early example of food-related media in Japan is the book *Tofu Hyakuchin*, a compilation of 100 tofu recipes that came out in the 18th century and was a bestseller in its day.

Flashing forward to the present, you will find plenty of manga about food. *Oishinbo*, starring a gourmet protagonist, has been serialized in a comic magazine for over 30 years, while *The Drops of God*, a manga about wine, is a hit overseas as well.

The 1990s TV show *Iron Chef* has spawned editions in the United States, England, Thailand, and several other countries. Each episode pits two chefs against each other in a cooking contest held in a kitchen built in the TV studio.

Japan's most legendary gourmet is probably the artist Kitaoji Rosanjin (1883-1959). Kitaoji was outspoken in his pronouncements about gastronomy as an artistic pursuit. A renowned potter, he also made ceramic vessels suitable for food.

Kurihara Harumi (1947-) is a cookery writer, media personality, and lifestyle coordinator regularly referred to as the "charismatic homemaker."

10

→

←

彼女のレシピ本の料理は、簡単に作れておいしいと評判で、英語版も出版
されています。伝統的な和食というより、各国料理の要素を採り入れた、
オリジナルの家庭料理です。

Notes

※ 23 豆乳をにがりなどの凝固剤を入れて、固めたもの。中国をはじめアジア各地で伝統的に食べられてい
るが、米等では日本語の tofu が定着。 ※ 24 2014 年 12 月現在、休載中。 ※ 25 2004 年、『Harumi's
Japanese Cooking』が、グルマン世界料理本賞にて「Cookbook of the Year」を受賞。生活雑貨やその
ショップ、レストラン等のプロデュースも手がける。

コラム 日本の食べ物あれこれ

漬物と梅干し	日本の漬物は、西洋のピクルスとはずいぶん味が異なります。食材を塩、ぬかみそ、しょうゆ（P. 236参照）、酒かす、こうじなどに漬けて発酵させるものと、浅く漬けて発酵させないものがあります。梅の実でつくる梅干しは、もっともよく食べられる漬物の一種。酸っぱくて、薬効があります。
そば	日本の代表的な細長い麺。そば粉でつくります。「ざるそば」は、冷えた麺がざるに乗っていて、だしをベースにした小鉢のつゆに、一口ずつ付けながら食べます。音を立ててすすって、噛まずに飲み込むのが、通の食べ方、あるいは江戸っ子風だという人もいます（のどごしがいいそうです）。大鉢に熱いつゆと麺、具がいっしょに入ったそばもあります。 そのほかの麺には、小麦粉でつくった太麺のうどんや、細麺のそうめんなどがあります。どれも、ねぎなどの薬味を添えます。
カレーライス	インド料理[26]がイギリス経由で日本に伝わるなかで、アレンジされたメニューだといわれています。茶色っぽくどろっと濃厚なカレーが、ごはんにかかっています。家庭ではたいてい肉、じゃがいも、玉ねぎ、にんじんなどの具を入れます。箸ではなく、スプーンで食べます。

Notes

※ 26 カレーという言葉はもともとインドになく、香辛料を使ったインドの煮込み料理を、西洋人がカレーと
総称し始めた。

Comment

疲れているとき、梅干しを食べるとほっとします。子どもの頃から、病気になると母がおかゆをつく
ってくれて、梅干しといっしょに食べていましたから。
When I'm tired, eating an umeboshi makes me feel better. I think it reminds me of
my childhood—when I was ill, my mother would make rice porridge for me and plop
an umeboshi in it.

The recipes in her cookbooks, which have also been published in English, have a reputation for easy and tasty cooking. Her style is an original form of home cooking that incorporates elements of various countries' cuisines more than it references traditional Japanese dishes.

Vocabulary

outspoken ｜率直な、遠慮のない	gastronomy ｜美食法
pronouncement ｜意見、見解	incorporate ... ｜…を含んでいる、組み込む

COLUMN **Odds and Ends of Japanese Food**

Tsukemono and Umeboshi	Though technically pickled, the varieties of tsukemono taste noticeably different from Western-style pickles. The vegetables may be immersed in salt, *nukamiso* fermented rice-bran paste, soy sauce (see p. 237), sake lees, or *koji* malted rice. Sometimes they are left long enough to ferment, and sometimes not. One of the most frequently consumed tsukemono is umeboshi, the salt-pickled fruit of the Japanese apricot (though *ume* is more often translated as "plum"). Extremely sour, it is prized for its medicinal benefits.
Soba	Japan's most ubiquitous noodle, *soba* is made with buckwheat flour. It is often eaten cold as *zaru-soba* served in a shallow bamboo basket (*zaru*). To eat zaru-soba you dip a mouthful at a time into a small bowl of **dashi**-based sauce, then lift it out and slurp it up. Some Japanese believe that slurping loudly and virtually inhaling the noodles without chewing them not only feels good in the throat but proves one's credentials as a true Edo-style soba connoisseur. Soba also comes in a hot broth, served in a large bowl with other ingredients. Japan favors other kinds of noodles as well, notably the thick wheat noodles called *udon* and the thinner variety known as *somen*. All are served with scallions and other garnishes.
Curry Rice	Curry rice is said to have reached Japan via the British as a modified form of Indian cuisine. The Japanese version of curry is a thick, gloppy brown sauce ladled over rice. Homemade curry typically contains meat, potatoes, onions, and carrots. Unlike most domestic dishes, it is eaten with a spoon, not chopsticks.

10

Vocabulary

pickled ｜ピクルス（塩漬け・酢漬け）にされた	ladled ｜おたまでよそった
inhaling ... ｜…を飲み込むこと、すFること	

09 すし

現在、海外でよく食べられている sushi といえば、酢飯の上に生の魚介などのネタ[27]を乗せてにぎる「にぎりずし」や、のり（黒いシート状の干した海藻）で細長く巻いた「巻きずし」ですね。日本にはほかにも、器に盛った「五目ちらし」や、薄い豆腐を揚げて袋状になった油揚げというもの[28]の中にシャリ（すし飯）を入れる「稲荷ずし」など、いろいろなすしがありますよ。

にぎりは、江戸時代に屋台の食べ物だったなごりか、手で食べるのが美味しいという人もいますが、現代的な回転ずし屋などでは、箸を使うことが多いです。しょうゆ（P. 236 参照）を少し、ネタに付けて食べます。ネタとシャリに挟まれた緑色のペーストは、植物の地下茎をすり下ろしたわさび[29]で、鼻につんとくる刺激があります。わさびは殺菌効果もあるといいますが、苦手なら「さびぬき」が注文できます。すしには、甘酸っぱいスライス生姜の漬物が添えられます。

海外では、ゴムやビニールの手袋をつけてすしを握る店が多いですね。修業に 10 年かかるような日本の本格的な店では、手袋はつけていません。職人の微妙な感覚を損なってしまうからだそうです。

Notes

※ 27　味付けや加熱調理してあるネタもある。　※ 28　稲荷の油揚げは煮付けてある　※ 29　わさびは日本原産。欧州原産のセイヨウわさびもある（horseradish ／根をすったものはローストビーフの薬味になる）。

料理／すし

10

すしを握る荒木水都弘
Sushi chef Araki Mitsuhiro at work, 2011
Photo: Kuma Masashi

⁰⁹ Sushi

The sushi currently eaten in many countries outside Japan tends to consist of either *nigiri-zushi*, the hand-shaped ovals of vinegared sushi rice topped with (usually raw) seafood, or *maki-zushi*, with the ingredients wrapped in long rolls of *nori*, a black dried seaweed cut into sheets. In Japan, other varieties of sushi are popular as well, especially *gomoku-chirashi*—ingredients mixed with rice—and *inari-zushi*—rice packed in small pouches made of thin-sliced, deep-fried tofu.

Perhaps as a holdover from the Edo-era days when nigiri-zushi was a fast food consumed at street stalls, many aficionados claim it tastes best eaten by hand. Nowadays, however, it is common—at conveyor-belt sushi bars, for instance—to pick up nigiri with chopsticks. Before you eat it, briefly dip the seafood topping in soy sauce (see p. 237). The green paste dabbed between the topping and the rice is grated wasabi, an indigenous root vegetable (often called "Japanese horseradish" in English) that is notorious for its powerful effect on the nasal passages. Wasabi is said to have antimicrobial properties, but if you don't like it, you can order your sushi without wasabi—"sabi-nuki." Sushi also comes with a side of sweet-and-sour flavored slices of pickled ginger (see p. 243).

Sushi chefs overseas often wear rubber or vinyl gloves. In Japan, they do not—at least not in authentic sushi establishments where a ten-year training regimen is the norm. According to the chefs, gloves interfere with the subtle sense of touch required to make fine sushi.

Vocabulary

wrapped in ... ｜…に巻かれた	dabbed ｜軽く塗られた
deep-fried ｜油で揚げた	notorious for ... ｜…で悪名高い、よく知られた
holdover ｜なごり、遺物	nasal passage ｜鼻の中
street stall ｜屋台、露天	antimicrobial ｜抗菌性の
conveyor-belt sushi bar ｜回転ずし屋	training regimen ｜修業法

世界をめぐるすし

日本に残るもっとも古いタイプのすしは、「なれずし」といって、魚を塩とごはんで乳酸発酵させてすっぱくしたものです。これは古代にアジア大陸から伝わった、魚の保存法が起源とされています。酢が普及してからは、現在のような酢飯のすしが発展しました。

にぎりの登場は意外に新しく、江戸末期のことで、当初は酢やしょうゆに漬けたり、加熱したりしたネタを使っていました。生魚のネタは、製氷が機械化した明治時代から普及し始め、冷蔵庫が普及してから一般的になりました。現在、人気の「回転ずし」は、1950年代に誕生しました。

かつて海外では、「日本人は生魚を食べる」と奇妙がられていたものですが、70年代アメリカで[※30]、スシ・バーがブームとなります。ネタをアボカドやカニかまに変え、のりをシャリの内側に巻き込んだ「カリフォルニア・ロール」は、この頃生まれました。今では世界各地の都市で、日本にない多彩な創作ずしが生まれています。

しかし、なかには日本人からみて、すしとは思えないsushiもあります。たとえば、酢めしでない飯を使っていたり……。2006年、日本政府が「海外日本食レストランの認証制度」を計画したときには、アメリカなどのメディアに「スシ・ポリス」がやってくるという記事が載り、その是非が論争となりました。この制度は結局、実施されていません。

一方、2010年には「全国すし商生活衛生同業組合連合会」が、生食を安全にあつかう技術を重視した、「すしアドバイザー」の認定制度を発足させています。

Notes

※30 日本で戦後に一般化した鉄板焼きも、60年代から海外の日本料理チェーンで普及している。

会席の焼物（型にこだわらないコース料理として）「伊勢えびと水なす白みそソース」
料理：小泉功二
Spiny lobster with eggplant and white miso sauce, a grilled dish for banquet-style
kaiseki with a contemporary twist. Chef: Koizumi Koji   Photo: Maekawa Akinori

懐石の八寸（木地の盆で、海のものと山のものが供される）   料理：柳原尚之（近茶流）
Hassun, a **cha-kaiseki** dish that presents "food from the sea and the land" on a square
wooden tray. Chef: Yanagihara Naoyuki   Photo: Kuma Masashi

『婦人画報』2012 年 7 月号より   From *Fujingaho* magazine (July 2012)

11

FASHION
ファッション

01 日本のファッション

日本の民族衣装として知られる**着物**は、今では、ほとんどの人が結婚式やお祭りなど、特別なときにだけ着るものとなっています。明治時代、日本政府は西洋列強と肩を並べようと、公的な服装の洋風化を推し進めたのです。そのとき男性は、**髷**（まげ）（P. 254 参照）を切ることが求められました。

私服はその後もしばらく着物が主流でしたが、第二次世界大戦後は、欧米のファッションが急速に流入・普及しました。

1960〜70 年代には、森英恵、山本寛斎などのデザイナーが、ニューヨークやパリのコレクションに参加し始めます。高田賢三の起こした「ケンゾー」ブランドは、世界の民俗衣装の要素を採り入れた、色鮮やかなスタイルで人気となりました。

やがて**三宅一生**、80 年代には**川久保玲**（コム デ ギャルソン）や**山本耀司**（ヨウジヤマモト、Y's）といった前衛的なデザイナーが、服の概念をくつがえす作品を打ち出して、世界のファッション界に衝撃を与えました。

当時は、日本の経済力がピークに達した時代で、日本人が「ルイ・ヴィトン」など海外の有名ブランド品を好んで買う傾向も、話題になりました。

90 年代頃から、若者たちのストリート・ファッション（P. 260 参照）が、海外のメディアで注目されるようになります。そして、「アンダーカバー」の高橋盾、「ア・ベイシング・エイプ」創設者の NIGO® といったストリート系のデザイナーが活躍し始めました。

一方、ノーブランドを打ち出す「無印良品（MUJI）」や、2000 年代からは廉価なファストファッション※1 の「ユニクロ」といったブランドも、海外展開を進めています。また近年は、世界的にエシカル・ファッション※2 への注目が高まっていますが、90 年代に活動を開始した、日本のフェアトレード※3・ブランド「ピープル・ツリー」はその草分けです。

Notes

※1 廉価なカジュアルウェアを、短期間で大量生産・販売するブランドや業態。　※2 エシカルの意味は「倫理的」。この場合、商品の製造や流通の仕方において、社会貢献や環境保全に留意したファッションを指す。　※3 おもに非工業国の生産者と、公正に取引（あるいは協働／支援）すること。

Comment

シンプルなデザインの MUJI は、海外ではよく **Zen** 的などといわれて、日本のイメージが強いようですね。日本ではむしろ、民族色を排したモダンなブランドと思われていますよ。
Muji's simple designs seem to be viewed as "**Zen**-like" and thus distinctively Japanese by consumers in other countries. Yet in Japan, people tend to think of it as a modern brand devoid of any native Japanese flavor!

⁰¹ Fashion in Japan

Legendarily Japan's definitive form of dress, the **kimono** is worn today mostly on special occasions, such as weddings and festivals. During the Meiji period (1868-1912) the Japanese government actively promoted the westernization of public attire as part of its campaign to make the country a peer in the eyes of the Western powers. It also called for men to cut off their *mage* topknots (see p. 255).

The kimono remained the norm in private wear for some time to come, but after World War II, Western fashions inundated Japan and became predominant.

In the 1960s and 1970s, designers like Mori Hanae and Yamamoto Kansai began participating in the New York and Paris collections. Takada Kenzo's brand, Kenzo, made a splash with its colorful blends of folk-dress elements from diverse cultures.

They were followed by such cutting-edge designers as **Miyake Issei** (Issey Miyake) and, in the 1980s, **Kawakubo Rei** (Comme des Garçons) and **Yamamoto Yohji** (Y's), all creators of clothes that upended conventional concepts of apparel and sent shockwaves through the world of fashion.

Around this same time, as the nation's economy reached its postwar peak, the Japanese acquired a reputation for indulging in purchases of goods by Louis Vuitton and other famous international brands.

With the 1990s came a growing interest by overseas media in the street fashions (see p. 261) of Japanese youth, as well as a rise to prominence of street-style designers like Takahashi Jun of Undercover and Nigo, founder of A Bathing Ape.

The 1990s also saw the "no-brand" brand Muji establish a foothold abroad, followed by the low-priced "fast-fashion" brand Uniqlo in the 2000s. People Tree, a fair-trade clothing brand launched in Tokyo in the 1990s, was a pioneer in the global ethical-fashion movement.

Vocabulary

legendarily｜伝説的に、よく知られているように	predominant｜広く行きわたっている
attire｜服装	upend ...｜…をくつがえす
make ... a peer｜…を匹敵させる、同等にする	conventional｜型にはまった、月並みな
call for 〜 to *do*｜〜に…することを要求する	a rise to prominence｜目立ち始めること
inundate ...｜…に殺到する	foothold｜足がかり、拠点

11

02 着物

着物は直訳すると「着る物」で、もともと衣類全般を指す言葉でした。今では、洋服が普及する前から日本で着られていたタイプの衣服が、着物と呼ばれています[4]。

着物は全身を覆うワンピースで、洋服のように立体的でなく、直線裁ちの布が接ぎ合わせてあります。前合わせで体に巻き付けるように着て[5]、ひもや布の帯だけで留めるのです。女性はたいてい幅の広い帯を、ウエストより高い位置に巻いて締めるので[6]、窮屈なようですが、着慣れた人は背筋が伸びて着心地がいいといいますよ。

襟もとにもポイントがあって、着物の下に着る長襦袢は、襟だけ見えるようにデザインされています。着物用の履物はどれもサンダル状で、木製のものを下駄、それ以外は草履[7]といいます。

伝統技法による手織りや手染めの絹の着物は、とても高価になっています。振袖といわれる未婚女性の晴れ着は、袖が1メートルほどもあり、全身で1枚の絵となるような絵柄が描かれています。また、華やかな帯の結び方も見せどころです。成人式や正月に着ることが多いのですが、一人で着られる人はほとんどいなくて、プロに頼んで着付けてもらいます。最近では、プリント地の着物やワンタッチの帯も増えていますね。

男性や既婚女性が着る礼服は、黒地で家紋が5カ所に入っています。男性はその上に、袴という太いズボンのようなもの[8]と、羽織という上着を着る。着物のなかで、もっともカジュアルに着られているのが夏の浴衣です。もともと素肌に1枚だけ着る綿や麻の着物で、花火大会や夏祭りのファッションとして親しまれています。旅館やホテルには、外出着でなく、湯上りや寝間着用の浴衣がよく置いてあります。

Notes

※4　一説によると、西洋では16世紀頃から日本の服装がキモノと呼ばれていた。西洋で、キモノはおもに部屋着として、ガウンのように着られてきた。　※5　前合わせで体に巻き付ける衣服は、東アジア全般にみられる。　※6　現在、女子の最高の衣装と考えられている十二単（じゅうにひとえ）には、このような帯はない。十二単は平安時代の高位女官の奉仕姿を指す、後世の俗称。当時、着る枚数は12枚とは限らなかった。　※7　皮、布、ビニール、イグサ、藁（わら）等が材料。　※8　行燈（あんどん）型というスカートのような型もある。

⁰² **Kimono**

A literal translation of *kimono* is "thing to wear," and indeed the word originally referred to clothes in general. Nowadays people use it for the type of clothing worn in Japan before Western attire became popular.

The kimono is a single piece of fabric that covers the entire body. Unlike more three-dimensional Western clothing, it consists of several pieces of straight-cut cloth sewn together. The wearer folds the kimono over itself in front and secures it with cords and a cloth sash called an *obi*. Women wear relatively broad sashes wound above the waist. Though the obi may appear tight and confining, wearers accustomed to them say that they support the spine and are quite comfortable!

The collar is a major focal point of the kimono, and the undergarment worn beneath it is designed to be visible only at the collar. The footwear accompanying kimono is always of the thonged sandal type—either *geta* wooden clogs, or *zori* sandals of other materials.

Silk kimono hand-woven and hand-dyed by traditional methods fetch extremely high prices. The festive *furisode* kimono worn by young unmarried women boast sleeves that may dangle down a meter or more, patterns that cover the entire fabric with a single picture, and colorful, elaborately tied obi. Kimono of this sort are frequently worn to coming-of-age ceremonies (at age 20) or during the New Year holiday. Few Japanese today are capable of putting on a full-dress kimono by themselves, so they must hire a professional kimono dresser for the occasion. Lately one sees more people wearing printed-pattern kimono and clip-on obi.

Formal kimono worn by men or married women typically display the family crest in five specific places against a black background. Men wear a *hakama* and a *haori*—a pair of loose pleated trousers and a half-coat—over the kimono.

The most casual version of the kimono is the summer-weight *yukata*. A thin robe made of cotton or hemp, the yukata is a trendy fashion item now, particularly for attending fireworks shows and other summer festivals. Hotels and traditional inns also provide guests with yukata to be worn after a bath.

11

Vocabulary

three-dimensional ｜立体的な、三次元の	**undergarment** ｜肌着［ここでは長襦袢］
fold ｜巻き付ける、まとう	**thonged sandal** ｜緒の付いたサンダル
broad ｜幅の広い	**dangle down** ｜ぶら下がる
wound ｜巻いた［原形は wind］	**clip-on** ｜クリップで留める＝ワンタッチの
collar ｜襟	**family crest** ｜家紋

03 扇子

扇子は古代の日本で発明されたといわれ、平安時代の遺物が現存しています。骨組みは竹や木製で、通常、その上に紙が貼られています。閉じてある扇子を開くときは、留めてある側を持って、親指でずらすように押します。扇子はあおいで涼を取るために使うだけでなく、冠婚葬祭などにおける儀礼的な持ち物にもなっています。また、**能**や日本舞踊（P. 124 参照）、**歌舞伎**、**落語**といった伝統芸能で、重要な小道具として使われています。

04 日本髪から茶髪へ

時代劇でみられるように、江戸時代の男性は、髷を結って額を剃りあげる髪型をしていました。髷の形は、身分や職業によって細かく分けられていました。また、その時代は女性たちも、凝った髪の結い方をしていました。ヨーロッパの宮廷で、高く盛り上げたカツラが流行ったのと時期が重なりますが、日本では自分の髪で結い、300 種類以上ともいわれるスタイルが出来ました。現在では、着物にも洋髪を合わせることがほとんどで、髷の男性は**相撲取り**だけ。時代劇のような女性の結髪は「日本髪」と呼ばれるようになり、**芸者**か一般の人では結婚式のときくらいしか、結わなくなりました。かつて日本では 1000 年近く、女性の髪は長い黒髪が美しいとされてきました。20 世紀後半になって、西洋のような明るい髪に憧れる美意識が生まれ、90 年代頃から男女ともに、髪を茶色などに染める人が増えました。

Comment

日本の美容院では外国にはないサービスがあって、よく珍しがられます。髪を切った後に肩を揉んでくれたり、顔をふく蒸しタオルを渡されたりするんですよ。
Japanese beauty salons offer some services evidently not found at their counterparts abroad. Among those that overseas visitors seem to find surprising are post-haircut shoulder massages, and hot towels for your face.

11

和装の結婚式
Wedding ceremony in kimono, 2014. The bride wears a Nihongami coiffure.
Photo: Muto Naomi

⁰³ Folding Fans

The *sensu*, a hand-held folding fan, was invented in ancient Japan, and Heian-era (794-1185) specimens still survive. The standard construction has paper stretched over a frame of bamboo or wooden ribs. To open a sensu, you grasp the closed end and push it open with your thumb.

The sensu is not only a tool for generating a cooling breeze, but an accessory for weddings, funerals, and other formal occasions. It is also an indispensable prop in such traditional performing arts as **Noh**, Nihon Buyo (see p. 125), **Kabuki**, and **Rakugo**.

Vocabulary

specimen｜見本、実例	indispensable｜欠くことができない、必須の
thumb｜親指	prop｜小道具
generate ...｜…を生む、発生させる	

⁰⁴ From Black Hair to Brown

As you can see in any samurai drama (see p. 209), men of the Edo period (1603-1868) shaved their foreheads and tied their hair up in a topknot, or *mage*. The style of the topknot varied with one's status and occupation.

Women of that same era wore their hair up in some very elaborate styles. Around the time that extravagantly tall wigs were in vogue with court ladies in Europe, Japanese women were getting their own hair arranged in over 300 (according to some accounts) different styles.

These days Western hairstyles predominate, even with wearers of traditional kimono. As for the topknot, it is seen only on **sumo** wrestlers. The term *Nihongami* (Japanese-style hair) now refers to the coiffures on women in period dramas; in the real world you are likely to see them only on **geisha**, or brides at weddings.

For nearly a millennium, long black hair was considered a benchmark for feminine beauty in Japan. But the latter half of the 20th century saw preferences shift toward the "brighter" hair colors associated with Westerners, and since the 1990s both men and women sporting dyed brown—or even blond—hair have become a common sight.

Vocabulary

extravagantly｜途方もなく	benchmark｜基準
account｜報告、記述	preferences shift｜好みが変化する
predominate｜優勢である、主流である	sporting｜誇示している、（見せびらかすために）
coiffure｜髪型［フランス語］	身に付けている

11

「日本ファッション」の衝撃
——三宅一生、川久保玲、山本耀司

70年代から「一枚の布」というコンセプトを打ち出している三宅一生は、布という素材の特質を原点から見直して、新しい布のまとい方を提案しつづけてきました。そして彼の登場で、現代ファッションは初めて、アートの文脈で語られるようになりました。

また彼は、日本の伝統的な職人技を尊重するとともに、繊維加工などの先端技術[9]を、早くから採り入れてきました。代表作「プリーツ・プリーズ」シリーズは、プリーツ加工の施された、とても軽い布でできています。その服は、小さく丸めて旅行鞄に入れてもプリーツがくずれないし、着る人の体型を選ばず、自在に伸び縮みするのです。

2007年には三宅の呼びかけで、東京にデザインの企画や提案を行うミュージアム「21_21 DESIGN SIGHT」が、開設されました。

川久保玲と山本耀司（写真 P. 266）はかつて恋人同士で、80年代パリで発表し始めた作品に通じるものがあったため、一緒に語られることが多い二人です。彼らは当時の黒色ブームの立役者と目されていて、それまで「死」や「闇」のイメージが強かった黒が、以降ファッションの基本色になりました。またその服は、布に穴を空けたり、破ったりの加工で、「ボロルック」といわれましたが、ゆったりしたシルエットは独特で、洗練されていました。彼らの服は、当時の自立した女性像の象徴でした。

山本耀司[10]は服作りを、「後ろ姿」から構想するといいます。90年代にはオペラ、2000年代には北野武監督映画の、衣裳デザインも手がけました。

川久保玲の近況としては、イギリスSPEEDO社の競泳用水着「レーザーレーサー」をデザインしています。そして2014年のパリ・コレクションでは、世界の時勢に呼応して、「反戦——でも静かに、無言で」[11]というテーマを掲げました。

Notes

※9 日本のハイテク繊維の開発力は、世界的に評価が高い。　※10 2009年には会社が経営破綻したが、投資を受け、新会社で事業を継続。このニュースで山本耀司の文化貢献度に注目が集まった。　※11 2015年春夏コム デ ギャルソン オム プリュスのコレクション。

The Impact of Japanese Fashion: Issey Miyake, Comme des Garçons, Yohji Yamamoto

Issey Miyake, as Miyake Issei is known overseas, introduced his "one piece of cloth" concept in the 1970s; since then he has continued to come up with new ways of wearing fabric that rethink the characteristics of cloth from the ground up. With Miyake's creations, fashion began to make an appearance in contemporary art contexts.

Miyake pays high regard to traditional Japanese craftsmanship, yet he has also pioneered the use of state-of-the-art fabric processing technology. His renowned Pleats Please series offers lightweight pleated garments that can be rolled up in a travel bag without losing their pleats, and will readily stretch or contract to fit any physique.

21_21 DESIGN SIGHT, a museum devoted to design projects and concepts that was a brainchild of Miyake, opened in Tokyo in 2007.

Perhaps because they were once romantic partners and are both known for the fashions they presented in Paris in the 1980s, Rei Kawakubo and Yohji Yamamoto (image on p. 266) often get mentioned in the same breath. Both were much enamored of the color black, which, thanks in no small part to their efforts, shed its connotations of death and darkness to become the go-to color of modern fashion. They are also associated with a style in which the fabric has been ripped or had holes poked in it, earning it the label "*boro* (ragged) look." Kawakubo's and Yamamoto's clothes were hailed for their loose-fitting yet undeniably sophisticated silhouette, and came to be identified with the image of independent women of the day.

Regarding his approach to clothing design, Yamamoto has famously declared that "a beautiful back makes a beautiful front." He has also been active as a costume designer—for opera productions in the 1990s, and for the films of director **Kitano Takeshi** during the 2000s.

Kawakubo recently made news as the designer of the LZR Racer line of competitive swimwear for Britain's Speedo. And in her 2014 Paris Fashion Week presentation, she responded to world events with a theme she described as "anti-war—but in a quiet way, with no words."

Vocabulary

pay high regard to ... | …を大いに尊重する	be enamored of ... | …に夢中になる
craftsmanship | 職人の技	shed ... | (幻想など) を捨てる［過去形も同形］
state-of-the-art | 最先端の、最新の	connotation | 含意、含み
lightweight | 軽い	be ripped | 破れる
brainchild | 発案、考え	be hailed for ... | …で称えられる
in the same breath | 同時に	undeniably | まぎれもなく、申し分なく

06 コシノ三姉妹と小篠綾子

コシノヒロコ、コシノジュンコ、コシノミチコの三姉妹は、70年代以降、そろって世界的なファッション・デザイナーとなったことで知られています。

また、三姉妹を育てた母親の綾子は、1930年代から洋服をデザインして仕立てる洋装店を経営していましたが、1988年、74歳にして「コシノ・アヤコ」ブランド[※12]を設立。92歳で没するまで、デザイナーを続けました。2011年には、その草分け的なキャリアと人生がテレビドラマ化されて、好評を博しました。

Notes

※12 60〜70歳代に向けたファッションを主軸に展開した。

07 カワイイ

「カワイイ」はもともと cute、adorable、sweet などと訳される言葉ですが、その意味は広がっています。おそらく80年代頃から、日本の女の子たちは、なにかとカワイイという言葉を使うようになりました。

たとえば、キティちゃんやピンクのフリルなど、小さいものや弱々しいものに対してカワイイというだけでなく、毒のあるものやグロテスクなものでも、感覚的に共鳴すればカワイイといいます。また高齢者や権威ある人についても、その主義主張は無視しつつ、親しみのもてる仕草やちょっとした失敗などに反応して、カワイイと言ったりします。

この傾向を、他人の庇護を得ようとする幼児性のアピールだとか、逆に成熟や既成概念を拒否する少女たちの、ひかえめな反抗だと指摘する人もいます。しかし、今では大人の女性も、気軽にカワイイと口にしますね。

そして最近は、海外の日本好きの間でも、kawaii という日本語が浸透してきました。彼らの kawaii は、「ポップで日本っぽくて、超キュート」といった意味合いで使われているようです。

Comment

最近、人気があるモデルで歌手の「きゃりーぱみゅぱみゅ」は、増田セバスチャンというアート・ディレクターがデザインした、カラフルでデコラティブな「カワイイ」ファッションを着ています。
Recently, the model-turned-singer Kyari Pamyu Pamyu has been wearing colorful, decorative "kawaii" fashions designed by art director Sebastian Masuda.

⁰⁶ The Koshinos

Three sisters, Koshino Hiroko, Junko, and Michiko, made news with their successive emergence as world-class fashion designers in the 1970s and 1980s. Their mother Ayako, who had run a dressmaker's shop designing and making Western clothing since the 1930s, launched her own brand, Koshino Ayako, in 1988 at the age of 74. She continued to work as a designer until her death at 92, and in 2011 a TV drama based on her life and pioneering career won plaudits.

Vocabulary

successive emergence ｜次々と頭角を現すこと	**win plaudits** ｜拍手喝采される［通例複数形］
launch ... ｜…を始める	

⁰⁷ Kawaii

Normally translated as "cute, adorable, sweet," *kawaii* is a term whose meaning has expanded of late. It was probably sometime in the 1980s that Japanese girls began describing all sorts of things as kawaii. They would apply the word not only to small, delicate-looking objects—**Hello Kitty**, pink frills, and so on—but to anything that struck their fancy on a sensory level, even the toxic or grotesque. They would also use kawaii as a comment on endearingly approachable or foolish behavior by the elderly or those in positions of authority, blithely ignoring what the individual was saying or stood for.

People have explained this habit as a juvenile attempt to appeal to others' protective impulses, or, conversely, as a low-key expression of rebellion by young girls against grown-up or established conventions. Nowadays, though, even adult women label things kawaii without a second thought.

In recent years the word has caught on among Japanophiles overseas. For them, kawaii appears to mean something that is extremely cute in a poppish, Japanese-y way.

(sidebar) FASHION / The Koshinos / Kawaii

11

Vocabulary

expand ｜広がる、拡大する	**impulse** ｜衝動、一時的な感情
of late ｜最近、近ごろ	**low-key** ｜ひかえめな
on a sensory level ｜感覚レベルで	**rebellion** ｜反抗、抵抗
toxic ｜毒がある	**without a second thought** ｜何のためらいもなく
endearingly ｜愛情をこめて	**Japanophile** ｜親日家、日本好き
blithely ｜平気で	**decorative** ｜装飾的な［英語には、日本のスラング「デコ」のような装飾過剰なイメージはない］
stand for ... ｜…を支持する	
juvenile ｜子どもじみた	

08 ハローキティ

「ハローキティ」は、リボンをつけた白い子猫の姿のキャラクターです。サンリオという会社が企画販売する、キャラクター・グッズに使われています。1970年代に登場した時は、少女向け商品だけでしたが、今では大人にも人気。ライセンス・ビジネスもさかんになり、同社によると100を優に越す数の国々で、小物やアクセサリーはもとより、介護用品や飛行機にいたるまで、年間5万種類ほどのキティグッズが展開されているそうです。レディー・ガガ、ブリトニー・スピアーズなど、キティファンを公言する著名人もたくさんいます。

キティは擬人化されていますが、無表情で口がありません。だからファンは、キティの気持ちを好きなように解釈できるのでしょう。また、キティをモチーフに美術作品を発表しているアーティストのトム・サックスは、「ハローキティは何も象徴していないアイコンだ」と語っています。

Comment

一時、キティは猫じゃなくて、「女の子」だって報道されて、騒ぎになってたね。結局どっちなのかは、曖昧みたいだけど……。

There was quite a commotion a while back when a news report came out that Kitty was not supposed to be a cat but a "little girl." It's still not clear exactly what she is...

09 少女たちのファッション ——ギャル、ロリータ、ゴスロリ

日本の若者のなかでも、派手なファッションとあっけらかんとした振る舞いで、1990～2000年代をピークに一大文化を形成したのが、「ギャル」（英語のgalからの借用語）と呼ばれる、10代の少女たちです。海外でも物珍しがられて、よく報道されましたね。

ギャル・メイクは一時、極端すぎる日焼けが話題になりましたが、やがて白い肌に移行。カラーコンタクトやつけまつげで目を強調し、髪を明るく染め、ネイルや携帯に、デコ・パーツをたくさん付けるのも典型です。しかし最近は、ひと目でそれとわかるファッションが下火になってきたので、ギャルを見たい観光客はがっかりするかもしれません。

また、日本の「ロリータ・ファッション」も、海外の人たちに注目されていますね。フリルやレースをたっぷり付けて、スカートをふくらませた、おとぎ話の少女のようなスタイルです。ロココなど前近代ヨーロッパのドレスに対する憧れを、形にしたものだと考えられます。

→

08 Hello Kitty

"Hello Kitty" is the name of a beribboned white kitten-like character seen on goods designed and sold by the Sanrio company. When they first appeared in the 1970s, Hello Kitty products had a target market of little girls, but today they enjoy the adoration of adults as well. Sanrio, which does a thriving licensing business, says that 50,000 different "Kitty Goods"—from accessories and other small items to nursing products and even airplanes—are sold each year in over 100 countries. Not a few celebrities, among them Lady Gaga and Britney Spears, have publicly declared themselves to be fans of Kitty.

Though Kitty is an anthropomorphic character, the iconic creature has no mouth and hence no facial expression. The idea is that fans can read any emotion into Kitty that they like. Or perhaps, to quote Tom Sachs, an American artist who has used Kitty as a motif in his work, "Hello Kitty is an icon that doesn't stand for anything at all."

Vocabulary

beribboned｜リボンで飾った	**anthropomorphic**｜擬人化された
thriving｜さかんな、繁盛している	**hence**｜だから、それゆえ

09 Girls' Fashions: Gyaru, Lolita, GothLoli

With their wacky fashions and carefree behavior, the teenage girls referred to as *gyaru* (from the English "gal") once formed a conspicuous youth subculture in Japan, peaking in the 1990s and 2000s. They were also an object of curiosity abroad, where they received quite a bit of media coverage.

Gyaru makeup was known at one time for its ultra-tanned look, but later white makeup became the norm. Adding to the look are colored contact lenses, false eyelashes, brightly dyed hair, and an abundance of "deco parts"—tiny decorative objects—glued to fingernails and cell phones. Nowadays, though, it's getting hard to find obvious examples of gyaru fashion on the streets—to the disappointment, one supposes, of gyaru-seeking tourists.

Another style favored by young Japanese women that has raised eyebrows overseas is Lolita fashion, which features lots of frills and lace, ballooning skirts, and other elements that make the wearer resemble a young girl in a fairy tale. The inspiration seems to be Rococo- or Victorian-era European clothing. Though the name derives from the seductive young heroine of Vladimir Nabokov's novel *Lolita*, if

➔

語源は魅惑的な少女を主人公とした、ナボコフの小説『ロリータ』ですが、日本のロリータ少女たちは、むしろ性的なイメージを忌避し、無垢な少女趣味を志向します。だから、男性の嗜好に応える「メイド服」（P. 158 参照）とは、混同されたくないといいます。2004 年の人気映画『下妻物語』は、このロリータと、「ヤンキー」と呼ばれる強面の不良（一昔前の）という、タイプの異なる少女二人の友情物語でした。

ロリータの派生ジャンルに、「ゴシック・ロリータ」（ゴスロリ）があります。「ゴシック」はもともと欧米にあったファッションで、「ゴシック小説」に出てくるドラキュラや魔女などをイメージした、黒っぽいスタイル[13]。ロリータにそのゴシックのテイストを合わせた、黒いけれど**カワイイ**ドレスが、日本発のゴスロリです。

Notes

[13] ゴシック・ファッションは、中世のゴシック建築等とは直接関係ない。ゴシック小説とは、18 世紀末〜19 世紀に流行った中世趣味の怪奇小説のこと。

ロリータの少女
Lolita girl, 2014
Photo: Miura Fumiko
Model: Tao Aya

10 制服

日本では 20 世紀前半に、セーラー服が女子の学校制服として定着しました。学園ものの映画やアニメを観ると、よく出てくるでしょう？　そこで描かれるセーラー服は、少女たちの若さや清純さだけでなく、ギャップとしての「反抗」や「色気」をも表現するアイテムになっています。

たとえば、1981 年の大ヒット映画『セーラー服と機関銃』では、女子高生

←

anything Japan's Lolitas eschew a sexual image in favor of that of an innocent maiden. Consequently they do not like to be confused with the "maid look" (see p. 159), which caters more obviously to male fantasies.

The popular 2004 film *Kamikaze Girls* tells a story of friendship between two young women who belong to oppositely-styled subcultures—one is a Lolita, the other a Yankii (a tough juvenile-delinquent look no longer much in fashion).

One offshoot of Lolita fashion is Gothic Lolita, or GothLoli for short. The black-heavy Gothic style originated in the West with images of vampires and witches from so-called Gothic novels. GothLoli is a Japanese invention that adds a touch of the Goth to Lolita with clothing that is black, yet **kawaii**.

Vocabulary

wacky | 奇抜な、風変わりな	**if anything** | むしろ
carefree | 屈託のない、のんきな	**cater to ...** | …の要求を満たす
ultra-tanned | 非常に日焼けした	**juvenile-delinquent** | 不良少女（少年）
raise eyebrows | 人を驚かせる	**offshoot** | 派生物

¹⁰ Schoolgirl Uniforms

The sailor outfit (a middy blouse and skirt) became the standard uniform for Japanese schoolgirls in the early part of the 20th century. You've no doubt seen them in films and anime set in schools. The sailor suit as depicted in those media is not merely a symbol of youth and innocence, but conversely suggests rebellion and even sex appeal.

The 1981 film *Sailor Suit and Machine Gun*, a major hit, features an unlikely heroine, a high-school girl who is also the head of a **yakuza** gang. One scene has her dressed in a sailor outfit while she sprays machine-gun bullets at random.

Japanese schoolgirls make numerous adjustments to their uniforms. At one time, skirts extended down to the ankles were a hallmark of delinquent girls. These days the miniskirted schoolgirl is a more typical sight.

During the 1980s and 1990s, a growing number of high schools switched to blazer-style suits. (For male students the standard outfit had been a stiff-collared black military-style uniform.)

Today schoolgirl suits are an icon of Japanese fashion, and even constitute their own category. Recent years have seen the appearance of "fake uniforms"—outfits picked out and purchased on their own by students and worn as a personal statement after school, or at schools

→

11

← のヤクザ組長というありえない設定の主人公が、敵対する組との抗争に向かい、セーラー服姿で機関銃を乱射するシーンがありました。

少女たちは、よく制服をアレンジして着ます。かつては、セーラー服のスカートを足首までの長さに伸ばすのが、不良少女の象徴でした。今ではむしろ、ミニスカートにする女子が多いですね。

80～90年代にかけて、日本の高校では、制服をブレザーに切り替える学校が増えました（男子は黒の詰襟が主流でした）。

近年、少女たちの制服は、日本のファッションのひとつの象徴、あるいはジャンルとなりました。数年前からは、「なんちゃって制服」も出ています――これはつまり、下校した後や、制服のない高校の生徒でも、自分で買った好きな制服ブランドの服を、私服として着るのです。

11 藍染めとジーンズ

藍染め[14]は古代から世界各地にありますが、19世紀の日本では、藍染めした木綿の衣服が広く普及していました。来日したあるイギリス人の化学者が、藍色を「ジャパン・ブルー」と呼んだほどです。藍で染めると布は強度が増し、防虫、殺菌などの効果もあるのです。

日本にはほかにも、繊細かつ多彩な色合いを持つ草木染めがありましたが、化学染料が発達した今では、わずかに継承されるのみとなっています。とはいえアートやエコロジーの文脈から、草木染めを見直す動きもあり、こと藍染めに関しては、高級ジーンズなど、新しいファッションへの展開が目立ちますね。

現代の日本で、ジーンズはカジュアルウェアというだけでなく、ファッション・アイテムとして定着しています。

国産ジーンズのブランドには、アメリカのヴィンテージ・ジーンズの技術を継承しつつ、日本なりに発展させた高級ジーンズを展開しているところがいくつかあって、その品質は、90年代頃から世界のジーンズ・ファンをうならせるようになりました。こうした日本のジーンズには、天然藍で染めたものもあるのです。

Notes

※14 染料に使う草は地域によって異なる。たとえばインドではインド藍（インディゴという色名の語源）、日本では中国から伝わったタデ藍が普及。沖縄では琉球藍。

←
that have no official uniform.

Vocabulary

outfit｜（ひと揃いの）服装	hallmark｜特徴
conversely｜反対に、逆に	stiff-collared｜かたい襟の［詰襟のこと］

¹¹ Indigo Dyeing and Jeans

Indigo dyeing has been practiced throughout the world since ancient times. By the 19th century, indigo-dyed cotton clothing had become prevalent in Japan—so much so that a visiting British chemist dubbed the color "Japan blue." Dyeing fabric with indigo makes it stronger and more resistant to insects, as well as killing bacteria.

Japan boasts other vegetable dyes that offer a diversity of subtle hues. Although their use has declined with the advent of chemical dyes, lately they have attracted renewed interest for artistic and environmental reasons. Indigo stands out for its appeal in the context of current fashion, and top-of-the-line blue jeans in particular.

Jeans in Japan today are not merely casual wear, but an enduring fashion item. Since the 1990s, certain Japanese brands have earned a reputation among jeans fans worldwide for their quality, adding their own special improvements to vintage American jeans technology. Natural indigo is used to dye some of these high-class Japanese jeans.

Vocabulary

prevalent｜広く行き渡った	advent｜出現、到来
resistant to ...｜…に耐性がある	top-of-the-line｜最高級の
boast ...｜…をもっている、誇る	enduring｜不朽の、長続きする
subtle hue｜繊細な色彩	

桃太郎 JEANS の『金丹』レーベルでは、経糸を天然藍で手染めするという。
The warp threads for Momotaro jeans (Kintan label) are hand-dyed with natural indigo.
Photo courtesy of Aibatake indigo-dye works

ヨウジヤマモトのドレス、1999 年春夏「ウェデ
ィング」コレクションより
Yohji Yamamoto's dress from the "Wedding"
collection, Spring-Summer 1999
Photo: William Palmer

12

ARCHITECTURE

建築

01 日本の建築とくらし

建築デザインは、日本がとびぬけて創造性を発揮している分野。世界各地の革新的なプロジェクトで活躍する建築家を、数多く輩出してきました（P. 278 参照）。

要因としては、近代以降、日本の伝統的な木造建築の原理が、国際的な建築デザインの方向性とうまくリンクできたせいかもしれません。たとえば桂離宮のような、屋外環境を取り込んだ空間のつくり方は、鉄やコンクリートを使った建築にも生かすことができます。

また、日本には腕のいい大工がいるおかげで、繊細なデザインが実現しやすいと、建築家たちは口をそろえます。

補足すると「建築家」[※1] は、近代になって西洋から日本に輸入された職業で、建物──特に芸術的な建物──の設計を担当します。施工は昔からの大工や、近代的な建設会社の仕事です。また、大工の棟梁や建設会社が、それぞれ伝統的な木造建築や、コンクリートのビルなどの、設計から施工までを一手に受けることもあります。

神社・仏閣の建造や補修をする「宮大工」は、卓越した木造技術で尊敬を集めていますが、希少になりつつあります。7世紀後半頃に建てられた奈良の法隆寺は、宮大工たちが補修を繰り返して、世界最古の木造建築となりました。

一方で日本の建物の大半は、数十年の利用を前提に、大量生産の建材で建てられています。

新旧の雑多なスタイルの建物が入り混じる、日本の都市風景は、刺激的なおもしろさを感じさせるかもしれません。それでも、20世紀後半以降の、土地利用の仕方やライフスタイル──都市の拡大と環境破壊、長期の住宅ローン返済など──は、問題が目立ってきています。

2011年の大震災と原発事故が契機となり、建築のありようを考える上でも、こうした根本的な課題へのアプローチを重視する声が高まっています（P. 286 参照）。

Notes

※1　日本において「建築士」は国家資格を取得した設計・工事監理の技術者を指すのに対し、「建築家」に資格制度はなく、定義は曖昧。

01 Japanese Buildings and Lifestyles

In the field of architectural design, Japan has demonstrated a creative flair that is second to none. Architects from this country have made their mark with innovative projects in many parts of the world (see p. 279).

One reason for this success may be that traditional Japanese principles of wooden building construction resonate with the direction taken by international architectural design in the modern era. Steel and concrete lend themselves well to the creation of spaces that interact with the outside environment, as exemplified by the **Katsura Imperial Villa**.

Architects are also in agreement that the presence of carpenters capable of exquisite craftsmanship makes it easier to bring demanding designs to fruition in Japan.

We should note that the job description of an architect—someone who designs structures, especially those with a monumental or artistic bent—is a modern import to Japan from the West. Building construction has long been the purview of carpenters or, in more recent times, construction companies. But a master carpenter (typically in the case of traditional wooden structures) or a contractor (for more modern buildings) may also handle the entire process from design on.

Miya-daiku—carpenters who specialize in building and repairing temples and shrines—are venerated for their superb skills with wood, but they are dwindling in number. Thanks to the repairs made by miya-daiku over the centuries, the Horyuji temple in Nara, built sometime around the late seventh century, endures today as the world's oldest wooden structure.

In fact, most Japanese buildings are made of mass-produced materials with the assumption that they will be used for a few decades at most. A typical Japanese cityscape, with its chaotic mix of old and new architectural styles, might look fascinating and fun. But since the latter half of the 20th century, Japan's land use policies and lifestyles have sparked serious concerns about such problems as urban growth, environmental destruction, and long-term housing debt. The devastating earthquake, tsunami, and nuclear accident of 2011 prompted discussions of the need for new approaches to architecture that address these fundamental issues (see p. 287).

12

Vocabulary

flair｜能力、才能
resonate with ...｜…と共鳴する
lend *oneself* to ...｜…に向いている
interact with ...｜…と影響し合う
bring ... to fruition｜…を実現させる

bent｜傾向、偏り
purview｜（仕事の）範囲
be venerated for ...｜…で尊敬される
dwindle in number｜次第に数が減る
spark ...｜…を引き起こす、…の引き金となる

⁰² 桂離宮とモダニズム

日本を代表する名建築・桂離宮^{※2}は、17世紀、京都の月の名所だった桂に、宮家の別荘として建てられました。雑木林に囲まれた**庭園**と織りなすように、開放的な木造建築が点在しています。御殿から池に面して突き出た竹製のベランダでは、木立の上にかかる月と、水面に映る月影がながめられます^{※3}。1930年代以降、桂離宮はブルーノ・タウト^{※4}などの建築家たちに称賛されて、世界的に知られるようになりました。やがて、その象徴する日本建築のシンプルな構成美——例えば、柱・梁などタテヨコ線のバランス、庭と屋内が一体化した空間、無駄な装飾の排除など——は、当時のモダニズム建築^{※5}の理論に通じる、普遍的なものだという説が広まりました。

しかし最近では評価のポイントが変わってきて、桂離宮の装飾的な要素が見直されたり、海外の人に愛される理由として、西洋的デザイン手法の影響——黄金分割や遠近法^{※6}など——が指摘されたりしています。

日本の簡素美の例とされるもうひとつの建築に、伊勢神宮があります。**神道**の最高位の神社ですが、その白木造りの社殿は、20年ごとに壊されて、新たに建て直されています。7世紀後半に、起源がさかのぼれるといわれているしきたりです。

また、日本の伝統建築はすべてがシンプルというわけではなく、きらびやかなものもあります。たとえば17世紀建造の日光東照宮は、今も極彩色のレリーフで彩られています。

Notes

※2 現在は宮内庁の管理で、申し込みによって見学できる。　※3 日本における月見の習慣の起源は不明だが、仲秋の十五夜の祭事は中国から伝わったとされている。　※4 ドイツから日本に亡命し、『日本美の再発見』などを著した建築家（1880～1938）。　※5 現在、世界中で主流の「鉄とガラスとコンクリートで作られたツルツルピカピカした箱のような建物」（藤森照信『日本の近代建築』より）。　※6 遠くに小さいものを配するなど、目の錯覚を利用して、距離感を強調する技法。

Comment

日本では、**わびさび**的な価値観の影響か、かつてはカラフルだったお寺などの伝統建築も、色落ちしたままに修復を留めている場合が多いですね。
Many once-colorful temples and other old buildings have been allowed to fade over time in Japan—perhaps due to the influence of the **wabi-sabi** values of antiquity and simplicity.

建築／桂離宮とモダニズム

12

[02] Modernism and the Katsura Imperial Villa

The Katsura Imperial Villa is one of Japan's most revered works of architecture. It was built during the 17th century in Katsura, a popular moon-viewing spot on the outskirts of Kyoto, to serve as a retreat for a branch of the imperial family. The estate's wooden structures are arranged about the grounds in an open configuration that blends with the **garden**, which is surrounded by woods. The bamboo veranda that extends from the main building toward the pond is an ideal vantage point from which to gaze at the moon over the trees and its reflection on the water.

The villa acquired an international reputation after architects like Bruno Taut began singing its praises in the 1930s. In time the Japanese architectural aesthetic of beauty in simplicity that it represents—such elements as the vertical/horizontal balance of pillars and beams, the unity of gardens and interior spaces, and the absence of superfluous ornamentation—came to be viewed by many as universal qualities that coincide with the theories of modernist architecture.

Lately, however, the decorative aspects of the villa have undergone a reappraisal, and the influence of such Western design techniques as perspective and the golden ratio has been cited as a reason for its popularity with non-Japanese.

Another structure frequently mentioned as embodying an aesthetic of simplicity is Ise Jingu, Japan's highest-ranking **Shinto** shrine. It has been a tradition to tear down and rebuild Ise's unvarnished wooden buildings every 20 years, a practice said to date back to the late seventh century.

Not all of Japan's traditional architecture is simple and plain. The Nikko Toshogu shrine, built in the 17th century, retains its ornate, brightly colored reliefs even today.

Vocabulary

on the outskirts of … ｜ …のはずれに	beam ｜ 梁
serve as … ｜ …として役立つ	superfluous ｜ 余計な、不要な
retreat ｜ 別荘	ornamentation ｜ 装飾
open configuration ｜ 開放的な配置	coincide with … ｜ …と一致する
vantage point ｜ 見晴らしの良い場所	unvarnished ｜ ニス等の仕上げ剤を塗っていない

12

⁰³ 日本庭園

日本の伝統的な庭園は、いわば理想郷の縮小版として発展しました。たとえば中国の伝説にある不老不死の蓬萊島や**仏教浄土**^{※7}、あるいは現実の景勝地などを、庭が象徴しているのです^{※8}。

庭園の形式はいくつかに分けられ、「池泉回遊式」といえば、海にみたてた池を中心に、緑のなかを散策できる庭園のことです。園内には起伏があって、くねった道が多く、あちこちに置かれた岩は、山や島などを表しています。岩は古来、畏怖の対象だったためか、自然のままの形が生かされています。

盆栽のように剪定された、樹や苔も生きた構成要素です。イギリス式庭園のようにカラフルな草花の花壇はあまり作らず、樹に咲く花や、秋の紅葉が季節を感じさせます。

池に流れ込むせせらぎや滝は、心地よい水音を奏でます。遠くの山などが、うまく景色に取り入れられているのは、「借景」という手法です。

日本庭園は、古代に影響を受けた中国庭園とよく混同されますが、現存している中国の伝統的な庭園は、壁で仕切ったり、巨大な奇岩があったりして、もっとドラマチックに設計されているようです。日本の回遊式庭園では、歩くにつれて木々の間から、別の風景が見え隠れするといった、なだらかな場面展開がよくみられます。

日本にはまた、池など水を使わない「枯山水」という独特の庭園形式があります（写真 P. 182）。岩の回りの白砂利に、ほうき目で水のような模様が付けられた庭を、写真などでご覧になったことはありませんか?

枯山水は、坐禅しながら眺める禅寺の庭として発展しました。近代になると、抽象的なアートとしても鑑賞されるようになり、モダンな枯山水が登場しました。

一方、回遊式庭園では近代以降、縮景に代わって、雑木林などを原寸大で再現するスタイルが増えました。

Notes

※7 初期の仏教には浄土の概念がないが、後に生まれた。　※8 「縮景」という。

建築／日本庭園

12

⁰³ Japanese Gardens

The classic Japanese garden evolved as a model of paradise in miniature. A garden might represent Horai, the fabled Isle of the Immortals known as Penglai in Chinese mythology, or Jodo, the Pure Land of **Buddhism**, or some other famous scenic spot that actually exists.

There are a number of formats of garden design. In one, the *chisen-kaiyu* style, paths circulate around a pond that symbolizes the sea, inviting strollers to savor the greenery surrounding the water. The paths will typically meander and undulate as they pass by strategically placed rocks that resemble mountains or islands. Perhaps because rocks were objects of awe in ancient Japan, they are preserved in their natural state in Japanese gardens.

Among the living compositional elements of these gardens are trees pruned in **bonsai**-like fashion and carpets of moss. Rarely will you see colorful flowerbeds in the manner of English gardens, but spring blossoms and autumn foliage on the trees vividly evoke the changing seasons.

Brooks or waterfalls flowing into the pond provide a soothing background music. Some gardens employ the *shakkei* (borrowed-view) technique of skillfully incorporating distant mountains or other features of the surrounding landscape into the garden's design.

Japanese formal gardens are often lumped together with those of China, which were an early influence. Chinese gardens that remain today, however, tend to use more dramatic elements, such as dividing walls and huge, oddly-shaped boulders. Japanese gardens, particularly those of the circulating variety, aim for more subtle transitions, with different scenes coming in and out of view through the trees as one walks along the path.

One style unique to Japan is the *kare-sansui* dry-landscape garden, which has no pond or other water features (image on p. 182). You may have seen photos of these gardens, with their expanses of white sand or pebbles raked around rocks in water-like eddies.

The dry-landscape garden was a genre developed by **Zen** temples for devotees to gaze upon. In modern times these gardens have earned appreciation as a form of abstract art, giving birth to contemporary *kare-sansui* designs. Meanwhile, a modern trend in circulating gardens is the use of full-size elements, such as entire groves of trees, in a departure from the traditional miniature-view concept.

12

Vocabulary

Isle of the Immortals｜蓬莱島 [the immortals は「不死の人々」]	undulate｜起伏する
stroller｜ぶらぶら散歩する人	compositional elements｜構成要素
meander｜曲がりくねる	in the manner of ...｜…の様式で
	be lumped together with ...｜…と一緒にされる

04 茶室

茶の湯（**茶道**）における茶室は、おもに小ささを旨とした、非日常的な空間になっています。草庵風の茶室では 4 畳半[※9]（一辺約 3 メートル弱の正方形）が基本（P. 282 参照）。少人数が畳の上に座って、落ち着いて時を過ごせるサイズです。

室内には通常、茶の湯を沸かす炉と**床の間**があります。また、茶室にいたる露地（茶庭）には、素朴な下草や飛び石、手や口を清める手水鉢^{ちょうずばち}などが配され、町中でも山居のような風情が演出されています。

もっと狭い茶室もあります。現存している最古の茶室「待庵」は、16 世紀の戦国武将・豊臣秀吉が、茶人・千利休に作らせた草庵で、主人と客が接するスペースは 2 畳しかありません。当時はそこで、政治的密談もしたのでしょう。客は壁の下方の「にじり口」という小さな開口部から、腰をかがめて出入りするのですから、気分が変わります。大小の窓からは、印象的な光が室内に差し込みます。

現代では、こうした伝統的な草庵風茶室のほかに、建築家が創意をこらした茶室も出現しています。たとえば藤森照信の「高過庵」（P. 290〜291）は、曲がった木の柱の上に不定形の小屋が乗っていて、はしごをかけて上ります。

Notes

※9 茶室の畳は京間。

05 城（天守）

戦国武将たちが激しい領地争いを繰り広げていた 16 世紀から、17 世紀の江戸時代初めにかけて、豪華な天守（天守閣）をもつ城[※10] が、列島の各地に建てられました。石積みの基礎の上に、瓦屋根の木造家屋のような形が、五層ほどにも積み重なったその姿は、今でこそ日本人にはなじみ深いものですが、最初期には、中国やヨーロッパなどの影響が顕著な無国籍風スタイルでした。当時はヨーロッパの船が初めて日本にやってきた時代にあたり、異文化の刺激が大きかったのでしょう。

歴史上、最初の天守は安土城（1579 年完成）

Photo: Miura Fumiko, 2014

→

建築／茶室／城（天守）

12

04 Teahouses

The house or room where tea ceremonies (see p. 189) take place is traditionally conceived as a small space that will foster a sense of detachment from the everyday world. Teahouses of the rustic *soan* (hut) style characteristically contain a square room four-and-a-half tatami mats (a bit less than three meters on a side) in area (see p. 283). This is considered the optimum size for a small number of people to sit on tatami and enjoy a tranquil, harmonious time together.

The tearoom will normally have a hearth for boiling water and a *tokonoma* alcove. The small garden through which one passes to get to it will contain a modest array of trees and shrubs, stepping stones, and a water basin for ritual rinsing of the hands and mouth. The effect is of leaving the city behind and entering a mountain retreat.

Some tearooms are extremely small. The oldest extant one, Taian, is a hut built in the 16th century by the tea master Sen no Rikyu at the behest of the warlord Toyotomi Hideyoshi. The space shared by the host and his guests consists of just two tatami mats. One can only guess at the secret political discussions that went on in that room. To enter, a visitor must edge forward on the knees through the *nijiriguchi*, a small doorway in the lower part of the wall—a procedure that is truly mood-altering. Sunlight filtering in from windows of diverse dimensions adds to the atmosphere.

In addition to traditional *soan*-style structures of this sort, Japan boasts a number of ingeniously designed teahouses by contemporary architects. One standout is Fujimori Terunobu's Takasugi-an (literally "too-high hut," image on pp. 290-291), an eccentrically shaped cottage built atop two crooked tree trunks. Visitors must climb a ladder to get to it.

Vocabulary

be conceived as ...	…として考案される	array	配置
foster ...	…を促進する	at the behest of ...	…の要請を受けて
a sense of detachment from ...	…から離れた感覚	ingeniously	独創的に
optimum	最適な	crooked	曲がった

05 Castle Towers

From the 16th century, when warlords fiercely vied for territory, and into the early 17th century under the Edo Shogunate, castles graced with magnificent towers were erected throughout the archipelago.

The archetypal Japanese castle—looking much like a tile-roofed wooden house, but with as many as five levels atop a stone foundation—is

➔

12

ですが、3年で焼失したので、いったいどんな形をしていたかは論争の的です。一説によると、屋根は五〜七層、最上部はまばゆい金色の外壁で、その下は朱色の八角堂、内部には4階分の吹き抜けがあったといいます。

日本各地に現在もみられる天守は、コンクリートで外部だけ復元[11] したものがほとんどですが、全国に12城、昔の姿を残すものがあります。

なかでも姫路城は、保存状態のよさと美しさで有名です（写真 P. 276）。しっくいの白さが映えるこの城は、シラサギが羽を広げる姿になぞらえてか、「白鷺城」とも呼び親しまれています。

Notes

※10 城のまわりに城下町が作られたことや、石積みの技術にも、日本の城の特徴がある。 ※11 平成になって木造の復元天守が建ち始めた。

Comment

天守閣の形から、私は戦国時代の大きなカブトやよろいを身に付けたサムライの姿を連想します。天守閣もカブトも、当時は実用性というより、権力を象徴する意味合いが強かったようですよ。
The shape of a classic Japanese castle tower always reminds me of the big curved helmets and armor worn by feudal samurai. They say, in fact, that both the castles and helmets of that era were more decorative than practical, their primary purpose being to project authority.

06 現代建築

1964年、日本の建築デザインの評価を飛躍的に高めたのが、東京オリンピックのときに建てられた国立代々木競技場でした。ハイテクな吊り屋根は寺院のシルエットのようなカーブを描き、柱がなく観戦しやすい内部空間も評判でした。設計の丹下健三は、戦後の記念碑的な建物や都市計画を次々と手がけた、日本の巨匠建築家です。

1960年代にはまた、日本の建築家グループが「メタボリズム」（新陳代謝）という重要な建築運動を発信しています。科学技術のもたらす未来が輝いて見えた時代を背景に、状況に応じて変わり続ける建築デザインが唱えられたのです。黒川記章・設計の「中銀カプセルタワービル」（1972、東京）は典型的メタボリズム建築で、交換可能なプレハブのカプセル住宅が、たくさん付いたタワーでした（実際に、カプセル住宅が交換されたことはありません）。

メタボリズムは科学技術信奉と批判されがちですが、当時としては先見的なリサイクルやエコシステムの提案も行われていて、その思想性を再検討する機運があります。

建築／城（天守）／現代建築

12

→

←

a familiar sight that most people consider quintessentially Japanese. Yet the earliest of these edifices were built in an exotic, eclectic style that shows a mix of influences from the Chinese and European architecture of the day. The first ships from Europe were arriving in Japan around that time, and foreign cultures were surely a major stimulus.

Japan's first castle with a full-fledged keep was Azuchi Castle. Built in 1579, it burned down only three years later and still inspires debate about what it actually looked like. According to one account the keep had five to seven stories, with the top painted a dazzling gold, a vermilion octagonal pavilion below that, and a four-story atrium inside.

The castle towers you see in Japan nowadays are nearly all concrete restorations of the exteriors alone, but twelve of the country's original castles remain standing. Himeji Castle (image on p. 276) is particularly famed for its well-preserved condition as well as its beauty. Its popular nickname, White Heron Castle, may be a homage to the white-plastered walls and roofs, which call to mind a bird spreading its wings.

Vocabulary

fiercely｜激しく、荒々しく	eclectic｜種々の要素が含まれた、無国籍の
vie for …｜…を奪い合う	full-fledged keep｜本格的な天守
be erected｜建てられる	atrium｜吹き抜け
quintessentially｜典型的に	white-plastered｜白いしっくいの

⁰⁶ Contemporary Architecture

The year 1964 was a watershed for Japanese architectural design, which soared in the estimation of international critics with the completion of the Yoyogi National Gymnasium, built for the Olympics held in Tokyo that year. Praise was lavished on its high-tech suspended roof, which described curves reminiscent of a temple, and its interior space, devoid of pillars and perfect for viewing sports events. Its designer, Tange Kenzo, is a giant among Japan's architects who contributed numerous monumental structures and urban-planning projects to the country's postwar landscape.

The 1960s saw the launch of Metabolism, a seminal movement by a group of Japanese architects. In an era when science and technology appeared on the verge of ushering in a bright future for all, the Metabolists called for a style of architectural design that would constantly change and adapt to different circumstances. The iconic Metabolist structure is the Nakagin Capsule Tower in Tokyo (1972). Designed by Kurokawa Kisho, it is composed of dozens of prefabricated, replaceable capsule units for residential use. (Actually, none of the capsules has ever been replaced.)

Metabolism is often criticized for its enthusiastic embrace of science

12

→

←

日本がバブル景気に沸いた 80 年代後半には建築ラッシュが起こり、列島各地に華やかで、時にキッチュなポストモダン建築[12] が建てられました。

その頃から現在までで、一番有名な日本の建築家は、むしろストイックな美意識の安藤忠雄でしょう。コンクリート打ち放しの壁面が、空や光、水などの外部環境を映し出すスタイルが、海外では日本的と解釈されるようです。

2000 年にオープンした、伊東豊雄・設計の複合文化施設「せんだいメディアテーク」は、21 世紀の建築名所となりました。ガラスの透明なビルの全層を、くねったチューブの柱が貫く姿は、重厚さを求める建築とは対極の軽やかさがあって、内部は人が自然に行き来する広場のような空間になっています。

近年、ヴェネツィア・ビエンナーレ国際建築展の金獅子賞[13] や、アメリカのプリツカー賞は、日本人建築家の受賞[14] が相次いでいます。

Notes

※ 12 機能主義的なモダニズム建築への反動で流行。装飾性の回復や折衷主義が特徴。

※ 13 伊東豊雄、SANAA（妹島和世と西沢立衛）、石上純也、篠原一男、日本館パビリオン賞（2012）。

※ 14 丹下健三、槇文彦、安藤忠雄、2010 年以降は、SANAA、伊東豊雄、板茂。

建築／現代建築

12

and technology, but the movement was also a pioneer for its time in advancing such concepts as recycling and ecosystems. The Metabolist philosophy is enjoying renewed interest of late.

Japan went through a building boom in the late 1980s, at the height of its economic bubble, and postmodern structures—often flamboyant, sometimes downright kitschy—popped up all over the country. Arguably the most visible force in Japanese architecture since that time, however, has been Ando Tadao, whose aesthetics lean more to the spartan. Ando's buildings feature bare concrete walls that reflect and react to spatial and environmental elements—air, light, water—in a style that foreign fans seem to view as distinctively Japanese.

Since opening in 2000, the Ito Toyo-designed Sendai Mediatheque, a multipurpose cultural center, has become one of the star attractions of 21st-century architecture. Twisting tubular pillars thrust through every level of the transparent glass-walled building, whose airy, playful ambience is the polar opposite of architecture that aspires to a dignified presence. The interior is a plaza-like space that encourages people to come and go at will.

In recent years Japanese architects have garnered one international prize after another, among them the Golden Lion of the Venice Architecture Biennale and the Pritzker Architecture Prize in the United States.

Vocabulary

watershed for …	…にとっての転換点	prefabricated	プレハブ（組立式）の
soar in the estimation of …	…の評価が高まる	flamboyant	飾り立てた
be lavished on …	…に惜しみなく与えられる	arguably	ほぼ間違いなく
reminiscent of …	…を連想させる	spartan	簡素な、厳しい［古代ギリシャのスパル
devoid of …	…がない	タ的な性質から。ここでは the spartan で抽象名詞
on the verge of …	…の寸前に	として使用］
usher in …	…をもたらす、導く	dignified presence	堂々とした存在感

左：日本を代表する建築家ユニット・SANAA（サナア／妹島和世＋西沢立衛）の設計による、NY(米)の「ニュー・ミュージアム・オブ・コンテンポラリー・アート」
Left: New York's New Museum of Contemporary Art, designed by the leading Japanese architectural unit SANAA (Sejima Kazuyo and Nishizawa Ryue), 2007
Courtesy of the New Museum, New York. Photo: Dean Kaufman

07 住宅

日本の家は、よく「木と紙で出来ている」、「空間をフレキシブルに使う」といわれます。

これについて解説すると、伝統的な家はまず、木の柱や梁を組んで家を支える構造になっています。そして、土などの壁だけでなく、紙貼りの引き戸でも部屋が仕切ってあるのです。

厚手の紙が貼ってある引き戸は「ふすま」※15といって、たいてい絵や模様が全面に描かれています。また、部屋の間のふすまを取りはらうと、大広間になります。一方「障子」といえば、格子状の木枠に白い薄紙が貼られた引き戸で、外光を柔らかく通します。庭に面した開口部には、古くは障子と、木の引き戸を並列させるのが一般的で――20世紀前半には、ガラスの掃出し窓も加わりますが――開け放すと家の内外がつながります。

日本家屋 Japanese traditional house with tatami room (below) and shoji
Photo: Sora – Fotolia.com

屋根については、茅葺きや板葺き※16は消えつつありますが、伝統的な瓦葺きは健在です。

家に入るときは、玄関で靴を脱いで、一段高い板張りの床に上がります。座敷（直訳は「シート敷き」）と呼ばれる部屋には、イグサで覆われた

畳という厚いマットが敷き詰めてあります。畳は人が寝られるくらいの90×180センチメートル前後※17。この畳の数が4畳半や6畳などと、部屋の大きさを決めるユニットとなっています。食事のときには低いテーブルを置いて畳の上に座り、寝る時にしまってあった布団を出して敷けば、部屋は多機能に使えます。

20世紀のうちに日本の家は大きく変わり、和洋折衷、寝食分離、合成素材を使ったプレハブ工法※18に向かいました。ニュータウンに立ち並ぶ「ハウスメーカー」が建てた家に入ると、ダイニングルーム・寝室などと、部屋の役割が分かれています（P. 284参照）。中高層の集合住宅も増えました。

→

⁰⁷ Residences

Two things you frequently hear about Japanese houses are that they are "made out of wood and paper" and are "flexible in their use of space." Traditional residences employ wooden beams and pillars for structural support. Rooms are divided not only by walls made of earth and other natural materials, but also by paper-covered sliding doors.

Doors made with thick, sturdy paper are called *fusuma*; these often have pictures or decorative patterns across their entire surface. You can remove the fusuma separating two or more rooms to create one large space. Another kind of sliding panel, *shoji*, has thin white paper stretched over a wood-lattice frame. The paper is translucent and lets a soft light into the room.

The side of the house that opens onto the garden has traditionally consisted of parallel sets of shoji and sliding wooden doors (glass doors became popular in the early part of the 20th century). When these panels are slid all the way open, the garden and the house become one.

Though roofs made of thatch or wooden shingles are fast disappearing, traditional tile roofing is alive and well.

When entering a Japanese house, you remove your shoes in the vestibule and step up onto a wooden floor. The rooms known as *zashiki* (literally "spread-out seating") are floored with thick rush mats called *tatami*. A single tatami mat measures approximately 90 by 180 centimeters, just large enough for a person to sleep on. Room dimensions are expressed in tatami units—six mats, four-and-a-half mats, and so on.

At mealtime people can sit on the tatami around a low table. At night they take futon bedding out of a closet and spread it on the tatami. Thus the *zashiki* is a multipurpose room.

The Japanese home underwent a dramatic transformation during the 20th century. Western-Japanese hybrids, separate sleeping and dining quarters, and prefab construction using synthetic materials all became common. When you enter one of the houses built by large corporate developers in Japan's suburban "new towns," you will find that the rooms have clearly defined functions—dining room, bedroom, and the like (see p. 285). Another change is the proliferation of high- and mid-rise apartment complexes.

Japan also has its share of idiosyncratic residences designed by architects or self-builders. Some of the most creative structures are not large mansions, but homes designed to take maximum advantage of small urban spaces.

→

12

←

建築家の設計やセルフビルド※19 などで、個性的な家もあります。大邸宅だけでなく、都会の小さな空間を生かすデザインも注目されています。

近年は古民家のよさが見直されていて、リフォームして住む人もいます。

Notes

※15 布張りのふすまもある。　※16 薄板で葺く柿葺や、ヒノキの樹皮で葺く檜皮葺（神社によく使われる）は日本独特。瓦は寺院建築とともに、大陸から伝わったとされる。　※17 地方によってサイズが違う。最近は新素材の畳が増えている。　※18 モダンデザインの歴史上、装飾を排し、可変性をめざしたプレハブ住宅が提案されたが、現在は各種の建築様式を借りたデザインの住宅が普及している。　※19 オーナーの自作による建築。

倉俣史朗デザインの「変型の家具」
Furniture in Irregular Forms, designed by Kuramata Shiro, 1970
Photo courtesy of Cappellini

08　家具

近代以前の日本では、日常生活のなかで椅子やベッドは使われていませんでした。高い床に敷いた畳自体に、座やベッドの役割があるからです（P.282 参照）。もちろん収納家具は古くからあって、飾り金具に特徴があるアンティークの和箪笥（たんす）は、海外でも人気です。

現代では同じ家のなかに、椅子を使う「洋室」と畳の「和室」の両方があります。

ただし日本の洋室は、欧米と違って土足で入らないので、背の低い家具──フロア・クッションや床置きライト──を配置するなど、ある意味で日本的なインテリアが工夫されています。

日本発のモダン家具としては、工業デザイナーの草分け・柳宗理が 1954 年に発表した「バタフライ・スツール」が、先駆的な名作として知られています。その後の家具・インテリアのデザイナーのうち、91 年に亡くなった倉俣史朗は、突出した存在でした。彼のデザインした家具や空間は、一見モダンに見えるのですが、じつは工業生産品でも手作業の工程が入っているなど、機能主義や画一主義へ与しない詩情を感じさせます。

←

Lately there has been a resurgence of appreciation for the virtues of older wooden houses, and more people are renovating and moving into them.

Vocabulary

sturdy｜じょうぶな	dimension｜寸法
wood-lattice frame｜木製の格子枠	have *one's* share of ...｜それなりに…がある
translucent｜半透明の	idiosyncratic｜個性的な
roof made of thatch｜茅葺き屋根	resurgence｜復活、再流行
vestibule｜玄関	

08 Furniture

Premodern Japan had no use for chairs or beds as everyday furnishings. Tatami mats laid atop elevated flooring served all seating and sleeping needs (see p. 283). But the Japanese have always used storage furniture. The antique chests of drawers known as *tansu*, with their decorative metal fittings, now find favor with homeowners abroad.

Contemporary Japanese houses may include both Japanese-style rooms with tatami floors and Western-style rooms where chairs are used. But the latter differ from rooms in actual Western houses, since people do not wear their shoes indoors. That custom has resulted in interior designs with a Japanese twist—large floor cushions and low floor lamps, for example.

Japan has also produced some innovative modern furniture. The pioneering industrial designer Yanagi Sori is still admired for one of the earliest such creations, the butterfly stool he invented in 1954.

After Sori, perhaps the most prominent furniture and interior designer of recent decades is Kuramata Shiro, who died in 1991. Kuramata's designs at first glance appear to be typically modern, but there are differences, such as the incorporation of handwork into the industrial production process. The spaces and furnishings he created reflect a poetic imagination that could be seen as the antithesis of functionalism or standardization.

Vocabulary

storage furniture｜収納家具	reflect ...｜…を反映する、示す
result in ...｜…という結果になる	antithesis of functionalism｜機能主義へのアンチ
twist｜工夫、味つけ	テーゼ、機能主義と正反対
be admired for ...｜…のために称賛される	

12

⁰⁹ 災害と持続可能性

日本は水や緑に恵まれた国ですが、一方で地震や津波、台風^{※20}、火山噴火などの災害が多発する、自然の厳しい地域でもあります。そのため木造建築では、古くから地震の揺れがうまく吸収できるような木材の組み方が工夫されてきました。また、1923年の関東大震災をきっかけに、鉄筋コンクリート造が普及しました。

1995年の阪神淡路大震災では、建築家・坂茂による、紙パイプを柱に使った仮設の住宅や教会が注目されました。紙パイプは、坂によると軽量なので移動や組立てがしやすく、防水・難燃加工も簡単だそうです。彼はこの「紙の建築」を、トルコ、インド、スリランカ、アメリカ、中国、イタリア、ハイチ、ニュージーランドなど、世界中の被災地で緊急支援に応用しています。

記憶に新しい2011年の東日本大震災では、自然災害だけでなく、原発の大事故が引き起こされてしまいました。難しい状況が続いていますが、エネルギーのインフラを含めた社会の持続可能性^{※21}については、より真剣に考えられるようになりました。

Notes

※20 英語の typhoon、hurricane、cyclone の違いを大まかにいうと、typhoon は北西太平洋、hurricane は北大西洋や北東太平洋、cyclone はインド洋や南太平洋にある強大な低気圧。cyclone は低気圧全般を指す際にも使われる。　※21 将来にわたって、人間が生存し活動できる条件や環境を保てるかどうかを指す。特に自然破壊や資源の枯渇が問題視されている。

Comment

最近はシェアハウスや、アーティストの坂口恭平が提案するモバイルハウスなどの住まい方も、今日的な関心を集めていますね。リスクが少なく、生活様式の変化に対応しやすいのです。
What with all the troubles homeowners face these days, people seem to be taking a fresh look at alternative, flexible, low-risk lifestyle concepts—share houses and the mobile houses proposed by artist Sakaguchi Kyohei, to name two.

建築／災害と持続可能性

12／

⁰⁹ Disasters and Sustainability

Blessed though it is with water and greenery, Japan is also a land buffeted by such destructive natural phenomena as earthquakes, tsunamis, typhoons, and volcanic eruptions. One consequence is that, over the centuries, the Japanese have developed methods of building wooden structures that can absorb the shaking of earthquakes. Since the Kanto Earthquake of 1923, reinforced concrete has also become a standard construction material.

When the Hanshin-Awaji Earthquake struck in 1995, architect Ban Shigeru attracted attention with his promotion of paper or cardboard tubing as a building material for temporary housing and churches. Paper tubing, Ban points out, is lightweight, easy to transport and assemble, and readily treated with waterproofing or flame retardant. His "paper architecture" has provided emergency shelter in disaster areas worldwide, including Turkey, India, Sri Lanka, the United States, China, Italy, Haiti, and New Zealand.

One catastrophe still fresh in the memory, the earthquake and tsunami of March 2011, involved not only a natural disaster but a man-made one, the nuclear accident in Fukushima. With the problems stemming from it still unresolved, this event has spurred intense debate about the sustainability of human society, including but not limited to our energy infrastructure.

Vocabulary

buffeted by … ｜…に翻弄される、巻き込まれる	waterproofing ｜防水
volcanic eruption ｜火山の噴火	flame retardant ｜防火
reinforced concrete ｜鉄筋コンクリート	stemming from … ｜…に由来する
cardboard tubing ｜ボール紙／板紙の筒	spur … ｜…を刺激する、促す
assemble ｜組み立てる	including but not limited to … ｜…を含むがそれに限らない
readily ｜すぐに、容易に	

12

日本の自然環境

日本の土地は、約70%が森林に覆われた山地です。そして雨が大量に降るので、急流の川や湖沼がたくさんあり、緑の山には地下水が蓄えられます。

樹種はもともと照葉樹林（常緑広葉樹林）の分布域が広かったのですが、原生林（手つかずの森林）はわずかとなりました。今では森林の約40%が針葉樹の人工林で、輸入木材が安価になってからは、それも荒廃しがちです。また日本は地形が変化に富んでいるため、生物多様性に恵まれ、固有種が比較的多い環境ですが、残念ながら絶滅危惧種が増えています。

もちろん、環境保全運動もあります。たとえば「鎮守の森」の保存や、「里山」再生運動。鎮守の森[22]とは、神社などが置かれて聖域として保たれてきた、土地本来の樹種が残る天然林[23]のことです（P. 170参照）。災害時には避難場所となり、手入れも必要ありません。里山とは里の近くの小高い雑木林で、江戸時代以来、人間が過剰な木材利用を抑えつつ、燃料（枝や下草）や肥料、山菜などを採って、持続的に開発・活用してきたところです。その多くはすでに宅地などに変わりましたが、近年、残された里山の機能が見直され、手入れや自然体験活動などが行われています。それから、日本で地道に実践されている「自然農」は、「耕さない／除草しない／農薬も肥料も使わない」を原則とする循環型農法で、海外のエコロジストたちにも大きな影響を与えています。

Notes

※22 明治時代の神社合祀で激減した。　※23 過去に伐採などで人の手が入っているが、自然に更新している森林。　※24 元は仏教用語で、神道と結びついた概念ともいわれる。

Comment

ケニアの環境保護活動家、故ワンガリ・マータイさんは、日本語から採った「モッタイナイ運動」を提唱し、Reduce, Reuse, Recycle + Respect を呼びかけました。モッタイナイ[24]は、wasteful という意味の日常的な言葉ですが、物事の価値は生かすべきという意識がベースにあります。
The late Kenyan environmental activist Wangari Maathai named her Mottainai Campaign to "Reduce, Reuse, Recycle and Respect" after an everyday Japanese word that means "wasteful." *Mottainai* is based on the notion of cherishing the value of all things.

Japan's Natural Environment

Forested mountains cover some 70 percent of Japan. This is a rainy country full of lakes, marshes, and fast-flowing streams, as well as stores of groundwater in mountainous areas.

Though much of the archipelago was once covered in broad-leafed evergreen forests, very little virgin timber remains. Today as much as 40 percent of the nation's forest consists of conifer plantations, but these have been largely abandoned due to the influx of cheap imported lumber.

With its richly varied topography, Japan is a mecca of biodiversity and indigenous species. Sadly, however, the list of endangered species is growing. Needless to say, the country is host to a number of environmental movements. Notable among these are the efforts to preserve sacred groves (*chinju no mori*) and revive *satoyama* woodlands.

Chinju no mori are natural groves that traditionally surround Shinto shrines. They are regarded as sacred spots and preserve the original vegetation, particularly tall old trees, of the region (see p. 171). They also serve as evacuation areas in the event of disasters, and require little or no maintenance.

Satoyama (literally "village hills") are woodlands in hilly areas outside farming villages. Since the Edo period (1603-1868), satoyama have been developed and maintained in a sustainable manner to provide nearby communities with fuel, fertilizer, and wild vegetables while preventing the overuse of wood resources. Housing developments have replaced most of Japan's satoyama today, but recent years have witnessed a reappraisal of the functions served by those that remain, and the spread of movements to maintain these woodlands or utilize them for nature-appreciation activities. Japan is also home to a small but active "natural farming" movement that espouses a closed-system form of agriculture with "no tilling, no weeding, no chemicals, no fertilizer." This method has had a significant impact on ecologists and organic farmers outside of Japan.

Vocabulary

conifer | 針葉樹   influx | 流入

12

茶室「高過庵」（長野県）
藤森照信・設計。二本の柱は、地元のクリ
の木。
Too-High Teahouse in Nagano, Japan,
designed by Fujimori Terunobu, 2004.
The two poles are local chestnut trees.
Photo: Masuda Akihisa

Geography
地理

日本一長い川：信濃川
Japan's longest river: Shinano River, 367 km

世界一長い川：ナイル川
World's longest: Nile River, 6,695 km

日本一大きな湖：琵琶湖
Japan's largest lake: Lake Biwa, 674 km²

世界一大きな湖：カスピ海
World's largest:
Caspian Sea, 374,000 km²

Sapporo ● Hokkaido

Pacific Ocean

Niigata ● Sendai
● Fukushima

Sea of Japan

Honshu

Kyoto ● ● Tokyo
Osaka Nagoya

Hiroshima

Fukuoka
Matsuyama

Nagasaki
Shikoku

Kyushu

日本一流域面積の広い川：利根川
Japan's largest drainage basin:
Tone River, 16,840 km²

世界一流域面積の広い川：アマゾン川
World's largest:
Amazon River, 7,050,000 km²

日本一高い山：富士山
Japan's highest mountain:
Mt. Fuji, 3,776 m

世界一高い山：エベレスト
World's highest: Mt. Everest, 8,848 m

Okinawa

Naha

▶ 日本列島

日本は島国です。アジア大陸の東側にある弓状の列島で、大きな島が４つ
あります。これら（沖縄本島を含む場合もある）を、日本人は「本土」と
呼んでいます。「島」というときは、その他 6,800 以上の小島を指すのです。
４島のうち最大の島を本州（メインの州という意味）といいます。本州は世
界で７番目に大きな島です。

Notes

---

* 北方四島、竹島（リアンクール岩礁、韓国名は独島）、尖閣諸島は、近隣国との間で領有権の問題がある。

国土面積：約 37.8 万 km² （そのうち約 60％が本州)

経緯度 （東経 / 北緯）：

東京 （首都）：139°44'E / 35°39'N   **那覇**：127°41' E / 26°13' N

北端 （択捉島）：148°45' E / 45°33' N* **南端**：(沖ノ鳥島) 136°04' E / 20°25' N

東端 （南鳥島）：153°59' E / 24°16' N   **西端**：(与那国島) 122°56' E / 24°26' N

▶ 東京の緯度は、アメリカの LA、中国の青島とほぼ同じ。

冬の気温 東京 1～2 月平均：6.0 ℃   **最低記録**：北海道・旭川 -41.0 ℃ （1902）

夏の気温 東京 8 月平均：28.6 ℃   **最高記録**：高知県・江川崎 41.0 ℃ （2013）

Total land area: 378,000 km² (Honshu covers about 60%)

Longitude and latitude (E/N):

Tokyo (capital): 139°44' E / 35°39' N   **Naha**: 127°41' E / 26°13' N

Northern tip (Etorofuto / Iturup Island): 148°45' E / 45°33' N*

Southern tip (Okinotorishima): 136°04' E / 20°25' N

Eastern tip (Minamitorishima): 153°59' E / 24°16' N

Western tip (Yonagunijima): 122°56' E / 24°26' N

▶ Tokyo's latitude is similar to that of Los Angeles (34°05' N) or Qingdao, China (36°04' N)

Winter temperatures:

Tokyo Jan.-Feb. average: 42.8°F / 6.0°C

Lowest record in Japan: Asahikawa, Hokkaido -41.8°F / -41.0°C （1902）

Summer temperatures:

Tokyo Aug. average: 83.5°F / 28.6°C

Highest record in Japan: Ekawasaki, Kochi 105.8°F / 41.0°C （2013）

データ出典：国土地理院、気象庁（平均気温は 2010～14 年の数値から算出）
Source: Geospatial Information Authority of Japan, Japan Meteorological Agency

Geography

▶ The Japanese Archipelago

Japan is a country of islands, a bow-shaped archipelago off the eastern coast of the Asian continent. It has four main islands (five if you include Okinawa), which make up what Japanese call their "mainland." When talking about "islands" they are referring to any of some 6,800 smaller islands that are also part of Japan. The biggest land mass is Honshu (meaning "main province"), which ranks as the seventh largest island in the world.

Notes

* There are several disputed islands: four northern islands held by Russia; Takeshima (Dokdo in Korean, also known as the Liancourt Rocks); and the Senkaku (Diaoyu in Chinese) Islands.

▶ 気候

日本は国土が南北に長いので、亜寒帯から熱帯まで変化に富む気候がみられますが、大半の地域は温帯に属しています。どの地域も四季の変化がはっきりしています。また、列島を縦断する山岳地帯の東と西（太平洋側と日本海側）でも、気候が大きく異なります。

日本海側は雪が多くて、新潟県などでは積雪量が7〜8メートルを超えるところもあります。南国の沖縄県では、雪が観測されたことはありません[※1]。また、太平洋側は多くの地域で、夏がとても蒸し暑くなります。近年は地球温暖化の影響か、さらに気温が高くなっています。

北海道、小笠原諸島以外では、初夏の6〜7月に、梅雨[※2]と呼ばれる雨期があります。

Notes

※1 1977年に沖縄県・久米島でみぞれが観測された。　※2 梅雨は東アジアの広域にみられる。

▶ 災害・自然環境→ p. 286、288

▶ 人

日本は単一民族の国だという意識を持つ人が多いのですが、日本人のDNAを調べると、たくさんの系統がみられ、太古からさまざまな地域の人々が、この列島に流入してきたことがうかがえます。北海道のアイヌ民族は、2008年に国会で先住民族と認められました。また、かつて琉球王国だった沖縄の人々や、その他いくつかのグループを民族ととらえる考え方があります。もちろん、近年に外国から帰化した人もいます。

WORLD CAFÉ **日本はせまい国?**

日本の面積は、世界194カ国中59番目。たとえばイギリスやドイツより広いのですが、アメリカや中国など、広大な国の影響が強いせいか、日本人は自分の国をよく、小さい国だといいますね。

一方、外国人がよく、日本はとても混雑しているところだというのは、部分的に当たっています。山地や森林が多く、人が住める場所が4%しかなくて、しかも都会に人が集中しているからです。

香港やパリもごく限られた地域は混んでいますが、東京など日本の都会は、広範囲に渡って人口密度が高いのです。

► Climate

The Japanese archipelago is long and narrow, and stretches from northeast to southwest. It therefore has a diversity of climates, ranging from subarctic to tropical, though most of the country is in the temperate zone. All of Japan enjoys four clearly defined seasons. The climate also varies noticeably between the Pacific Ocean side and the Sea of Japan side, to the east and west respectively of the mountains that run the length of the country.

The Sea of Japan side gets the heaviest snowfall, with seven or eight meters or more accumulating in some parts of Niigata Prefecture. By contrast, Okinawa at the southwestern end of the archipelago has never recorded a snowfall. Much of the Pacific side experiences hot, humid summers—nowadays even more so, perhaps due to global warming. Except for Hokkaido in the north and the Ogasawara Islands in the far south, the entire country has a rainy season in June and July.

► Disasters, Natural Environment → pp. 287, 289

► People

Many Japanese think of their country as ethnically homogenous, but a check of Japanese DNA reveals a diversity of ethnic origins. This suggests that people from many different places have migrated to the archipelago over the millennia. In 2008 Japan's Parliament recognized the Ainu of Hokkaido as an indigenous people. A number of other groups, notably Okinawans (whose homeland was once a separate country, the Ryukyu Kingdom), can also be viewed as ethnic groups. People arriving from overseas in more recent years have also acquired citizenship, of course.

Data

日本の人口：1 億 2,700 万人／世界 10 位（総務省『世界の統計 2014』より）
日本全国の人口密度（1 km²あたり）：343（2010 年、国勢調査）
東京 23 区の人口密度：14,473 ／豊島区　20,880（2014 年、東京都総務局統計部）
香港の人口密度：6,650 ／人口密集地域　57,120（2013 年、香港政府）

Population: 127,000,000 (ranking 10th in the world)
Density in Japan (people per km²): 343
Density in Tokyo's 23 wards (people per km²): 14,473 (Toshima Ward: 20,880)
Density in Hong Kong: 6,650 (most densely populated district: 57,120)

Periods of Japanese History
日本史時代区分

＊日本の時代区分は諸説あり、これはその一例です。
＊Opinions vary on the demarcation of these periods.

時代区分	時代		内容
原始	旧石器時代 （–c. 14,000 BC）		
	縄文時代（新石器時代） （c. 14,000–800 BC）		▶ 日本列島が出来たのは、約1万2000〜1万3000年前。それまではアジア大陸と地続きでした。 ▶ 多様な集団がこの地に流入し、それぞれに文化圏を形成。なかでも縄文文化は特徴的でした。
古代	弥生時代 （c. 800 BC–250 AD）		▶ 新たな渡来人が、本格的な水稲農耕の技術をもたらしました。
	古墳時代 （c. 250–600）		▶ 古墳（丘状の権力者の墓）が各地に作られた時代。ヤマト王権が勢力を拡大。 ▶ 6世紀中頃、仏教が公式に伝来。 ▶ 中央集権国家へ（東北北部など列島の北と南を除く）。
	飛鳥時代 （592–710）		▶ 7世紀後半には、それまで倭などと呼ばれていた国名が、日本と定められました（当初の発音はヤマト、ニッポン、ジッポンと推測される）。
	奈良時代 （710–794）		▶ 律令制が整った時代。また、唐（中国）から、シルクロードの文化がさかんに輸入されました。
中世	平安時代 （794–1185）		▶ 王朝文化の華やかな頃。京都（平安京）が、日本の都として栄えました。 ▶ 武士の登場。 ▶ 中国の硬貨が流入し、商品経済が発達しました。
	鎌倉時代 （1185–1333）		▶ 平安末期以降、武士が国家を運営する時代に。
	建武の新政 （1333–1336）		▶ 天皇を中心とした新政権が起こるも、2年余りで崩壊。
	室町時代 （1336–1573）	南北朝時代 （1336–1392）	▶ 公家と武家の文化が融合し、茶の湯や能楽などの原型ができました。
		戦国時代 （1493–1590）	▶ 乱世が続く時代。 ▶ ヨーロッパとの交易開始。キリスト教の伝来。
近世 （近代前期）	安土桃山時代 （1573–1603）		▶ 豊臣秀吉が全国を支配下に。

Who Were the Samurai?

The word *samurai* refers to family-based armed groups or individual warriors, skilled in the military arts, who were active between the 10th and 19th centuries. During the peaceful Edo period, samurai served as politicians or bureaucrats.

武士（侍）とは、10〜19世紀の武芸を身に付けた戦闘集団（家族共同体）、あるいは戦闘員。戦さのなくなった江戸時代には、政治家や役人のような存在でした（英語で武士／侍は、samurai として辞書に載っている。日本の歴史上、「侍」という言葉は上級武士を指した時期があるが、日本でも現在、武士と侍を同じ意味で使うことが多い）。

▼ **Periods of Japanese History**

Ancient Japan	**Japanese Paleolithic** (–c. 14,000 BC)	
	Jomon (Japanese Neolithic) (c. 14,000–800 BC)	► The Japanese archipelago formed around 12,000 to 13,000 years ago. Until then it was connected to the Asian continent. ► Various groups of people migrate to the region, establishing different culture zones. The Jomon culture is particularly distinctive.
	Yayoi (c. 800 BC–250 AD)	► New arrivals from the continent bring with them techniques of large-scale paddy-rice cultivation.
Classical Japan	**Kofun** (c. 250–600)	► Large burial mounds known as kofun are built for rulers in various regions. The territory under Yamato rule expands. ► Buddhism officially arrives in Japan in the mid-6th century. ► Formation of a centrally governed state (excluding northeastern Honshu and the northern and southern ends of the archipelago).
	Asuka (592–710)	► In the late 7th century the state, which had been called "Wa" by other countries, starts formally using the kanji of its current name. The pronunciation at the time may have been Yamato, Nippon, or Jippon (Nippon and Nihon are used today).
	Nara (710–794)	► The Ritsuryo legal system is established. Silk Road culture flows into the country from Tang-Dynasty China.
	Heian (794–1185)	► The golden age of court culture, when Heiankyo (Kyoto today) flourishes as the royal capital. ► Samurai make their appearance. ► Chinese coins enter the country as a commodity economy develops.
Feudal Japan	**Kamakura** (1185–1333)	► Samurai run the state from the late Heian period on.
	Kenmu Restoration (1333–1336)	► A new emperor-centered government is formed but collapses in less than three years.
	Muromachi (1336–1573) **Nanboku-cho** (1336–1392) **Sengoku** (1493–1590)	► Court culture and samurai culture merge, giving birth to such arts as tea ceremony and Noh theater. ► Years of war and social turmoil. ► Trade with Europe begins, and Christianity arrives.
Early Modern Japan	**Azuchi-Momoyama** (1573–1603)	► Toyotomi Hideyoshi places the entire country under his rule.

Notes

飛鳥時代以降、奈良、平安、鎌倉、室町、江戸は、政治拠点の地名が、時代区分名になっています。また安土・桃山時代は、当時の城にまつわる由来からこう呼ばれています。

The Asuka, Nara, Heian, Kamakura, Muromachi, and Edo periods are named after the location of the political center during each era. Azuchi-Momoyama refers to castles built by the two dominant rulers of the period.

明治以降、天皇の即位時に元号が変わる制度となり、元号によって明治時代、大正時代等と呼ばれています。

Since the reign of Emperor Meiji, era names have changed with the accession of each new emperor and have come to be used as period names. To date these eras are Meiji, Taisho, Showa, and the current Heisei.

近世 (近代前期)	江戸時代 (1603–1868)		▶ 徳川政権が約300年続きます。海外との行き来が厳しく制限され、身分制度が敷かれました。歌舞伎や浮世絵などの大衆文化が栄えました。
近代	明治時代 (1868–1912)		▶ 明治維新により武士階級が廃止され、天皇を中心とした近代国家に。日本における産業革命の時代で、生活は欧米化に向かいました。
	大正時代 (1912–1926)		▶ 自由主義運動が規制され、軍国主義が色濃くなる時代。
現代	昭和 (1926–1989)	戦前期	▶ 1941〜45年、アジア太平洋戦争。
		戦後期 GHQ占領期 (1945–1952**)	▶ 戦後に制定された新憲法には、戦争の放棄と武力の不所持を謳った平和主義が盛り込まれました（9条）。 ▶ 1950〜70年代にかけて、高度経済成長期。 ▶ 1980年代後半〜90年代初頭、資産価格が実体以上に高騰し、バブル景気といわれました。
	平成 (1989–)		▶ 2011年、東日本大震災／福島第一原子力発電所事故。

（左余白・縦書き）▼ 日本史時代区分

Tenno (Emperor) and Shogun

"Emperor" is the traditional translation for *tenno*, the monarch of Japan. The emperor is part of a hereditary line that extends back to the ancient past. Today's emperor has no political power and is defined by the Constitution as the "symbol of the State and of the unity of the people." The shogun was a military commander of the samurai class during the premodern era; the title no longer exists. From the Kamakura through the Edo periods, with rare interruptions, the shogun, appointed by the emperor, was the political ruler of Japan.

天皇と将軍

日本には、古代からつづく世襲制の天皇がいます（emperor※3は日本で、「天皇」の訳語として定着しています）。現在の天皇は政治権力をもたず、憲法でその地位が「国と国民統合の象徴」と規定されています。一方、将軍とは、前近代に存在した武士のなかの軍事司令官のことで、今はもういません。鎌倉時代〜江戸時代には、一時期を除いて、将軍が政治のトップで、天皇が将軍を任命していました。

Notes

※3 英語のemperorは元々「帝国のトップ」という意味で、「将軍」の訳語と受けとめられることがある。かつては「天皇」の英訳にmikadoという言葉も使われた（19世紀イギリスで、『The Mikado』というオペレッタが人気を博した）。

Early Modern Japan	**Edo** (1603–1868)		► For nearly 300 years the Tokugawa Shogunate rules Japan from Edo (now Tokyo). Contact with other countries is suppressed and a rigid class system enforced, but popular culture (such as Kabuki and ukiyo-e) thrives.
Modern Japan	**Meiji** (1868–1912)		► The Meiji Restoration abolishes the samurai class and replaces the Shogunate with an emperor-centered modern state. Japan enters its industrial revolution and lifestyles begin to westernize.
	Taisho (1912–1926)		► Liberal movements are suppressed and militarism comes to the fore.
Contemporary Japan	**Showa** (1926–1989)	**Prewar** **Postwar** Postwar Occupation (1945–1952**)	► The Asia-Pacific War (1941–45). ► The new Constitution enacted after the war includes the pacifist Article 9, which renounces war and the maintenance of armed forces. ► The country enjoys rapid economic growth from the 1950s to the 1970s. ► Extreme asset inflation from the late 1980s into the early 1990s earns this period the nickname "bubble economy."
	Heisei (1989–)		► The East Japan Earthquake occurs on March 11, 2011, accompanied by a devastating tsunami and the Fukushima nuclear accident.

日本列島における日本の範囲の変せん

Changes in Japan's Land Area on the Japanese Archipelago

擦文時代～アイヌ時代
Satsumon period ～
Ainu period

鎌倉時代
Kamakura
period

グスク時代～
三山時代
Gusuku period ～
Three-Kingdom
period

江戸時代
Edo period

琉球王国 Ryukyu Kingdom
(1429 ～1879 ／
薩摩支配 Satsuma rule
1609 ～1872)

明治時代
Meiji period

Notes

明治時代以降、アジア太平洋戦争時まで日本は台湾、南樺太、朝鮮半島、関東州（遼東半島先端部 等）、南洋諸島を統治し（満州国も支配下に置く）、戦中の一時期は中国本土の一部や東南アジア等を占領していた。
** 第二次世界大戦後、伊豆諸島、トカラ列島、奄美群島、小笠原諸島、沖縄県はアメリカに統治され、それぞれ 1946 年、52 年、53 年、68 年、72 年に日本に返還された。

From the Meiji period up to the end of the Asia-Pacific War, Japan ruled Taiwan, Sakhalin, the Korean Peninsula, the Kwantung Leased Territory, and the South Pacific Mandate. Manchuria was also under its control. During the war it occupied a part of China and Southeast Asia as well.
** After the war, the Izu, Tokara, Amami, and Ogasawara Islands and Okinawa Prefecture were ruled by the United States. They were returned to Japan in 1946, 1952, 1953, 1968, and 1972 respectively.

AFTERWORD

ポスト311の日本で──あとがきに代えて

私たちがある国の文化を語るのは、どのようなときでしょうか。まずは、違う国で生まれ育った友人や恋人同士が、あるいは結婚によって家族になった人たちが、お互いを知り合うための会話が思い浮かびます。「日本では（あなたの国では）、どうなの？」といった質問は、今日もどこかで繰り返されていることでしょう。

一方、文化の違いは、残念ながら友好的でない場面でもテーマになります。この本を書く上で、文化人類学の資料をいくつか参考にしましたが、その成果は、戦時下の敵国に対する戦略を練るために、利用されてきた側面があります。私自身は無条件な平和主義者のつもりですが、すべてのことは、もろ刃の剣でしょうか。

まえがきでも述べたように、文化の実相は多様で、国境線だけで分けられるものではありません。しかし、たまたまこの国で起きている何かをピックアップして語ると、それが国全体のイメージになってしまうかもしれない──執筆中には、そんなジレンマがありました。

特にすばらしいとされる（あるいは私が評価する）物事を取り上げた部分については、「日本文化」を好きになってほしいという気持ちだけで、解説したわけではありません。

たとえば日本で洗練された、料理の技法とか、建築における空間のあり方、俳句のリズムなどに興味を持つ人が世界のどこかにいて、明日から自分の作品や生活に取り入れることがあるかもしれない。そのためには、表面的な概要だけでなく、「質」をもテーマにしたいのです。読者のとらえ方は自由ですけれど、最初からエキゾチズムだけを流通させるような態度は、むなしいと思うからです。

また本書では、日本で起こっていることの問題点にも触れています。それでは「日本ブランド」に傷がつくといわれるかもしれませんが、人間社会の出来事は、どこかに普遍性があると感じます。グローバル化している今日では特に、世界中の人々に共有される問題が多いのではないでしょうか。「他人事じゃないよ」──そう応える人が、地球の裏側にもみつかることでしょう。

本書の企画が立ち上がったのは、もう5年も前のことです。日本のポップカルチャーなどが世界的に注目を集めていた時期で、思えば私の日本や世界に対する見方も楽観的でした。

2011年3月11日に起こった、東日本大震災と未曾有の原発事故は、日本の現代史の転換点だったと思います。日本は信じていたほど安全ではなかったことに、私をふくめて多くの人が気づきました（もっと前から気づいていた人はいたのでしょう）。

どういうことかというと、第二次世界大戦後の日本は、憲法で戦争の放棄を宣言した国です。しかしあの戦争の終わりにみた放射能の悪夢を、また経験することになるとは。しかも、今なお見えにくい形で……。また、あれから急速に、政治でも文化においても、「永久に」誓ったはずの平和主義さえ、形骸化が危ぶまれる状況が起こってくるとは……。

それでも、本書の各章で一つひとつに触れてはいませんが、2011年以降、反原発や反戦をテーマにした音楽や漫画、映像……そうした作品もたくさん生まれています。

広島、長崎、福島といった地名が有名になってしまったこの国は、警告と未来へのヒントを乗せた文化が、発信される場所でもあるということでしょう。

本書のテーマは、国の名前でくくった文化の話ですが、ちょっとしたお国自慢はどこの人でもするものの、攻撃的なナショナリズムに著者は賛成していません。むしろ「日本文化」という言葉は、単なるきっかけでいいと思っています。

私は時に自分を無力と思う一人ですが、何かのご縁で知り合った編集者や翻訳者、その他のスタッフのみなさんと、小さな「文化摩擦」を繰り返しながら、その先にみえるものへの期待を失わずに、この本が出来上がりました。受け取った読者のみなさんのまわりでは、どのような会話や文化が展開されていくのでしょうか。

2014年12月

三浦史子

Afterword: From Post-3.11 Japan

On what occasions do we talk about the culture of a particular country? One that comes to mind is get-acquainted conversations with friends, colleagues, or lovers who were born and raised in a land other than our own. At this moment, somebody somewhere is surely asking the question, "What's it like in your country?"

Unfortunately, cultural differences are also a popular topic in settings that are not at all friendly. In writing this book I have referred to texts on cultural anthropology, and some of their findings have actually been used against enemy countries during wartime. Although I call myself an unconditional pacifist, one might say that all knowledge is a double-edged sword.

As I wrote in the foreword, cultures are diverse things and do not divide neatly along national boundaries. But when we talk about phenomena that happen to have occurred in Japan, it is all too easy to generalize them into images that apply to the entire country. That is one of the dilemmas I have faced in writing these chapters.

When I bring up something that is celebrated (or that I think is remarkable) about Japan, it is not simply in the hope that people will become enamored of my country. I picture someone in another country with an interest in certain cuisine techniques, or the sense of space in Japanese wooden buildings, or the rhythmic features of haiku, which they can incorporate into their own life or work. For that reason, I have tried not only to provide an overview, but to touch on more essential aspects or realities of Japanese culture that would interest people both here and overseas. Readers are free to view them as they like, but my intention is not to promote cultural images for their exotic value.

I have also discussed problems that occur in Japan. Some might say that raising such issues damages the Japan "brand," but the experiences of human society are universal, aren't they? Particularly in our current era of globalization, people around the world share many of the same problems. By acknowledging them we are more likely to find people on the other side of the planet who will respond, "You are not alone."

The plans for this book first took shape five years ago. At the time, the whole world seemed fascinated by Japanese pop culture. In hindsight, my own attitude toward Japan and the world at large was rather optimistic. The East Japan Earthquake of March 2011, and the unprecedented nuclear accident that followed, were a turning point in contemporary Japanese history. The disasters made many people, including myself, realize that Japan was not as safe as we had believed (granted, others had realized that much earlier).

Consider that postwar Japan was a nation whose Constitution renounced war. Yet here we were reliving the radioactive nightmare that the country had experienced at the end of World War II... and the worst of it is still invisible. Since then, moreover, the threat to our country's vow of pacifism "forever" has only accelerated, both politically and culturally.

At the same time, while I could not cite them in every chapter, the years since 2011 have witnessed the birth of a great number of antinuclear and antiwar works in music, manga, film, and other media. That Hiroshima, Nagasaki, and Fukushima have become such well-known place names indicates that Japan is also the birthplace of a culture that offers both warnings and hints for our future.

The theme of this book is the culture associated with a particular country. We all may indulge in innocent boastful talk about our homeland, but this writer does not condone aggressive nationalism. I am happy if the term "Japanese culture" serves as no more than a point of entry for exploration.

Like many of us, I sometimes feel powerless against the problems we face today. But together with the editors, translators, and other staffers I had the fortune to meet, we managed to complete this book—while negotiating various small "cultural clashes"— without losing sight of our expectations for what lies ahead. I look forward to learning what conversations and cultural phenomena arise among our readers.

Miura Fumiko

December 2014

REFERENCES
おもな参考文献

01

『日本の音』小泉文夫（平凡社）

『日本音楽がわかる本』千葉優子（音楽之友社）

『カラオケ化する世界』ジョウ・シュン 他（青土社）

『日本民謡辞典』編：仲井幸二郎 他（東京堂出版）

『音楽は自由にする』坂本龍一（新潮社）

『歌謡曲の構造』小泉文夫（冬樹社）

『J-POP 進化論』佐藤良明（平凡社）

『い〜じゃん！ J-POP だから僕は日本にやって来た』マーティ・フリードマン（日経 BP 社）

02

『境界の美術史』北澤憲昭（ブリュッケ）

『奇想の系譜』辻惟雄（筑摩書房）

『もっと知りたい伊藤若冲』佐藤康宏（東京美術）

『中国絵画史事典』王伯敏（雄山閣）

『漆百科』山本勝巳（丸善）

『民芸』監修：濱田琢司 他（プチグラパブリッシング）

『日本近現代美術史事典』監修：多木浩二、藤枝晃雄（東京書籍）

『日本の伝統』岡本太郎（光文社）

『日本・現代・美術』椹木野衣（新潮社）

『オノ・ヨーコという生き方 WOMAN』アラン・クレイソン 他（ブルースインターアクションズ）

『SUPERFLAT』村上隆（マドラ出版）

『創造力なき日本』村上隆（角川書店）

『運慶』根立研介（ミネルヴァ書房）

『円空と木喰』本間正義（小学館）

『ジャポニスム入門』編：ジャポニスム学会（思文閣出版）

『ジャポニスム——幻想の日本』馬渕明子（ブリュッケ）

03

『図説 漫画の歴史』清水勲（河出書房新社）

『ニッポンマンガ論』フレデリック・L・ショット（マール社）

『マンガ産業論』中野晴行（筑摩書房）

『マンガはなぜ面白いのか その表現と文法』夏目房之介（日本放送出版協会）

『ジャパナメリカ 日本発ポップカルチャー革命』ローランド・ケルツ（武田ランダムハウスジャパン）

『テヅカ・イズ・デッド』伊藤剛（NTT 出版）

『フランスのマンガ』山下雅之（論創社）

『マンガ名作講義』青山南 他（情報センター出版局）

『アジア MANGA サミット』編著：関口シュン、秋田孝宏（子どもの未来社）

『世界コミックスの想像力』小野耕世（青土社）

04

『日本文学の歴史』ドナルド・キーン（中央公論社）

『日本文学史』小西甚一（講談社）

『源氏物語の結婚』工藤重矩（中央公論新社）

『『古事記』神話の謎を解く』西條勉（中央公論新社）

『世界文学のスーパースター夏目漱石』ダミアン・フラナガン（講談社インターナショナル）

『世界は村上春樹をどう読むか』編：柴田元幸、沼野充義、藤井省三、四方田犬彦（文藝春秋）

『ライトノベル「超」入門』新城カズマ（ソフトバンク新書）

『ライトノベル☆めった斬り！』大森望 他（太田出版）

『なぜケータイ小説は売れるのか』本田透（ソフトバンク新書）

05

『比較文化的に見た日本の演劇 / Japanese Theater』野間正二（大阪教育図書）

『（英語版）日本演劇ガイド』ロナルド・カヴァイエ、ポール・グリフィス、扇田昭彦 他（講談社インターナショナル）

『演劇のことば』平田オリザ（岩波書店）

『能って、何？』松岡心平（新書館）

『土方巽全集』土方巽 他（河出書房新社）

『新宿末広亭』長井好弘（アスペクト）

「ベルエポックと「ゲイシャ」——文学の中のジャポニスム」堀江珠喜『大阪府立大学紀要』第 41 巻

「女性・異文化：フィンランドにおけるゲイシャのイメージ」植村友香子『言語文化と日本語教育』第 21 号

06

『アニメーション学入門』津堅信之（平凡社）

『日本アニメーションの力』津堅信之（NTT 出版）

『（英語版）外国人のためのヲタク・エンサイクロペディア』パトリック・ウィリアム・ガルバレス（講談社インターナショナル）

『最新アニメ業界の動向とからくりがよ〜くわかる本』谷口功、麻生はじめ（秀和システム）

『アニメ文化外交』櫻井孝昌（筑摩書房）

『折り返し点 1997〜2008』宮崎駿（岩波書店）

『戦闘美少女の精神分析』斎藤環（筑摩書房）

『デジタルゲームの教科書』（ソフトバンククリエイティブ）

『デジタルコンテンツ白書 2014』監修：経済産業省商務情報制作局（デジタルコンテンツ協会）

『オタクはすでに死んでいる』岡田斗司夫（新潮社）

『オタク・イン・USA』パトリック・マシアス（太田出版）

『ル・オタク フランスおたく物語』清谷信一（講談社）

『キャラクターとは何か』小田切博（筑摩書房）

『BT 美術手帖』2013 年 6 月号／特集 初音ミク

07

『日本人のための宗教原論』小室直樹（徳間書店）
『日本人はなぜ無宗教なのか』阿満利麿（筑摩書房）
『ポストモダンの新宗教』島薗進（東京堂出版）
『一個人』2013年9月号／特集 日本の新宗教入門
『武士道の逆襲』菅野覚明（講談社）
『戦場の精神史』佐伯真一（NHK出版）
『切腹 日本人の責任の取り方』山本博文（光文社）
『切腹の話』千葉徳爾（講談社）
『わび・さび・幽玄』編：鈴木貞美（水声社）
『日本美を哲学する』田中久文（青土社）
『ただ坐る』ネルケ無方（光文社）
『矛盾だらけの禅─悟りを求めるアメリカ人作家の冒険』ローレンス・シャインバーグ（清流出版）
『ラフカディオ・ハーン』太田雄三（岩波書店）
『日本事物誌』バジル・ホール・チェンバレン（平凡社）
The Myth of Japanese Uniqueness, Peter N. Dale, Croom Helm
『イデオロギーとしての日本文化論』ハルミ・ベフ（思想の科学社）
『『日本文化論』の変容』青木保（中央公論新社）
『人間を幸福にしない日本というシステム』カレル・ヴァン・ウォルフレン（毎日新聞社）

08

『芸術と社会』監修：山本正男（玉川大学出版部）
『日本の家元』林忠彦（集英社）
『日本の芸道六種』桑田忠親（中央公論新社）
『茶の湯といけばなの歴史』熊倉功夫（左右社）
『茶の湯の歴史』神津朝夫（角川選書）
『〈お茶〉はなぜ女のものになったか──茶道から見る戦後の家族』加藤恵津子（紀伊國屋書店）
『日本の伝統美とヨーロッパ』宮元健次（世界思想社）
『いけばな辞典』大井ミノブ（東京堂出版）
『前衛いけばなの時代』三頭谷鷹史（美学出版）
『まっしぐらの花─中川幸夫』森山明子（美術出版社）
『香と香道』編：香道文化研究会（雄山閣）
『香三才』畑正高（世界文化社）
『盆栽との対話』森前誠二（亜紀書房）
『創作盆栽に挑む』加藤三郎 他（日本放送出版協会）
『武道の誕生』井上俊（吉川弘文館）
『武道』編：二木謙一 他（東京堂出版）
『武道を生きる』松原隆一郎（NTT出版）
『yawara 知られざる日本柔術の世界』山田實（BABジャパン）
『ここまで知って大相撲通』根間弘海（グラフ社）
『大相撲の経済学』中島隆信（東洋経済新報社）

09

『日本映画は生きている』黒沢清 他（岩波書店）
『日本映画史100年』四方田犬彦（集英社）
『日本映画史』佐藤忠男（岩波書店）
『映画館と観客の文化史』加藤幹郎（中央公論新社）
『日本映画はアメリカでどう観られてきたか』北野圭介（平凡社）

『日本映画の国際ビジネス』（キネマ旬報社）
『時代劇映画の思想』筒井清忠（ウェッジ）
『やくざ映画とその時代』斯波司 他（筑摩書房）
『ヤクザ1000人に会いました!』鈴木智彦（宝島社）
『七人の侍と現代』四方田犬彦（岩波書店）
『ヒバクシャ・シネマ』編著：ミック・ブロデリック 訳：柴崎昭則、和波雅子（現代書館）
『素晴らしき円谷英二の世界』矢島信男 他（中経出版）
『大島渚と日本』四方田犬彦（筑摩書房）
『物語』他、北野武自叙伝シリーズ（ロッキング・オン）
『Kitano par Kitano』北野武 他（早川書房）

10

『日本料理の神髄』阿部孤柳（講談社）
Food of Japan, Shirley Booth, Interlink Books
『もち』渡部忠世、深澤小百合（法政大学出版局）
『英国一家、ますます日本を食べる』マイケル・ブース（亜紀書房）
『春夏秋冬 料理王国』北大路魯山人（中央公論新社）

11

Japan Fashion Now, Valerie Steele et al., Yale University Press
『美容文化論』千村典生、村澤博人（日本理容美容教育センター）
『無印良品の「改革」』渡辺米英（商業界）
『世界カワイイ革命』櫻井孝昌（PHP研究所）

12

『日本の近代建築』藤森照信（岩波書店）
『図説 日本建築のみかた』宮元健次（学芸出版社）
『日本─タウトの日記』ブルーノ・タウト（岩波書店）
『つくられた桂離宮神話』井上章一（弘文堂）
『日本の庭園』西沢文隆 他（中央公論新社）
『日本庭園』小野健吉（岩波書店）
『中国の庭園』木津雅代（東京堂出版）
「庭園構成から見る中国的空間の特質」西本吉輝
『藤森照信の茶室学』藤森照信（六耀社）
『現代日本建築家列伝』五十嵐太郎（河出書房新社）
『メタボリズムの発想』黒川記章（白馬出版）
『日本民家の造形』川村善之（淡交社）
『日本住居史』小沢朝江 他（吉川弘文館）
『図説・近代日本住宅史』内田青蔵 他（鹿島出版会）
『英語版スモール・スペース』アズビー・ブラウン（講談社インターナショナル）
『1971→1991 倉俣を読む』鈴木紀慶（鹿島出版会）
『3・11後の建築と社会デザイン』編著：三浦展、藤村龍至（平凡社）
『原発と建築家』竹内昌義 他（学芸出版社）
『鎮守の森』宮脇昭（新潮社）
『鎮守の森は甦る』上田正昭 他（思文閣出版）

Appendix

『DNAでたどる日本人10万年の旅』崎谷満（昭和堂）
『日本人になった祖先たち』篠田謙一（日本放送出版協会）

ACKNOWLEDGMENTS

本書の執筆・制作にあたっては、多くの方々にご協力いただきました。原稿の一部をお読みいただき貴重なアドバイスを下さった小沼純一氏、村井寛志氏、ケリー・ベノム氏、取材上、重要な情報をご提供いただいた山口秋月氏、西本太郎氏、木下亮氏、また本書の翻訳者、アラン・グリースン氏からも得がたい情報をいただき、いくつかの項目は彼との議論を通して練り直しました。それから、この本を的を射た美しい形に仕上げてくださったアート・ディレクター、藤本やすし氏とデザイナーの山﨑隼氏。そして編集者の西田由香氏は、立ち上げから紆余曲折を経て刊行に至るまで、忍耐強くこの企画を支えてくださいました。その他の制作・営業に携わるみなさま、友人たちや家族……。すべての方のお名前をここに記すことは控えますが、みなさまへの深い感謝を表します。

I would like to express my special thanks to Konuma Jun'ichi, Murai Hiroshi, and Carey Benom, who read parts of the script and gave me significant advice; Yamaguchi Shugetsu, Nishimoto Taro, and Kinoshita Ryo, who provided me with important information; Alan Gleason, who not only translated the book but also gave me valuable information and discussed some of those topics with me; art director Fujimoto Yasushi and designer Yamasaki Hayato, who beautifully visualized the book; editor Nishida Yuka, who patiently cooperated with me from the start of the project; as well as the other staff, my friends and family, and all of those who helped me in a variety of ways to produce this book. — The Author

PROFILES

著者紹介

三浦史子 (みうらふみこ)

山口県生まれ。芸術、デザインの理論と実践を学んだ学生時代から、カメラを手に世界各地に旅する。商業建築のインテリア企画設計職、文化・芸術関連書籍／雑誌の編集者、国際ジャーナリストのリサーチ・スタッフ等を経ながら、フリーランスで雑誌に記事と写真を発表する。アーティストや科学者、宇宙飛行士等、これまで数百人にインタビュー。また、テーマとして「文化の移動」に興味をもち、ハワイの日系移民文化についての取材も。著書に、ルポ『フェア・トレードを探しに FAIR TRADE TRAIL』(2008 年／スリーエーネットワーク)がある。

About the Author

Miura Fumiko was born in Yamaguchi Prefecture, Japan. While studying the theory and practice of art and design at university in Tokyo, she began traveling to various parts of the world, and later spent a year in London. In Japan she has worked as a commercial building interior designer, a book and magazine editor on culture and the arts, a researcher for overseas journalists on international issues, as well as a nonfiction writer and photographer. She has interviewed hundreds of people, ranging from artists to scientists to astronauts. Her interest in the migration of cultures has inspired her to study such phenomena as the Japanese immigrant culture of Hawaii. Among her publications is the book *Fair Trade Trail* (3A Corporation, 2008), an inquiry into the fair trade movement around the globe.

翻訳者紹介

アラン・グリースン

米国生まれ。少年時代を東京で過ごす。長唄や八重山民謡といった伝統音楽を学ぶため 20 代で日本に戻り、同時期に翻訳家としてのキャリアをスタート。以来、日本の音楽、美術、演劇、歴史、政治等、さまざまなテーマの翻訳・編集に携わる。漫画の翻訳も多数手がけ、広島への原爆投下を描いた漫画『はだしのゲン』の英語版では、全 10 巻の編集を担当した。現在もまた東京在住で、美術館・アート情報のウェブマガジン「Artscape Japan」(英語版) や、日本文学を海外に紹介するサイト「Books from Japan」の編集者・ライターとして活動中。

About the Translator

Alan Gleason was born in the United States and spent his childhood in Tokyo, Japan. Returning to Tokyo in his twenties to study traditional Japanese and Okinawan music, he also began working as a translator. Since then he has translated and edited many works on Japanese music, art, drama, history and politics. He has also translated numerous manga, and served as editor of the English translation of the internationally acclaimed manga series *Barefoot Gen*, a ten-volume account of the atomic bombing of Hiroshima. He currently lives in Tokyo, where he edits and writes for the web magazine *Artscape Japan* and the Japanese literature website *Books from Japan*.

デザイン	山﨑 隼＋Cap
翻訳協力	パメラ・ミキ
編集協力	足立恵子
DTP 組版	奥田直子

英語で日本文化の本　The Japan Culture Book

2015 年 2 月 5 日	初版発行
2017 年 3 月 5 日	第 3 刷発行
著　者	三浦史子
	© Miura Fumiko, 2015
訳　者	アラン・グリースン
	English translation © Alan Gleason, 2015
発行者	堤 丈晴
発行所	株式会社 ジャパンタイムズ
	〒 108-0023 東京都港区芝浦 4 丁目 5 番 4 号
	電話　(03) 3453-2013 ［出版営業部］
	振替口座　00190-6-64848
	ウェブサイト　http://bookclub.japantimes.co.jp
印刷所	図書印刷株式会社

本書の内容に関するお問い合わせは、上記ウェブサイトまたは郵便でお受けいたします。
定価はカバーに表示してあります。
万一、乱丁落丁のある場合は、送料当社負担でお取り替えいたします。
ジャパンタイムズ出版営業部あてにお送りください。

Printed in Japan　　ISBN978-4-7890-1580-6